TEMPLE OF PEACE

BAKER SERIES IN PEACE AND CONFLICT STUDIES

Edited by Ingo Trauschweizer

The European Union: From Jean Monnet to the Euro
edited by Dean Kotlowski

Failed States and Fragile Societies: A New World Disorder?
edited by Ingo Trauschweizer and Steven M. Miner

Temple of Peace: International Cooperation and Stability since 1945
edited by Ingo Trauschweizer

temple of peace

International Cooperation and Stability since 1945

Edited by INGO TRAUSCHWEIZER

OHIO UNIVERSITY PRESS
ATHENS

Ohio University Press, Athens, Ohio 45701
ohioswallow.com

Paperback edition © 2022
Paperback ISBN: 978-0-8214-2493-3

Printed in the United States of America
Ohio University Press books are printed on acid-free paper ∞ ™

31 30 29 28 27 26 25 24 23 22 21 5 4 3 2 1

Library of Congress Cataloging-in-Publication Data
Names: Trauschweizer, Ingo, editor.
Title: Temple of peace : international cooperation and stability since 1945 / edited by Ingo Trauschweizer.
Description: Athens : Ohio University Press, 2021. | Series: Baker series in peace and conflict studies | Includes bibliographical references and index.
Identifiers: LCCN 2020048197 (print) | LCCN 2020048198 (ebook) | ISBN 9780821424407 (hardcover) | ISBN 9780821447321 (pdf)
Subjects: LCSH: International cooperation—History—20th century. | International cooperation—History—21st century. | International organization—History—20th century. | International organization—History—21st century. | World politics—1945–1989. | World politics—1989–
Classification: LCC JZ1318 .T39 2021 (print) | LCC JZ1318 (ebook) | DDC 341.7—dc23
LC record available at https://lccn.loc.gov/2020048197
LC ebook record available at https://lccn.loc.gov/2020048198

CONTENTS

INTRODUCTION

INGO TRAUSCHWEIZER

The postwar liberal international order, upheld by organizations such as the United Nations (UN) and alliances such as the North Atlantic Treaty Organization (NATO), seemed to ensure decades of relative stability in international relations.[1] Not that wars did not break out, and all too many people died in conflicts large and small, but some forty-five years after the end of World War II, observers could claim that Europe had experienced its longest stretch of peacetime since the fall of the Roman Empire. Indeed, to some scholars it appeared that war itself had become obsolescent and man less prone to violence.[2] Armed conflicts in the 1990s, from the violent breakup of Yugoslavia—including a vicious reminder that ethnic cleansing was not a phenomenon of an archaic past—to genocide in Rwanda sent stark warnings that the structures that had helped keep the great powers off one another's throats in the Cold War era did not guarantee peace and stability for all.[3] Koreans, Vietnamese, as well as many Africans, Latin Americans, South Asians, and Middle Easterners could have told observers in the West that the system they celebrated had never brought them peace in the first place.[4] And yet the world of the great powers had seemed more stable in the decades after the downfall of Adolf Hitler and the bombing of Hiroshima and Nagasaki. And, of course, the UN and NATO, as well as other supranational bodies such as the European Union, tried to extend their reach and project their positive impact into the twenty-first century.

Looking back from the twenty-first century, we often take the emergence and evolution of international organizations in the wake of World War II's devastation for granted, and we lose sight of negotiations and nuances that defined the inner working of the postwar order. The UN developed from the wartime coalition against Nazi Germany and had an early founding document in the August 1941 Atlantic Charter, though the UN itself came into being only in 1945 and some of its founders saw it more as guardian of an old order than guarantor of the new.[5] Linked to the framework of collective security were the Anglo-American–run World Bank and International Monetary Fund, which derived from discussions at Bretton Woods in New Hampshire and Dumbarton Oaks in Washington, DC, in 1944 and 1945.[6] Equally linked was the definition of human rights and the pursuit of war criminals in international military tribunals.[7] As Elizabeth Borgwardt notes in chapter 1, collective security, economic stability, and the rule of law were the underpinnings of the new order. Yet all of this was a negotiated process that required compromise. After all, liberal democracies and communist dictatorships had to sign on to the same shared principles, and each side could block the other by veto power in the UN Security Council.[8]

NATO was an even less natural outgrowth of the wartime coalition, not least because it was aimed at deterring the Soviet Union but also because it tied the United States to Europe in its first peacetime military alliance. Postwar strategists and diplomats had not planned for that outcome. At least until 1948, George C. Marshall, the wartime chief of staff turned secretary of state, intended to follow the course of his adviser George Kennan and put the promise of economic recovery at the center of US strategy for stability in Europe. Yet crises between East and West had already taken hold in the northern tier of the Middle East, the eastern Mediterranean, and Berlin, and soon the Soviet acquisition of atomic weapons, the victory of communist forces in the Chinese Civil War, the outbreak of the Korean War, and resulting fears in Europe all combined to turn a political statement—the North Atlantic Treaty of April 1949—into a full-blown military alliance.[9] NATO members could claim to work under the umbrella of the UN, but even in the first half-decade after the war, postwar order had already shifted from promises of cooperation to formation of hostile camps.

For Europeans the postwar system brought considerable stability, albeit at the cost of lack of freedom and stunted economic development in the communist east, and for the United Kingdom, the Netherlands, Portugal, and France the retreat from empire, sometimes in bloody wars. Much of the rest of the world could celebrate decolonization and the emergence of new states—the UN grew from fifty-one founding members to seventy-six by 1955, 117 by 1965, 144 by 1975, and 193 by 2011—but also saw protracted political crises, wars, violence, and often abject poverty as the UN struggled to build or keep peace.[10] Frequently, the members of the Security Council—the United States and the Soviet Union but also China, the United Kingdom, and France—intervened in what was then called the Third World, sometimes with military means in wars as destructive as the one in Vietnam.[11] The discrepancy of peace, security, and stability in some parts of the world and warfare, violence, and poverty in others led some observers to theorize about a "zone of peace" in the affluent world.[12] At the end of the Cold War, it seemed that conflict potential was shrinking, but it soon appeared that neither the UN nor military alliances had the means to counter crises of the 1990s and 2000s efficiently. The struggles of the UN in the nascent Republic of the Congo in the 1960s, explored in this volume by Alanna O'Malley, were thus a harbinger of things to come.

Today one may point at President Donald Trump as the embodiment of the critique of the international system and perhaps even, at least in his rhetoric, as a return to isolationist tendencies of an earlier era, but he is hardly alone: the world scene has not appeared this unsettling since the 1930s. The crises of the twenty-first century run deep: terrorist attacks and the war on terror, lethal civil wars such as the one in Syria, refugee streams in the millions, the seeming strain on democratic systems even in Europe, emboldened regional actors such as Iran and North Korea that pose significant threats, and powers such as Russia and China that pursue agendas sharply opposed to the tenets of the postwar order.[13] Under this weight, the pillars of the liberal order have borne massive strain, and they might yet bend or break. Of course, disagreement, at times sharp, within NATO over burden-sharing is nothing new; instead, it has been at the center of debates about the alliance's future since the 1950s, a point noted by both Seth Givens and Stephan Kieninger.[14] Equally so, politicians in the United States from time to time raised questions about whether American payments to the UN were worth the cost. Those voices grew louder in the 1980s and again in the 2010s. By the end of 2019, even before the onset of the all-consuming covid-19 crisis, Western European leaders disagreed on the state of NATO: France's president, Emmanuel Macron, complained about the "brain death" of the alliance, with US and European interests completely separated, but German chancellor Angela Merkel and NATO secretary-general Jens Stoltenberg emphasized areas of cooperation, Stoltenberg even going so far as to suggest there was now the largest set of joint initiatives under way.[15]

Where do we stand some seventy-five years after the end of World War II? Britain's wartime prime minister—by then opposition leader—Winston Churchill referred to the UN framework as "the temple of peace" in his 1946 speech in Fulton, Missouri, which is typically identified by his remark about the "iron curtain," and he maintained there and elsewhere that alliances could help provide necessary stability so that free people could prosper, both economically and politically.[16] The history of the West since 1945 could be read in that fashion. Does it still apply? The pillars of international order remain in place, but in a world defined as much by populism and protest, leaders in the United States no longer seem inclined to allow the country to serve as the indispensable power in an alliance framework that is built on shared values, human rights, and an admixture of hard and soft power. Perhaps rising powers will step in, but as of mid-2020, fears of anarchy in the international system seem to outweigh such hopes.[17] In this book, nine scholars and practitioners of diplomacy explore that issue. At the conference in spring 2019 where they debated in person, retired admiral James Stavridis, former commander of NATO and US Southern Command, opened the proceedings with an impassioned plea for the continued importance of international cooperation and of organizations such as UN and NATO. Even though the pace of their operations may be frustrating, it is much better, Stavridis held, to work through issues with great conflict potential in their conference rooms than engage in the field of battle, in whatever dimension (land, sea, air, space, cyberspace) that might take place in the future.[18] Even though there is a great deal of skepticism in these pages, we could all agree that for all its flaws, international cooperation in the past seven decades has been a boon to peace and stability.

In the first chapter, Elizabeth Borgwardt describes what she terms Franklin Roosevelt's "New Deal for the World," a grand strategy that extended beyond the national interests of the United States and embedded American goals in deeper international foundations. Key elements of this process, she notes, were the founding of the UN itself but also the international military tribunals at Nuremberg and Tokyo and other structures that linked economics and the need to provide aid for the restoration of war-torn countries to establish the promise of prosperity that served to underwrite postwar stability. Collective security negotiated at the UN Security Council, economic stability provided by World Bank and International Monetary Fund, and accountability to legal structures, Borgwardt argues, served as the crucial tools. Seth Givens follows up with a chapter on the emergence of NATO's command structure and the role played by the alliance's supreme commanders as soldiers and diplomats. This was particularly critical, Givens notes, because NATO was the embodiment of the new transatlantic relationship that served to promise security as well as prosperity. Cooperation among former enemies, once West Germany joined in the mid-1950s, was not always easy, and NATO was from the outset beset by questions of fair burden-sharing, concrete concerns over nuclear war, a pessimistic assessment that most of Western Europe could not be defended on the ground, and the ever-present tensions between Atlantic and continental orientations that eventually found their expression in crises precipitated by French president Charles de Gaulle in the 1960s. It was in these stormy seas, Givens holds, that the steady hand of Dwight Eisenhower and his successors at NATO's military headquarters became particularly important. Armin Grünbacher completes the set of chapters on the initial underpinnings of the system. Grünbacher considers European-American economic cooperation through the surprisingly understudied lens of the Organization for European Economic Cooperation (OEEC), which is typically overshadowed by the luster of the Marshall Plan. He acknowledges that there were other factors that explain the growth in economic productivity across Western Europe in the 1950s—notably the European Coal and Steel Community, which would later grow into the European Economic Community—but Grünbacher holds that the contribution of the OEEC was quite important and should not be overlooked. If nothing else, he notes, its inner workings offer a window into how Europeans and Americans negotiated the practical processes of their cooperation.

The middle chapters of the book consider the evolution and performance of the UN and NATO as well as Australia's perspective on regional stability in Asia and the Pacific region. On the latter, Laura Seddelmeyer argues Australia learned in the 1960s and 1970s that it had to carve out its own role as a regional power or, as she calls it, a "neighborhood power." Australia may have seemed far removed from the Cold War's hot spots, but the war in Vietnam and the grave crisis in Indonesia—very much within Australia's perceived buffer zone—combined with the United Kingdom's gradual retreat from most positions east of Suez forced Canberra to act more assertively in defense of national interest and regional stability. While Australia provided for a degree of stability in the Pacific and Indian Oceans, neither the UN nor NATO were particularly effective outside of the Northern Hemisphere. As Alanna O'Malley shows, the UN's response to the Congo Crisis in the first half of the 1960s underscores its difficulties addressing the crises of the Cold War and decolonization, but she also illustrates the decisive leadership of UN secretary-general Dag Hammarskjöld and the role of the organization as actor, incubator of ideas, and forum for discussions that could diffuse tensions. The UN mission to the Congo, O'Malley concludes, had multiple dimensions that went well beyond peacekeeping, and the UN more generally contributed to the dismantling of empires both on the ground and, perhaps even more so, in people's minds.

Considering the changing nature of warfare, Steven Metz explores the evolution of insurgency and revolutionary people's war in three waves since Mao Zedong put into practice his blueprint in China in the 1930s and 1940s. Maoist insurgency aimed to take over the state, it was typically defined by Marxist ideology (though it could also be nativist), and it unfolded in the classic model of three phases (mobilization and consolidation of political ties, guerrilla warfare, and conventional and larger-scale operations). This, of course, bedeviled Western states in the Cold War from Vietnam and Algeria to the Americas, and it posed challenges to an international order written for states with a near monopoly of war. The second wave, ongoing in some areas, came to the fore in the 1970s and 1980s; it featured transnational and nonstate actors and straddled both sides of the line between organized violence and organized crime. Motivation could be commercial, religious, or ideological, and most insurgent groups still intended to control territory and claim political power. In the third wave, now only beginning, Metz perceives a "network-and-node" organization model, and he fears that twenty-first-century insurgents may no longer be intent on claiming power in the same ways, which would make it much harder to combat their strategy.

Stephan Kieninger shows that NATO managed to muddle through its own political crises from the mid-1960s into the post–Cold War years but also that policies that were enacted helped transform Western Europe. Some of the issues that bedeviled the alliance were similar to earlier concerns: uncertainty about what exactly constituted effective deterrence, what was the proper balance of conventional armament (in the early 1960s pushed by the John F. Kennedy administration) and nuclear weapons, and who should pay how much for the security of Western Europe and the North Atlantic. A new item of disagreement, or at least mild distrust, included détente, a foreign policy approach of engagement with the Soviet Union that was defined rather differently in Washington, Bonn, and Paris. But, as Kieninger notes, from the Harmel Report of 1967 forward, wherein NATO placed détente next to deterrence as a twin strategic goal, the allies found ways to address their disagreements satisfactorily, and the alliance adapted in the Euromissile Crisis of the late 1970s and early 1980s and again in eastward expansion and engagement of Russia in the 1990s.

The final pair of contributions strike a more alarmed and pessimistic tone. Mary Nolan expands on the cultural decline of the Atlantic partnership, which negatively affects both NATO and the UN. Her pessimistic reading of the present is rooted in the recognition of an erosion of shared values since at least the 1970s, which now finds expression in the unilateralism of Donald Trump, the rejection of Trump and his unilateralism by most European allies, and the populist turns in Hungary, Poland, and elsewhere. Nolan concludes that the liberal postwar order and its core agreements are under sustained and very serious assault. Equally, retired ambassador Jennifer Brush, an expert in the politics of the former Soviet Union and the Balkans, offers little optimism. She sees Russian president Vladimir Putin at the center of the assault—unlike Nolan, Brush considers this more outside attack than internal rot. The problem, as both Brush and Nolan imply, is that the UN is powerless in the face of such fracturing and the pillars that have upheld the Pax Americana no longer seem sound. Nolan, in particular, concludes that the world has changed since 1945 and that politics, economics, and ideologies are very different today. In other words, structures that were fitted to crises of the 1930s and 1940s may no longer work in the 2020s, even if there were more widespread agreement on core principles. Collectively, the authors in this volume seek to address questions of how the liberal international order was built and maintained and what challenges it has faced, and they offer perspectives on what could be lost in a post-American world.

NOTES

1 John Lewis Gaddis, *The Long Peace: Inquiries into the History of the Cold War* (New York: Oxford University Press, 1987).

2 John E. Mueller, *Retreat from Doomsday: The Obsolescence of Major War* (New York: Basic Books, 1989); Steven Pinker, *The Better Angels of Our Nature: Why Violence Has Declined* (New York: Viking, 2011).

3 Mary Kaldor, *New and Old Wars: Organized Violence in a Global Era*, 3rd ed. (Stanford, CA: Stanford University Press, 2012).

4 Paul Chamberlain, *The Cold War Killing Fields: Rethinking the Long Peace* (New York: Harper, 2018).

5 Mark Mazower, *No Enchanted Palace: The End of Empire and the Ideological Origins of the United Nations* (Princeton, NJ: Princeton University Press, 2009).

6 Benn Steil, *The Battle of Bretton Woods: John Maynard Keynes, Harry Dexter White, and the Making of a New World Order* (Princeton, NJ: Princeton University Press, 2013).

7 Universal Declaration of Human Rights (1948), https://www.un.org/en/universal-declaration-human-rights/; Telford Taylor, *The Anatomy of the Nuremberg Trials: A Personal Memoir* (New York: Knopf, 1992).

8 David L. Bosco, *Five to Rule Them All: The UN Security Council and the Making of the Modern World* (New York: Oxford University Press, 2009).

9 Ingo Trauschweizer, "An Alliance by Default: Marshall and the North Atlantic Treaty," in *George C. Marshall and the Early Cold War: Policy, Politics, and Society*, ed. William Taylor (Norman: University of Oklahoma Press, 2020).

10 For UN membership, see "Growth in United Nations Membership, 1945–Present," United Nations, accessed November 8, 2019, https://www.un.org/en/sections/member-states/growth-united-nations-membership-1945-present/index.html.

11 Odd Arne Westad, *Global Cold War: Third World Interventions and the Making of Our Time* (Cambridge: Cambridge University Press, 2005).

12 Azar Gat, *War in Human Civilization* (Oxford: Oxford University Press, 2006), 570–637.

13 For an argument that links new and older forms of warfare as a threat to Western conceptions of world order, see David Kilcullen, *The Dragons and the Snakes: How the Rest Learned to Fight the West* (New York: Oxford University Press, 2020).

14 Seth A. Johnston, *How NATO Adapts: Strategy and Organization in the Atlantic Alliance since 1950* (Baltimore, MD: Johns Hopkins University Press, 2017); Timothy A. Sayle, *Enduring Alliance: A History of NATO and the Postwar Global Order* (Ithaca, NY: Cornell University Press, 2019).

15 "Merkel weist NATO-Kritik von Macron zurück," *Der Spiegel*, November 7, 2019, https://www.spiegel.de/politik/ausland/nato-angela-merkel-weist-kritik-von-emmanuel-macron-zurueck-a-1295417.html.

16 Winston Churchill, "The Sinews of Peace," speech at Westminster College, Fulton, Missouri, March 5, 1946, International Churchill Society, https://winstonchurchill.org/resources/speeches/1946-1963-elder-statesman/the-sinews-of-peace/; David Reynolds, *In Command of History: Churchill Fighting and Writing the Second World War* (New York: Basic Books, 2005), 133–34.

17 For perspectives on a multipolar world, see Fareed Zakaria, *The Post-American World: Release 2.0* (New York: W. W. Norton, 2011), and Amitav Acharya, *The End of American World Order,* 2nd ed. (Cambridge: Polity, 2018). For a pessimistic perspective on both international relations and domestic repercussions, see Timothy Snyder, *The Road to Unfreedom: Russia, Europe, America* (New York: Tim Duggan Books, 2018).

18 "Stavridis Discusses National Security Risks, Opportunities at Baker Peace Conference," *College of Arts and Sciences Forum,* Ohio University, April 3, 2019, https://www.ohio-forum.com/2019/04/stavridis-presents-thoughts-on-national-security-risks-and-opportunities-in-baker-peace-conference-keynote-address/.

CHAPTER 1

The New Deal as Grand Strategy

Constructing the Postwar Institutional Order

ELIZABETH BORGWARDT

"There should have been a Secretary of the Future," the novelist, social critic, and World War II veteran Kurt Vonnegut once mordantly observed. Any putative secretary of the future in the US executive branch would in effect be a "grand strategist"—gaming out long-term big-picture scenarios not only linked to a vision of the national interest but also designed to shape the responses of allies and rivals alike.[1]

Yet President Franklin Delano Roosevelt, often criticized as a hasty, improvisational, and short-term thinker, served in certain ways as his own secretary of the future in the World War II era. By 1941, FDR and his key advisers were distilling some hard-won wisdom from their trial-and-error approaches in devising what became known as the New Deal and applying it to the world's burgeoning international crises. They were also aiming to sidestep many of the perceived mistakes of President Woodrow Wilson at the end of World War I.[2]

The key, for Roosevelt, was a New Deal–inspired set of ideas and institutions that animated a capacious reframing of the national interest.[3] Internationalizing the New Deal meant reconfiguring the playing field of world politics in three broad institutional realms:

- *Collective security* through the United Nations (UN), especially the UN Security Council
- *Economic stability* through the Bretton Woods institutions as originally conceived (including the International Monetary Fund and the World Bank) and also through subsidiary organizations of the UN such as the International Labor Organization
- *Rule of law institutions* addressing concerns about accountability notably through the Nuremberg and Tokyo war crimes trials, at one point intended to pave the way for a permanently sitting International Criminal Court, as well as through a revived International Court of Justice (for interstate disputes not of a criminal nature)

These three institutional pillars are what contemporary international relations specialists generally mean when they refer to "the postwar international order."[4] What made this institutionally focused scaffolding into "grand strategy"—as opposed to just a fancy term for long-term planning—was the way any resulting improvement to the functioning of the international order was dependent on negotiation and diplomacy. The strategic element is the necessity of anticipating and accommodating how others will likely—or even just possibly—react. Proposals needed to be crafted in order to advantage one's own side, to be sure, but also to benefit other players enough for them to say "yes."[5]

All three sets of institutions also involved what social scientists like to call a certain "cabining" of sovereignty for the sake of this essential coordination and cooperation. It is precisely these three postwar pillars that have been energetically hewed away by the policies and personnel of the Donald Trump administration. While conservative Republicans in the United States have long been intent on rending the fabric of the domestic New Deal, the Trumpian order of Republican operatives is equally as focused on ending the New Deal as grand strategy, with its attendant institutional expressions of US leadership worldwide.[6]

There is no claim here that this liberal institutional ordering is in any way ideal. As any number of critics have been quick to highlight, by the 1970s New Deal social liberalism had become free-market neoliberalism, quite explicitly abandoning any kind of aspirational economic justice orientation along the way. Nevertheless, recent Trumpian attacks on these three institutional pillars are still a terrible idea, as our study of history suggests here.

GRAND STRATEGY AS "SECURITY"

Many of the programs of FDR's New Deal had sought to expand the boundaries of security at home, based on the perceived lessons of the early years of the Great Depression. One explicit purpose of Social Security was to help to short-circuit civil unrest, for example. Yet for the most creative New Deal administrators, security meant much more than simply stability. Expanding the capacity of a widening swath of Americans to participate in a more prosperous and hopeful future may indeed have served to stabilize capitalism. But widening these circles of inclusion was also intended to entrench—and even to improve upon—the practice of democracy. Many of these New Deal programs were designed to sand down some of the sharpest edges of the spiking inequalities generated by the free-enterprise system.[7]

To be sure, the domestic New Deal programs aimed at expanding opportunities and improving standards of living also starkly reflected the limits of the American social imagination. Social Security programs made a point of excluding agricultural and domestic workers, for example—that is to say, segments of the economy with high proportions of African American participation. Electrification programs tended to benefit rural areas, while many youth employment programs generally assisted urban dwellers, but in both cases Black exclusion was the norm, by design. Southern senators, in particular—virtually all of them Democrats in this era—often explicitly demanded fencing out African American citizens as a price of "party solidarity" and white political participation in FDR's reformist initiatives.[8]

Just because New Deal programs sought to expand the idea of "security" to encompass economic and social security—within the arguably rather crabbed demographic confines referenced above—did not mean that the concept was therefore confined to domestic dimensions, however. Such a perspective would discount the powerful anxieties glowering on the international horizon in the unsettled strategic landscape of the late 1930s. Whether Americans looked out over the Atlantic or the Pacific late in the interwar era, the idea of "security" had never exclusively been economic or domestic.[9]

By the time the United States joined the ongoing war effort, devastation across the European landscape and the economic leverage offered by America's wartime boom combined to make the United States a willing leader in designing New Deal–style models for multilateral institutions for the postwar era. Charles Merriam, a political science professor working for the National Resources Planning Board (NRPB), observed in 1941 that

> there are two great objectives of democracies in the field of world relationships:
>
> 1. The security of a jural order for the world in which decisions are made on the basis of justice rather than violence.
> 2. The fullest development of the national resources of all nations and the fullest participation of all peoples in the gains of civilization.[10]

The linkage of these two sets of objectives in "world relationships" as a matter of public policy was a direct outgrowth of the perceived lessons of New Deal.

Lawyers and other Roosevelt administration officials who participated in the drafting and negotiating the terms of the UN Charter, the Bretton Woods charters, and the Nuremberg Charter later in the war often communicated among themselves and with other departments and officials, both in the United States and overseas, about what they thought they were doing and why. They tended to describe themselves as architects drawing up constitutive blueprints that would fill in concrete content behind abstract statements of freedoms and rights, using institutions to entrench and extend order, prosperity, and legitimacy. As a 1944 editorial in *The Nation* proclaimed, "Only a New Deal for the world, more far-reaching and consistent than our own faltering New Deal, can prevent the coming of World War III."[11]

"FREEDOM FROM FEAR AND WANT"

As early as the summer of 1940, FDR had been asked at a press conference how he might "write the next peace." He began to speak about this New Deal–infused agenda as a set of war aims, most notably in his January 1941 "Four Freedoms" State of the Union address and in his joint statement with British prime minister Winston Churchill, the "Atlantic Charter" of early August 1941.

In his Four Freedoms speech, Roosevelt described "four essential human freedoms" as needing to take effect "everywhere in the world" for true security to be possible. He called for "the protection of human rights—everywhere in the world." FDR elaborated: "Freedom means the supremacy of human rights everywhere. Our support goes to those who struggle to gain these rights or keep them."[12]

One noteworthy dimension of the Four Freedoms speech was accordingly its international scope. Presidential adviser Harry Hopkins noted that the repeated phrase "everywhere in the world" was perhaps too ambitious, "cover[ing] an awful lot of territory, Mr. President." He warned, "I don't know how interested Americans are going to be in the people of Java." "I'm afraid they'll have to be someday, Harry," a ruminative Roosevelt reportedly replied. "The world is getting so small that even the people in Java are getting to be our neighbors now."[13]

Later that year, Roosevelt was seeking to capitalize on the favorable attention the Four Freedoms speech had attracted by propounding, in his words, "some kind of public statement of the objectives in international relations in which the Government of the United States believed." The president indicated he was seeking to use the framework of the Four Freedoms to advance the cause of "keeping alive some principles of international law, some principles of moral and human decency" in both the United States and world public opinion. Although he was of course a lawyer himself, this was unusual language for Roosevelt, who rarely spoke about international law explicitly.[14]

The resulting Atlantic Charter soon became best known for its resonant evocation of the earlier Four Freedoms speech, a phrase about establishing a particular kind of postwar order —a peace "which will afford assurance that all the men in all the lands may live out their lives in freedom from fear and want." An early British draft of the proposed joint declaration described the document as a list of "certain principles which [Roosevelt and Churchill] both accept for guidance in the framing of their policy and on which they base their hopes for a better world." The Atlantic Charter purported to sketch a postwar world in broad strokes, calling for self-determination of peoples, freer trade, and several New Deal–style social welfare provisions. Released as a four-hundred-word telegram, the document also mentioned establishing "a wider and permanent system of general security"—the first reference in a bilateral document at this "high political" level to what would become the UN organization—as well as arms control and freedom of the seas.[15]

One of the more eyebrow-raising aspects of these proclamations was simply their timing: it was a rather risky step to be meeting with a foreign leader and invoking a postwar world, however aspirational, months before the United States was actually in the war. FDR was mindful that "the isolationists at home were screaming bloody murder," leading him to go so far as to leave behind a decoy Secret Service officer fishing in the Cape Cod Canal—complete with cigarette holder, pince-nez, and Fala the dog—while the president departed in secret for the site of the Atlantic Conference off the coast of Newfoundland. Sensitive to these American political constraints, British negotiators offered successive drafts that avoided formal treaty language or the suggestion of a military alliance.[16]

What legal scholar Edward Laing has called the Atlantic Charter's "flexible constitutional essence" also served as a focal point for movements promoting an expanded role for multilateral institutions. The Atlantic Charter prefigured the collective security articulated in the UN Charter, the rule-of-law orientation of the Nuremberg Charter, and even the Keynesian approach of the Bretton Woods charters. As noted, early planning memos for subsequent, detailed blueprints such as the charters of the UN, Nuremberg, and Bretton Woods all drew their inspiration and in many cases their broad provisions from the Atlantic Charter.[17]

The Atlantic Charter was part of an effort on Roosevelt's part to prepare the American public for an increasingly activist, multilateral foreign policy. In 1943, he expressed exasperation with what he perceived as his critics' literalism and negativity: 'I am everlastingly angry at those who assert vociferously that the four freedoms and the Atlantic Charter are nonsense because they are unattainable," commented FDR, in a peroration he wrote himself for a speech marking the end of the First Quebec Conference in August 1943. The president continued testily, "If these people had lived a century and a half ago they would have sneered and said that the Declaration of Independence was utter piffle."[18]

A number of US postwar planners did indeed seek to siphon off some drams of legitimacy from America's founding documents, at least rhetorically. Some analogized the Atlantic Charter to the Declaration of Independence and the subsequent set of more detailed institutional charters to the Constitution. Just as the young FDR had been an avid consumer of the strategic sea-power theories of Alfred Thayer Mahan (which drew heavily on analogies to ancient Rome), so too were these young New

Dealers designing road maps for the future by tracing over parchments from the past.

Roosevelt-hating journalist John Flynn wrote scornfully that the Atlantic Charter was a "fake document" that was "nothing more than a publicity stunt." Moreover, anti–New Dealers and anti-interventionists were by no means the only critics. By the end of the war, images of "war aims" and "what we are fighting for" had contributed to creating and raising expectations about the justice and legitimacy of any proposed postwar order in the United States and abroad. People around the world who heard or read FDR's words were inspired by them and often adapted speeches' underlying ideas to support their own struggles against racism, in favor of economic justice, or in support of more thoroughgoing international cooperation.[19]

As with the programs of the domestic New Deal, these initiatives aimed at a new postwar architecture may be defined as much by their omissions as by their inclusions. Their capacious designs and often ambiguous rhetoric ducked problems of colonial legacies and economic justice, as various energized constituencies had of course noted from the very beginning. The editor of a West African newspaper asked, "Are we fighting for security of Europeans to enjoy the four freedoms while West Africa continues on prewar status? We naturally feel we are entitled to know what we are fighting for, and are anxious to know what our position is to be in the coming new world order."[20]

This postwar institutional order may be framed as somewhat analogous to the domestic New Deal: it was both progressive and conservative, forward-looking and backward-looking, imaginative and hidebound, inflating and constricting global citizenship at the same time. Some critics of these postwar institutions have asserted that injustice and inequality were, in essence, baked into the cake of the postwar international order. Other critical voices in the United States—styling themselves "nationalists" or "unilateralists"—have continued to argue that these institutions simply gave away too much cake to others. Liberal internationalists, by contrast, have framed the weaknesses of these institutions as a kind of frosting that could somehow be scraped away and replaced. But the analogy itself highlights where both approaches are somewhat off-kilter: international systems are dynamic. They are not cakes; they are not any kind of object. Their dynamics reflect values and leadership, and when the values, leadership, and surrounding cultures alter, so do the workings of the systems.

THE MAXIMALIST VISION: "A NEW DEAL FOR THE WORLD"

Political scientists Daniel Duedney and John Ikenberry have recently referenced these "liberal internationalist organizations and regimes" of the New Deal as a kind of "third founding" for the United States.[21] In their estimation, "the greatness of the United States during the 'American Century' rested on a set of institutional foundations, both domestically and internationally." They continue: "At home, the Roosevelt revolution forged the modernized government that re-established economic growth, political legitimacy, and social peace. Abroad, the Roosevelt Administration, in winning World War II, established the United States as the pre-eminent great power in the international system and started putting into place the panoply of international organizations and regimes that make up the postwar liberal international order."[22] Historian Carol Anderson offers the important reminder that in addition to eliding the New Deal's exclusion of issues of racial justice on the domestic front, these kinds of sweeping assessments also map similar exclusions onto the Global South. It was nevertheless Roosevelt's personal vision, as well as the vision of others on the left wing of the New Deal, that such a social democratic system was premised on expanding to become more inclusive over time.[23]

More than this: ambitious international visions for security, stability, and accountability drew power from domestic ambitions. As legal scholar Cass Sunstein frames it, "the threat from Hitler and the Axis powers broadened the New Deal's commitment to security and strengthened the nation's appreciation of human vulnerability." In another section of his Four Freedoms speech, FDR had spelled out his ideas about the "basic things expected by our people of their political and economic systems." This list served as the basis for a more elaborate "Economic Bill of Rights" devised by one of the most aggressively progressive of the New Deal agencies, the NRPB, and widely reprinted in a pamphlet titled *Our Freedoms and Rights.* Charles Merriam, the NRPB's vice-chair, offered a summary of these "fundamentals which underlie a democratic program guaranteeing social justice" in his 1941 Godkin Lecture on Democracy at Harvard University. This Economic Bill of Rights, which included a right to education, health care, "a job at a fair wage," and "equal access to minimum security," was summarized by Merriam with the pious hope that "some day [*sic*] it will dawn upon us that all of the clauses in the Preamble to the Constitution are worth fighting for."[24]

Such a "renewed summation of the New Deal," in the words of another one of Roosevelt's speechwriters, marked what Sunstein explains as "a basis for a broadened understanding of what a nation would do if it were genuinely committed to ensuring the 'security' of its citizens. The threat to security from abroad was a reason to strengthen and rethink the idea of security at home." And vice versa: the maximalist multilateralist vision in the early World War II years had included a robust UN system capable of repelling aggression and a full World Trade Organization, along with the Nuremberg and Tokyo trials, which were meant to lead the way to a permanently sitting International Criminal Court. FDR saw the postwar UN as possibly having its own air force to constrain and punish aggressors. John Maynard Keynes's early drafts of the Bretton Woods institutions saw the World Bank and International Monetary Fund as global engines to reduce economic injustice. Francis Biddle, the primary American judge at the main Nuremberg trial, wrote to President Harry Truman in 1946 that "the time has now come to set about drafting a code of international criminal law" that would "reaffirm the principles of the Nuremberg Charter" and lay the groundwork for a permanently sitting international criminal court.[25]

By 1949, however, this maximalist vision had diminished considerably, at home and abroad. In one sense, perhaps this is a tale of institutional declension. On the international plane, grandiose visions such as a robustly functioning UN based on the sovereign equality of all states, a Bretton Woods system that would actually support development, and a permanently sitting International Criminal Court had given way to a series of paler and less ambitious measures, often bounded in both time and scope.

A set of miniaturized institutions had emerged as muffled echoes of these ambitious wartime blueprints: an ambitiously multilateral UN Relief and Rehabilitation Association (UNRRA) was wrapping up by 1947; substantial Marshall Plan aid to former European Allies (and not including the Soviet Union) was US-based and as much an instrument of geopolitical dominance as an aid to postwar reconstruction. Twelve slightly anemic subsequent Nuremberg trials were run exclusively by the Americans in 1946–49, in the wake of the flagship International Military Tribunal. The Bretton Woods agreement ginned up a wheezing mechanism of the General Agreement on Tariffs and Trade instead of Keynes's earlier vision of a more robust World Trade Organization, and regional security organizations such as the North Atlantic Treaty Organization

(NATO) grew up alongside the universalist UN as a partial replacement for an increasingly sclerotic UN.[26]

The expansive briefs of these postwar organizations quickly fell victim to rapidly changing circumstances. The UN Charter, for example, was out of date before the ink was dry on its fifty signatures. The charter and the resulting UN were unable either to anticipate or to respond in agile ways to three of the most tectonic shifts of the immediate postwar era. First, the advent of the most virulent phase of the Cold War—which might be dated from Winston Churchill's 1946 "Iron Curtain" speech—quickly reconfigured the international diplomatic landscape. Second, rapid decolonization meant that the initial pro-US majority in the UN General Assembly soon evaporated. Third, of course, was the advent of the nuclear age. International legal scholar José Alvarez has noted the irony of how "the United Nations, intended to institutionalize an effective collective security system, [became] the greatest state-producing device in the history of the world." The design of the UN had been hobbled by the unwillingness of its great-power founders to address the legacies of colonialism, economic injustice, or other violations of human rights with any vision of what it might mean for "democratizing" winds to blow both at home and abroad.[27]

Ambitions for the social democratic provisions of the New Deal were shrinking on the home front as well. The aspirations of the Economic Bill of Rights, discussed above, collided with the realities of an increasingly Republican-dominated Congress. Rather than an expansion of democracy—improving the well-being of an ever-wider swath of US citizens and the prospect for their participation—the key provisions of the Economic Bill of Rights emerged instead as a social welfare program: the Servicemen's Readjustment Act of 1944. Veterans were an easier sell to conservatives as "deserving" citizens who had sacrificed for the homeland. Better known as the GI Bill of Rights, the legislation included funding for mortgage assistance, education, business loans, medical care, and extended unemployment assistance. The GI Bill was in effect a shriveled version of the New Deal Economic Bill of Rights, with an echo of the latter's mission of increasing economic stability through reducing inequality. Roosevelt had envisioned various categories of civilians becoming eligible for GI Bill–type benefits over time in an ever-widening circle of inclusion, a process labeled "social citizenship" by the sociologist T. H. Marshall. To be sure, the veterans' program was a significant commitment: by 1948, almost half of US enrollees in higher education were GI Bill beneficiaries. As Ira Katznelson summarizes it, "no other New Deal initiative had as great an impact on changing the country."[28]

Nevertheless, part of the point of the GI Bill as enacted was exclusion. The price of its approval had been appeasing southern legislators with a system of local administration for the benefits, for example, which meant in practice that assistance to African American veterans was slowed to a trickle. Women veterans as well as those discharged dishonorably, or those discharged on an "undesirable" basis (often homosexuals), were also routinely denied. As historian Margot Canaday has argued, the workings of the GI Bill reinforced the image of the normative "first class" American citizen as male, white, and straight.[29]

And even this constricted demographic was a wee bit suspect, at least if those included were poor. Anxieties lingered from the World War I era that returning servicemen might turn into "roving armies of jobless veterans" like the ill-fated Bonus Army veterans who marched on Washington to demand early payment of a promised bonus during the Depression. Conservative legislators believed that rewarding veterans for their roles as breadwinners and family men would domesticate them in desirable ways, whereas extending benefits to others in need risked undermining the "moral fiber" of the country, in the words of one opponent of the New Deal, by encouraging "laziness," in the words of another such skeptic. Just as the Marshall Plan symbolized how far the United States had moved on from true multilateralism, so too the GI Bill suggested "how much further [Congress] had moved from New Deal aspirations to distribute state resources broadly among its citizenry," in Canaday's incisive assessment.[30]

PRESENT AT THE DESTRUCTION

The twenty-first-century incarnations of FDR's domestic opponents have been focused on dismantling the enduring legacies of the New Deal. What Donald Trump's former adviser Steve Bannon has called the "deconstruction" of the administrative state has long been a feature of some Republican agendas. Early policies have included inaugurating a poorly designed "Muslim ban," hollowing out the State Department, cutting various cabinet-level agencies, reducing taxes for the superwealthy, eviscerating public health and education programs, gutting the Voting Rights Act, deregulating polluters and predatory lenders, and building a wall to exclude outsiders—Trump's signature initiative—including asylum seekers.[31]

Reducing equality and access to resources while turning a blind eye to corruption is part of a process that is of course not limited to the United States. The United Kingdom, Hungary, Poland, Brazil, the Philippines, Nicaragua, Venezuela, and Russia, among others, are also slipping downward in what one investigative nongovernmental organization calls its "Freedom Index." Rather than a post–Cold War vision of democracy triumphant, the breakup of the Soviet Union seems to have resulted in rivulets of corruption and oligarchic practices seeping throughout the industrialized world—or perhaps more accurately, such practices becoming more widespread and acceptable where they already existed. That these aspects of the Russian model would prove to be more generalizable than the much-vaunted spread of democratizing forces is one by-product of abandoning equality as a focus for domestic policy.[32]

In the United States, this antigovernmentalism and whole-cloth opposition to the New Deal order at home is also reflected in a rending of the institutional fabric abroad. Ikenberry notes that "as their prospects dim, the willingness of the American public to support an ambitious American role in the world is understandably in decline." Once again, the outside reflects the inside. Fighting "globalists" has entailed withdrawal from the Paris climate accord, the Iran nuclear deal, the Intermediate-Range Nuclear Forces Treaty with Russia, as well as expressing a generalized hostility to multilateral institutions such as the UN, the International Criminal Court, and even NATO. Under the banner of "America First"—once the title of anti-Semite Gerald L. K. Smith's 1943 political party—Trump officials moved quickly to spin a narrative reframing human rights concerns as obstacles to national security interests, promoting what reporter Jackson Diehl has called "values-free foreign policy." Yet it is increasingly clear that support for perpetrators of massive human rights abuses further fuels anti-Americanism and highlights the role of the United States as an ever-more-unreliable ally. Or, as Ikenberry tartly summarizes it: "All across the horizon of international problem-solving and institution-building, the radical Right has diminished America's ability to lead."[33]

The pillars of collective security, economic stability, and rule of law support the edifice contemporary analysts are referencing when they say that the Trump administration is attacking the structure of the postwar order. Political scientists write of the "stickiness" of institutions, and these institutions, flawed as they are, nevertheless had the staying power to outlast the Cold War. It is precisely this stickiness that Trump and his associates are working to unglue. In their eager degradation of norms, institutions, and the careers of experienced personnel, Trump's policies are not serving to "drain the swamp," in the words of another well-known campaign slogan. Rather, this eager undermining of diplomacy and collaboration is rapidly draining away the very resource that one of FDR's Republican opponents, Wendell Willkie, described as "a gigantic reservoir of good will" toward the American people. "As I see it," Willkie elaborated over seventy-five years ago, "the existence of this reservoir is the biggest political fact of our time."[34] A parched and polluted puddle may soon be all that is left.

Inevitably, debates continue to unfold about the value of history—or, more specifically, the value of historians as commentators on contemporary affairs. Historians themselves often resist distilling "lessons of the past" as such a framing risks a too-thorough deracination from important context (see, for example, the ubiquitous and all-purpose "Lessons of Munich"). An objection to instrumentalizing the past elides the fact that on some level what we remember about the past is already instrumentalized by our choosing to memorialize it in books, statues, and museums.

Analysts of the past who steep themselves in the development of ideas, institutions, and practices of a variety of historical contexts may help us all critique, adapt, and apply interpretive principles in a variety of changing circumstances. The seemingly hegemonic power exerted by a regime of legal, institutional, and administrative ordering may be less about actual force and more about "its capacity to persuade that the world described in its image and categories is the *only* attainable world," in the words of legal historian Robert Gordon. A deeper understanding of the origins, theory, and deployment of the concepts and terms that underlie today's international politics may sharpen the caliber of analysis and—at least potentially—expand the moral and policy imagination to envision other worlds. All good history does this.[35]

A number of what we might call "prescriptive principles" emerge from this chapter's framing of the outward projection of the New Deal as grand strategy. This label is carefully chosen for its implicit limits: prescriptive ideas are meant at most as default suggestions, to be weighed and then adapted or dismissed as circumstances warrant. Even more provisional than the older notion of "rules of thumb"—now presumably disfavored for its unsavory gender history—prescriptive principles may help to navigate the shifting boundary between wider applicability and relevant context, between universality and rootedness, between norms and facts.

First of all, we have the prescriptive ideas that FDR and his staff took from their own assessments of the perceived failures of the World War I era—a time when many of them were already active participants in policy-making. Among other guidelines, numbers of them (Harold Ickes, Henry Morgenthau Jr., and Adolf Berle, to name a few) distilled the following, according to their public papers and memoirs:

- **Mistakes were made:** American planners in the World War II era communicated quite openly about the settlement in the wake of World War I as serving as a kind of reverse playbook or mirror image of sound policy and diplomacy. Bluntly, World War I had led to World War II, and so that earlier postwar order was self-evidently not very robust, in their eyes. In trying to salvage a usable past from the previous twenty-plus years, some of them arguably overcompensated: if earlier responses were "soft-hearted" or "sentimental," then New Dealers had to be sure to seem hard-headed and pragmatic—to the exclusion of many useful approaches from the earlier era.

- **Start planning for the peace during the war:** A weary postwar society is predictably going to want to demobilize and resume "normal" civilian life as soon as possible. Calls to win the war "first" before figuring out postwar architecture ought to be avoided; postwar plans already on the shelf before the war actually ends will likely be more influential. Accordingly, such planning was well under way by 1942 by at least thirty-five governmental agencies, not to mention many more private groups (clergy, industrial and trade associations, other civil society groups).

- **Make your peace plans sticky:** In the World War I era, a Democratic president's postwar plans were undone to a large degree by domestic opposition spearheaded by angry Republicans shut out of the process. Wilson did not bring a single Republican with him to the Paris Peace Conference, for example. By contrast, Roosevelt moved quickly to include domestic rivals in postwar planning, most notably by taking the venerable Republican statesman Henry Stimson into his cabinet as secretary of war.

- **Develop supportive public opinion through an "influential middle":** Attention and resources are well deployed when devoted to setting goals for armed conflict that will appeal to ordinary people. The domestic propaganda model from World War I relied more on slick advertising and deference to local leaders, such as the "Four Minute Men," who delivered short and well-vetted speeches in movie theaters and other crowded places. By contrast, the Office of War Information adopted an already popular series of images, not originating with a government agency, to serve as the visual symbol for war bond campaigns: Norman Rockwell's *Four Freedoms* series famously served to process abstractions in a way that was meaningful to many citizens who would normally have little or no interest in foreign affairs.
- **Ideas can be a powerful hook:** A newly expanded role for public opinion also meant that publicity campaigns might also become hostages to their own inspirational rhetoric: a State Department initiative to cultivate interest and enthusiasm for a new UN organization meant that an early draft of its charter, known as the Dumbarton Oaks conversations, was widely read in schools, by church groups, by women's organizations, and by other civil society groups. Many of these entities promptly expressed their disappointment at the draft's silence on human rights issues and on decolonization, among other perceived weaknesses and problems. Although this widely expressed discord was clearly annoying to State Department officials, even their half-hearted attempts to address some of these critiques in the final version of the UN Charter helped make it (a little) stronger than it might otherwise have been.

Second, we have a set of prescriptive principles that numbers of subsequent historians have drawn from the World War II reordering, which might include:

- **Spread around decision-making authority—even just a little:** British negotiators at the Bretton Woods conference would occasionally ask why the representatives of so many "small" nations were present; American organizers would joke about "inviting along the Cubans for the cigars." Racist jocularity aside, some of the more junior staff clearly understood that the willingness to consult with others before deciding was not a giveaway of authority but rather a sign of strength. One weakness of the League of Nations system, for example, had been that parties without much of a stake in the system had every incentive to kick over the table.

- **You can invest in future stability:** Keynesian ideas about "investing" in prosperity and stability for future, longer-term benefits were reflected at least partially in the 1948 Marshall Plan, for example, where short-term aid helped rebuild the postwar economies of some US allies. Marshall Plan aid bound many of the allied states in Western Europe more firmly into the US orbit, but its legislation would arguably never have passed in subsequent congresses where even Marshall aid would likely have been framed as an unwarranted "giveaway" of US resources.
- **Institutions are more effective when they are both forward- and backward-looking:** Even with all its flaws and shortcomings, the main Nuremberg trial of 1945–46 was arguably one of the more successful pieces of denazification policy. By contrast, the very similarly designed Tokyo trial of 1946–49 is usually judged more harshly. Among myriad reasons for this contrast, one is that the Tokyo process traded away too much legitimacy in its eagerness to create a governable Japanese ally (e.g., in refusing to try the Japanese emperor). This orientation toward the Pacific region's Cold War future interfered with the trial's ability to address past injustices.
- **Pluralism and inclusivity are strengths:** In the 1940s, State Department officials in particular were irritated by calls for what we would now call "inclusivity," many of which were intended more as window dressing than anything. Still, there were some gestures, such as including women and African Americans among the advisers to the US delegation to the San Francisco Conference to negotiate the UN Charter. American propagandists understood on some level that pluralism was an important component of the values that made the United States different from, and superior to, the values of the Third Reich. The formula of the World War II–era "buddy movie" suggested

as much: the Iowa farm boy and the tough Brooklyn kid may have overcome their differences in the foxhole, even if it was still a bridge too far to include an African American pal in the mix in a still-segregated army. Part of what made the Nazis weak, by contrast, was their crabbed vision of citizenship and belonging.

- **What might the unintended consequences be?** Just because you look to the future does not mean you can predict the future. The example of the UN Charter's inability to take into account a changing international landscape suggests that retooling/reviving ideas about social democracy that once captured the imaginations of many Americans is only one part of a new approach to policy that must address climate change, flows of migrants and money, and pandemics—all inherently transnational phenomena that will need robust, coordinated, strategic management.

And finally, we have a growing roster of possible prescriptive principles historians and other analysts are distilling in real time from our post–Cold War and increasingly populist moment:

- **Norms collapse more easily than they are built:** Institutions may be "sticky," as noted above, but they are not infinitely sticky. As cultures shift, so too do norms. Cultural change can help to degrade pernicious norms and laws such as the exclusion of lesbian, gay, bisexual, and transgender people from the full rights of citizenship. Yet veterans and Holocaust survivors from the World War II era, among others, have been noting of late that norm erosion can also work to degrade a favorable environment for civility, pluralism, and even democracy. Politics as usual may be frustrating or even boring, but that does not mean that reality show–style politicking is a good substitute.

- **Forgetting about inequality is a huge problem,** both domestically and internationally. As a recent report from the International Committee for the Red Cross worried, attention to spiking inequality from Appalachia to Gaza is imperative lest the Four Freedoms become the Four Famines. We seem to need to periodically relearn the lesson that the most important builders of democracy are well-fed, well-educated, and employed citizens with a stake in their own society.

- **Forgetting about accountability is also a huge problem,** both domestically and internationally. The study of history helps here again as well. In the United States, giving up on accountability in the Reconstruction era helped to usher in the era of Jim Crow, underlining the need to "clean the wound" before transitional justice—or any kind of justice—might help to heal a postconflict society. In Cambodia, Prime Minister Hun Sen argued that "poking at the wound" of past atrocities is a bad idea; the Trump administration's early move to abolish the Office of Global Criminal Justice similarly suggested that shrugging and moving on would be its preferred approach to reckoning with past injustice. An old wound may not always hurt, but it weakens the body politic.
- **Cultivating allies matters:** Many of Britain's Brexiteer diplomats seemed surprised by the United Kingdom's isolation and diminished bargaining power once they made it clear that Britain was no longer part of the future of the European Union. Similar disappointments may be in store for US diplomats fresh from lecturing South Korea and Japan to pull up their socks and support "their own" security. If China were to seize Taiwan, for example, as the former has long threatened, stalwart Pacific Rim allies may soon be in high demand.
- **Leadership also matters:** Such thinking has been a signal contribution of Yale University's Brady-Johnson Program in Grand Strategy. In an era where quantifiable indicia of success dominate the academic analysis of politics, the risk that what cannot be counted therefore "doesn't count" is, sadly, unquantifiable. The motivating power of a Green New Deal, for example, may draw as much from inspirational leaders who help people look to the future as it does from the specifics of promising-sounding programs.

"IMMUNE FROM THE GREAT CATARACT OF NONSENSE"

The Greek historian Dionysius famously asserted that "history is philosophy teaching by examples." In addition to helping us expand our own political imaginations, the study of history may also offer some analytic distance and perspective on our own contemporary assumptions, approaches, and aspirations.

In what might serve as a bookend to the Vonnegut quote about planning for the future that opened this chapter, the British novelist, poet, and literary critic C. S. Lewis wrote, "Most of all, perhaps, we need intimate knowledge of the past." He continued: "A man who has lived in many places is not likely to be deceived by the errors of his native village: the scholar has lived in many times and is therefore in some degree immune from the great cataract of nonsense that pours from the press and microphone of his own age."[36] In other words, studying the past may help citizens, scholars, and officials alike to serve as our own "secretaries of the future." Vonnegut's quote was actually part of a drawing in some hitherto unpublished notebooks. As part of the self-same image, the novelist and political commentator also offered a sobering reminder of the costs of failing to factor in the perceptions of other parties that will inevitably affect the outcomes of any strategic planning, however intricate or bold. His admonition about how "there ought to have been" a secretary of the future is etched on the side of a bomb plummeting toward earth—too late for the planning, too late for the future.

NOTES

1 Kurt Vonnegut, *Armageddon in Retrospect: New and Unpublished Writings on War and Peace* (New York: G. P. Putnam's Sons, 2008), n.p. but near 47.

2 On FDR as improvisational, see Warren F. Kimball, *The Juggler: Franklin Roosevelt as Wartime Statesman* (Princeton, NJ: Princeton University Press, 1994). On FDR as seeking to avoid the perceived mistakes of Woodrow Wilson, see Elizabeth Borgwardt, *A New Deal for the World: America's Vision for Human Rights* (hereafter *NDFW*) (Cambridge, MA: Belknap Press of Harvard University Press, 2005), especially ch. 1, "The Ghost of Woodrow Wilson."

3 Roosevelt and his advisers tended to use the term "New Deal" very loosely—as did their many enemies—to refer to "the duty of government to use the combined resources of the nation to prevent distress and to promote the general welfare of all the people." On expanding the idea of national security, see Borgwardt, *NDFW*, 7ff.

4 See, e.g., Or Rosenboim, *The Emergence of Globalism: Visions of World Order in Britain and the United States, 1939–1950* (Princeton, NJ: Princeton University Press, 2017), and Daniel Deudney and G. John Ikenberry, "Unraveling America the Great," *American Prospect* 11 no. 5 (March 15, 2016).

5 See especially Roger Fisher's *Beyond Machiavelli: Tools for Coping with Conflict* (coauthored with Elizabeth Borgwardt and Andrea Schneider) (Cambridge, MA: Harvard University Press, 1994), an elaboration on the approaches presented in his *Getting to Yes: Negotiating Agreement without Giving In* (coauthored

with William Ury and Bruce Patton), 2nd ed. (New York: Penguin, 1991), and based on Fisher's consulting experience on conflicts in El Salvador, Guatemala, Cyprus, Iran, and elsewhere.

6 On the cabining of sovereignty, see Kal Rustiala, "Sovereignty and Multilateralism," *Chicago Journal of International Law* 1, no. 2 (2000) (revised as UCLA School of Law, Law-Econ Working Paper No. 2000–01, last revised May 19, 2017). On the early days of the Trump administration's relationship to the neoliberal world order, see Wolfgang Streeck, "Trump and the Trumpists," *Inference: International Review of Science* 3, no. 1 (2017).

7 Kiran Klaus Patel, *The New Deal: A Global History* (Princeton, NJ: Princeton University Press, 2016), reminds us that many of these New Deal social welfare programs were inspired by European models. See also Wolfgang Schivelbusch, *Three New Deals: Reflections on Roosevelt's America, Mussolini's Italy, and Hitler's Germany, 1933–1939* (New York: Picador, 2006), and Daniel Rodgers, *Atlantic Crossings: Social Politics in a Progressive Age* (Cambridge, MA: Belknap Press of Harvard University Press, 1998).

8 Patel, *Global New Deal,* 74; Ira Katznelson, *Fear Itself: The New Deal and the Origins of Our Time* (New York: Liveright 2013); Barton J. Bernstein, "The Conservative Achievements of Liberal Reform," in *Toward a New Past: Dissenting Essays in American History,* ed. Barton J. Bernstein (New York: Pantheon, 1968).

9 Borgwardt, *NDFW,* 7; Schivelbusch, *Three New Deals* (on projecting power as part of a New Deal aesthetic), introduction and ch. 5, "Public Works."

10 Quoted in Borgwardt, *NDFW,* 52.

11 Freda Kirchwey, "A Program of Action," *The Nation,* March 11, 1944, 300.

12 Franklin Delano Roosevelt, "Annual Message to Congress, Jan. 6, 1941," available online in text and audio at http://www.americanrhetoric.com/speeches/fdrthefourfreedoms.htm. For text of the 1941 Atlantic Charter, see the appendix to Borgwardt, *NDFW.*

13 Sherwood, *Roosevelt and Hopkins,* 231.

14 Hadley Cantril, letter of March 20, 1941 (to Anna Rosenberg for the President), quoted in Borgwardt, *NDFW* at 21, 29.

15 Sherwood, *Roosevelt and Hopkins,* 350.

16 "1st British Draft" in FDR's handwriting, dated August 10, 1941, Franklin D. Roosevelt Presidential Library, Hyde Park, NY.

17 Edward Laing, "Relevance of the Atlantic Charter for a New World Order," *Indian Journal of International Law* 29, no. 3/4 (December 1989): 298–325; George B. Galloway, *Postwar Planning in the United States* (New York: Twentieth Century Fund, 1942). On the Bretton Woods charters as Keynesian, see, e.g., Benn Steil, *The Battle of Bretton Woods: John Maynard Keynes, Harry Dexter White and the Making of a New World Order* (Princeton, NJ: Princeton University Press, 2013).

18 FDR quoted in Samuel Rosenman, *Working with Roosevelt* (London: Rupert Hart-Davis, 1952), 387.

19 John T. Flynn, *The Roosevelt Myth* (New York: Devin-Adair, 1948), 386. On various groups adopting FDR's rhetoric for their own purposes, see Borgwardt, *NDFW,* 34–35. For a discussion of some analogous expectations raised in various quarters around the world by Woodrow Wilson's World War I–era aspirational rhetoric, see Erez Manela, *The Wilsonian Moment: Self-Determination and the International Origins of Anticolonial Nationalism* (Oxford: Oxford University Press, 2009).

20 "From the editor of the *North African Pilot* to Mr. Winston Churchill, November 15, 1941," quoted in George Padmore, "Nigeria Questions Intent of Atlantic Charter," *Chicago Defender,* January 31, 1942. See also Carol Anderson, "A New Deal for (Most of) the World," review of Elizabeth Borgwardt, *A New Deal for the World,* H-Peace, H-Net Reviews, August 2006, https://networks.h-net.org/node/19206/reviews/19341/anderson-borgwardt-new-deal-world-americas-vision-human-rights.

21 Daniel Duedney and G. John Ikenberry, "Unraveling America the Great," *American Interest* 11, no. 5 (March 15, 2016).

22 Duedney and Ikenberry, "Unraveling America." The first two foundings were the framing of the Constitution, premised on the sovereignty of the people, and the expansion of citizenship heralded by the Reconstruction Amendments in the wake of the American Civil War.

23 Anderson, "New Deal for (Most of) the World." On Roosevelt's preferences, see Margot Canaday, *The Straight State: Sexuality and Citizenship in Twentieth-Century America* (Princeton, NJ: Princeton University Press, 2012), 143–44.

24 Cass Sunstein, *The Second Bill of Rights: FDR's Unfinished Revolution and Why We Need It More than Ever* (New York: Basic Books, 2004); National Resources Planning Board, "After the War—Toward Security: Freedom from Want," September 1942, President's Secretary's File (PSF), Postwar Planning, Franklin D. Roosevelt Presidential Library, Hyde Park, NY. See also James T. Kloppenberg, "Franklin D. Roosevelt: Visionary" (review of Borgwardt, *New Deal for the World,* and Sunstein, *Second Bill of Rights*), *Reviews in American History* 34 (December 2006), 509–20, and Borgwardt, *NDFW,* 51–52.

25 Rosenman, *Working with Roosevelt,* 264; Sunstein, *Second Bill of Right.* Biddle quoted in Elizabeth Borgwardt, "'Constitutionalizing' Human Rights: The Rise and Rise of the Nuremberg Principles," in *The Human Rights Revolution: An International History,* ed. Akira Iriye, Petra Goedde, and William Hitchcock (Oxford: Oxford University Press, 2012), 75.

26 On UNRRA, see Jessica Reinisch, "Internationalism in Relief: The Birth (and Death) of UNRRA," *Past and Present* 210, supp. 6 (January 2011): 258–89. On the Marshall Plan, see Ben Steil, *The Marshall Plan: Dawn of the Cold War* (New York: Simon & Schuster, 2018). On the subsequent Nuremberg trials, see Kevin Jon Heller, *The Nuremberg Military Tribunals and the Origins of International Criminal Law* (Oxford: Oxford University Press, 2012). On the Bretton Woods institutions, see Benn Steil, *The Battle of Bretton Woods: John Maynard Keynes, Harry Dexter White, and the Making of a New World*

Order (Princeton, NJ: Princeton University Press, 2013), and Eric Rauchway, *The Money Makers: How Roosevelt and Keynes Ended the Depression, Defeated Fascism, and Secured a Prosperous Peace* (New York: Basic Books, 2015). On NATO, see Timothy Andrews Sayle, *Enduring Alliance: A History of NATO and the Postwar Global Order* (Ithaca, NY: Cornell University Press, 2019).

27 Winston S. Churchill, "The Sinews of Peace" (Iron Curtain speech), Westminster College, Fulton, MO (March 5, 1946), audio available at winstonchurchill .org; José E. Alvarez, "Multilateralism and Its Discontents," *European Journal of International Law* 11, no. 2 (2000): 395; Mark Mazower, *No Enchanted Palace: The End of Empire and the Ideological Origins of the United Nations* (Princeton, NJ: Princeton University Press, 2009). Critical analysts of international law and politics such as Mazower and Samuel Moyn have joined such venerable critics as Richard Falk and Noam Chomsky to warn that a predatory neoliberalism was the point of many of these ideas from the very outset. See generally Ibrahim J. Gassama, "A World Made of Violence and Misery: Human Rights as a Failed Project of Liberal Internationalism," *Brooklyn Journal of International Law* 37, no. 2 (2012): 407–58. Other equally trenchant critics such as Martti Koskenniemi are starting to reframe some of the harshest critiques as somewhat overstated. See, e.g., Martti Koskenniemi, "The Many Faces of Sovereignty: Introduction to Critical Legal Thinking," *Kutafin University Law Review* 4, no. 2 (2017): 282–91.

28 On "deserving" citizens, see Canaday, *Straight State,* 142, 144. T. H. Marshall quoted in Canaday, 140; Katznelson quoted in Canaday, 141. See also Kathleen J. Frydl, *The GI Bill* (Cambridge: Cambridge University Press, 2009).

29 Canaday, *Straight State,* 141.

30 Canaday, 152, 168, in a chapter that includes an extensive discussion of the "domestication" of returning servicemen.

31 See Brian Beutler, "Steve Bannon Is Not Your Friend," *New Republic,* August 22, 2017, and Roger Cohen, "The Desperation of Our Diplomats: Why Is Trump Hollowing Out the State Department?," *New York Times,* July 28, 2017.

32 "Democracy in Retreat 2019," with the subsection "The United States in Decline," noting that the countries with the closest tallies to the United States on its metrics are Belize, Croatia, Greece, Latvia, and Mongolia. Freedom House Report, freedomhouse.org/report/freedom-world/freedom-world-2019. See also Franklin Foer, "Russian-Style Kleptocracy Is Infiltrating America," *The Atlantic,* March 2019.

33 Diehl quoted in Sarah B. Snyder, "Is the Trump Administration Abandoning Human Rights?," *Washington Post,* July 2, 2017. Duedney and Ikenberry, "Unraveling America the Great."

34 Wendell L. Willkie, *One World* (New York: Simon & Schuster, 1943), 284.

35 Robert W. Gordon, "Critical Legal Histories," *Stanford Law Review* 36 (January 1984): 109; italics added. On historians as commentators on contemporary events, see Moshik Temkin, "Historians Shouldn't Be Pundits," *New York*

Times, June 26, 2017, and Julian Zelizer and Morton Keller, "Why (Some) Historians Should Be Pundits," *The Atlantic,* June 26, 2017. On the additional dimensions to the analysis of policy that may be offered by the study of history, see, e.g., Margaret MacMillan, *The Use and Abuse of History* (London: Profile, 2010).

36 C. S. Lewis, *The Weight of Glory and Other Addresses* (New York: Macmillan, 1949), 50–51. The excellent essay by Cian O'Driscoll, "Divisions within the Ranks? The Just War Tradition and the Use and Abuse of History," *Ethics & International Affairs* 27, no. 1 (2013): 47–65, led me to the Lewis quote and the one from Dionysius.

CHAPTER 2

SACEUR as Statesman

Politico-Military Leadership in NATO, 1951–67

SETH GIVENS

The North Atlantic Treaty Organization is the manifestation and guarantor of the liberal order that the West built in the wake of World War II, based on the concept of collective security and economic interdependence of like-minded nations. It was and remains an alliance formed to prevent war, and yet it is more than just a military alliance. NATO was, after all, a response to a European belief that US involvement in the continent's affairs beyond just an economic program or military aid was necessary to resist an overwhelming Soviet military and political threat to Western order.[1] The supranational basis of NATO became the foundation for the restoration of Europe, providing stability that underwrote economic and political recovery.

In his influential 1962 work *NATO: The Entangling Alliance,* Robert Osgood argued that the organization is inherently politico-military for three reasons: its military posture is political warfare in a test of wills, its members subordinate independent control of their own forces in exchange for consultation and cooperation, and its strategy is the means by which allies exert political influence on their enemies and each other.[2] As NATO's highest military authority, the supreme allied commander Europe (SACEUR) is the expression of this politico-military intersection. While at once a military leader, strategist, logistician, tactician, public relations agent, and business manager, any one of the SACEURs from 1951 to 1967 was also a diplomat and statesman. Interacting with national leaders and their cabinets as an official without nationality, these five generals forged a new role in a grand experiment of international politics, as proconsuls who answered to a multinational body. This chapter analyzes who the first SACEURs were, how they waged political warfare and acted as diplomats, and the ways in which they steered NATO in the pursuit of international cooperation and collective security. Doing so helps us understand a foundational era of the postwar order, from 1949 to 1967, when generals were also statesmen.

EISENHOWER (APRIL 2, 1951–MAY 30, 1952)

In the mere fourteen months that Dwight Eisenhower served as SACEUR, he helped transform NATO from a concept into a military alliance, giving form to the mutual defense arrangements that the Western powers envisioned when they signed the Brussels Treaty in March 1948 and the North Atlantic Treaty in April 1949.[3] He did so through contingency plans and organization as well as forming Supreme Headquarters Allied Powers Europe (SHAPE), the alliance's military command structure. Yet he also played a pivotal role in convincing Western capitals to invest in their defense at a time when the public worried about triggering another cataclysmic war. Aware that he was involved in "the most delicate military task of [his] career" and doing more than building a Western army, he constructed an ideology of common defense by urging alliance members to overcome their national aspirations, mistrusts, and resentments.[4] These challenges required the forthrightness of a military leader and the political vision and diplomatic skill of a statesman.

In an unprecedented example of transatlantic cooperation, it was a broad consensus among the twelve founding NATO members that led to Eisenhower becoming the inaugural SACEUR. By the end of 1950, Western capitals realized the global threat of communism necessitated building a NATO force that answered to a permanent multinational headquarters.[5] The Soviets now had nuclear weapons, and United Nations (UN) troops were in retreat in Korea. In the United States, isolationists opposed allocating manpower and money for the defense of Western Europe. European nations still struggled economically from the effects of World War II, and few governments could agree on how to defend territory that stretched from the Arctic Circle to the Mediterranean. If Josef Stalin's Soviet Union decided to invade Western Europe, those nations had no NATO command structure. Its ten army divisions and 370 aircraft were also a paltry defense against Moscow's 175 divisions and 14,000 aircraft.[6] European leaders concluded that only Eisenhower and his experience of holding together a multinational force during World War II was equipped for the challenge.

Eisenhower did not agree. He believed the intense lobbying from Europe and the White House for him to lead SHAPE was because no one had faith that the experiment would work.[7] Nonetheless, he accepted the position—taking a leave of absence from his presidency of Columbia University in January 1951—and became the concurrent commander of United States European Command (EUCOM). Fortifying words from US leaders likely offered little comfort. President Harry Truman warned Eisenhower that he would face "imponderable forces" like "pride of race and blood" and "national jealousies." W. Averell Harriman advised him that his "job will be far more civil than it is military."[8] After New Year's Day 1951, Eisenhower left New York for Europe, soon meeting leaders of every NATO member nation. He listened to European concerns and communicated his confidence in their ability to meet the manifold challenges.

When Eisenhower assumed command in April, he had two immediate tasks: to build a headquarters and to formulate defense plans. Rather than creating SHAPE out of whole cloth, he used existing staffs and structures. In 1948, the five Brussels Treaty nations—the Benelux countries, Britain, and France—had formed the forerunner to NATO, the Western Union Defense Organization (WUDO), though it had no troops or authority in peacetime. As one NATO officer put it in 1956, all that stood between the Red Army and the English Channel during those days "was a group of committees."[9] The WUDO had spent its energy drafting plans. Crucially, those contingencies and the group's organization provided SHAPE with an already functioning international staff that had contemplated important questions about defense.[10]

Eisenhower chose Field Marshal Bernard Montgomery as his deputy supreme commander, allaying fears that the Americans would dominate the body. For chief of staff, he selected Lt. Gen. Alfred Gruenther, US Army, his former deputy chief of staff during the invasion of North Africa. Choosing subordinate commanders for the three regional commands required a delicate balance between military necessity and allied parochial and political concerns. The British wanted one of their officers to lead NATO's maritime commands. The French, mistrusting the British and West Germans, insisted one of their generals lead NATO forces on the continent.[11] Eisenhower knew the importance of the central sector from both a military and political perspective and took personal control of Allied Forces Central Europe but then appointed two Frenchmen, Marshal Alphonse Juin and Vice Adm. Robert Jaujard, as his land and naval commanders. Lt. Gen. Lauris Norstad, US Air Force, served as air commander. Recognizing Britain's traditional role as a naval power, Eisenhower made Adm. Patrick Brind commander in chief of Allied Forces Northern Europe, though London would have preferred the Mediterranean command. To overcome national divisions, he urged everyone within SHAPE to develop a higher patriotism for cause and alliance.[12]

Eisenhower had to convince NATO members that a defense of Europe was possible—a tough sell so soon after two devastating wars. He toured Europe tirelessly, meeting with national leaders and their cabinets.[13] Expanding allied contributions to NATO would have an obvious military effect of providing SHAPE with manpower, but it had the more important political effect of tying together the alliance members. Though a Soviet rout of allied forces from the German frontier to the English Channel was a possibility, Eisenhower and most American officials believed the overriding threat to Europe was the political disintegration of the West. In a bid for political conquest, Moscow supported its active subversion of governments with threats of force. The leftist movements in Italy and France gaining momentum assisted Stalin's meddling.[14] His principal task, then, was to build confidence in NATO as an Atlantic military alliance that could deter Soviet aggression and domestic political aggravation. Doing so would provide Europeans with a sense of security and therefore an alternative to acquiescing to Moscow's threats. Eisenhower believed that European political integration would follow military integration—a European army would set the foundation for a United States of Europe. The concept of NATO therefore rested on power politics, at the center of which was its military chief.[15]

Eisenhower knew that his public and private comments had to advance the political and economic unification of Europe.[16] In this regard, his biggest test as SACEUR came in trying to sell the idea of West German rearmament and inclusion in NATO.[17] He understood that a settlement of the

German question had to be found within a European framework. Whatever that solution was, NATO would underwrite it. This fell into line with the Truman administration's containment strategy, which sought to avoid German neutrality through revitalizing the country and incorporating it into Western political and military structures.[18] Since 1945, US officials had desired a capable Europe that would permit an American extrication from the continent. German involvement in European defense and politics became the linchpin in that plan. The idea did not pick up momentum until fighting began in Korea in June 1950, however, which recast European defense in a global light.[19] As SACEUR, Eisenhower argued that the United States could not be "a modern Rome guarding the far frontiers with our legions if for no other reason than because these are *not,* politically, *our* frontiers."[20] The French ultimately outmaneuvered Eisenhower and the Americans on the German question with the European Defense Community (EDC), a modified version of Paris's bid in late 1950 to create a supranational European army that maintained French sovereignty and German suzerainty.[21] Though the EDC was France's explicit attempt to control Bonn's rearmament, Eisenhower claimed success on the grounds that the organization reinforced SHAPE.[22]

Eisenhower's time as SACEUR culminated with the first North Atlantic Council (NAC) meeting at Lisbon in February 1952.[23] There the new supreme political body of NATO set an ambitious goal for the alliance at fifty army divisions, four thousand aircraft, and 704 combat vessels by year's end and double those numbers by 1955. Greece and Turkey also joined NATO during the conference, expanding the alliance to fourteen members. For Eisenhower, these goals were illustrative pledges from members to build the force structure for which he had lobbied. He therefore left Europe in May 1952 having accomplished turning NATO from a concept into an alliance. His successors would have to deal with the details of implementation. A paragon of integrity during World War II who demanded the separation of military and political authority within a large coalition, as SACEUR Eisenhower so effectively merged the two that it became difficult to separate them.

RIDGWAY (MAY 30, 1952–JULY 11, 1953)

Matthew Ridgway succeeded Eisenhower as SACEUR on May 30, 1952. He was an excellent field commander whose efforts stabilizing the UN effort in Korea convinced Truman he would succeed in Europe, but Ridgway struggled in his new role as a politico-military leader. He was sincere but blunt and lacked patience or inclination for diplomacy. The key feature of the Ridgway era was that of a leader who, despite his best efforts to focus on military matters, could not escape the political and economic issues facing him, from EDC ratification to European economic difficulties and sensitivity to American influence and power.[24]

It was not supposed to be that way. Apart from deciding force goals, the NAC had agreed at the Lisbon Conference to organizational changes that would delineate political and military authority. Permanent representatives with the rank of ambassador were to replace council deputies who had limited scope and power since their introduction in May 1950 and lead national delegations in permanent session in Paris.[25] To manage the growing civilian agencies and staff in the NAC, the allies agreed to create the position of secretary-general to serve as chief international diplomat. As head of the International Secretariat and chairman of the NAC, the secretary-general ostensibly would give SHAPE the ability to focus on military issues. The first secretary-general, Lord Ismay, was capable and accomplished but did not aspire to control NATO.[26] Even if he had had such desires, the intertwined politico-military nature of the alliance meant that national leaders still required nearly constant consultation with the SACEUR. The result was that Ridgway found himself in more fraught political territory than he desired.

As a harbinger of Ridgway's time as SACEUR, the Europeans made it known that they preferred the affable and diplomatic Gruenther as Eisenhower's successor. They did not doubt Ridgway's accomplishments on the battlefield—indeed, that was one of the reasons they were wary of him. His martial background concerned Europeans that the new SACEUR would pursue war, not peace.[27] Chairman of the Joint Chiefs of Staff (JCS) Omar Bradley had recommended Ridgway to the White House, though, and Truman wagered that SHAPE had put together a competent team. Truman thought that Gruenther, who continued to serve as deputy, could make up for Ridgway's political shortcomings.[28]

Ridgway spent June 1952 traveling and meeting with allied leaders. His task was to put flesh on the bone of the alliance but not before taking on issues of command that grew out of the expansion of NATO. In Southern Europe, Ridgway had to modify the command structure to accommodate Greece and

Turkey.[29] This was easier said than done, as he had to take into consideration how the expansion in the theater would affect Britain's prestige in the Mediterranean. Contrary to popular narratives about the postwar order, the British still retained considerable power on the world stage and were not yet a junior partner to the United States.[30] The British argued at the December 1952 ministerial meeting that the Mediterranean and the Suez Canal were crucial to their empire. They chafed at serving under an American, Adm. Robert B. Carney, and lobbied for a new, British-led command coequal to the SACEUR and the position of supreme allied commander Atlantic (SACLANT), which NATO created in January 1952 with an American at the helm. It was one of Ridgway's most trying diplomatic tasks, as talks involved Churchill and Truman with their defense ministers. The two sides compromised, making the new British-led command subordinate to SHAPE.[31]

On the question of where to place the Greek and Turkish forces, current command structures would have them under the commander of Allied Land Forces Southern Europe (LANDSOUTH), an Italian general with headquarters in northern Italy who answered to the commander of Allied Forces Southern Europe (AFSOUTH). This stretched the lines of communication a thousand miles, and also put the new NATO allies under command of a people they had fought during World War II. Ridgway's solution was to create a whole new subcommand, Allied Land Forces Southeastern Europe. The issue necessitated Ridgway making multiple trips to Italy, Greece, and Turkey. This was not insignificant, since it meant acting as an intermediary between old enemies who were now the anchor of NATO's southeastern line. He ultimately succeeded and managed a public relations and diplomatic feat when he oversaw a meeting near the Greek-Turkish border that resulted in senior officers shaking hands.[32]

In Central Command, issues of friction over personalities and national ambition remained. During his conversations with Eisenhower after arriving in Paris in May 1952, Ridgway criticized Central Command for being the only command led by a triumvirate. Eisenhower explained that this was "a reflection of politics" and Ridgway must understand that being SACEUR required military knowledge but also "a great amount of diplomacy."[33] Marshal Juin and French officials still coveted the position of commander of Central Europe Command, which Eisenhower had taken for himself. Knowing that commanding NATO's central front would put undue strain on SHAPE in the event of war, Ridgway stepped aside and promoted Juin.

He also promoted Lauris Norstad from commander of Allied Air Forces Central Europe to SHAPE as air deputy, satisfying the US Air Force, which wanted someone who could request the use of Strategic Air Command from the SACEUR.[34]

With SHAPE's organizational problems mitigated, Ridgway concentrated on ensuring that the allies carried out their promises about force levels.[35] The NAC had agreed that NATO would reach twenty-five combat-ready divisions and twenty-five reserve divisions by the end of 1952, giving Ridgway seven months to accomplish the objective. Economic factors prohibited governments from increasing their defense budgets, however. To spur further investment, Ridgway publicly cajoled NATO members to fulfill their pledges. Like Eisenhower, Ridgway looked to the West Germans to make up the allied shortfalls but managing the EDC ratification was just as difficult as haranguing the capitals about force goals. Here Ridgway's lack of political experience came to the fore. Selling the EDC and German rearmament to a hostile France was overly ambitious, especially when the French were still undertaking a concerted effort to restore their leadership in Europe.[36]

Ridgway's command reorganizations and force goals had antagonized allied politicians along the way. He stood in stark contrast to Eisenhower, whose infectious optimism, charisma, and persuasive powers had captivated European leaders. Some of this was the result of a misunderstanding of Ridgway's soldierly bearing, but it was also a misreading on his part about the nature of being SACEUR. He viewed Eisenhower's job at SHAPE "primarily a political one" and his "essentially military."[37] He failed to realize that these tasks could never be divided. This explains why some of his actions—such as surrounding himself with American staff officers—had the inevitable outcome of angering Europeans.[38] Two coinciding events led to his replacement. First, Stalin's death in March 1953 had made Europeans feel less vigilant about defending against an impending Red Army attack. Second, Eisenhower won the 1952 US presidential election, paving the way for the former SACEUR to select the person he had wanted to succeed him all along.

GRUENTHER (JULY 11, 1953–NOVEMBER 20, 1956)

Alfred Gruenther's ascendency placated irritated Europeans. It also came at a critical time for the transatlantic alliance, which appeared it could collapse after only five years. He had worked at SHAPE since its inception and therefore understood that NATO was a victim of its own success. While European leaders wondered why they had been so worried in the first place, Gruenther reminded allies that the perceived improvement in East-West relations was not the result of a Soviet change of heart but Western strength. "We can stand criticism," he once said, "but we cannot stand indifference."[39] European apathy was also a product of circular logic regarding American atomic weapons. If NATO could not raise enough divisions and therefore had to rely on those weapons for defense, then why, the Europeans asked, should they still contribute expensive conventional forces? Articulating the continued necessity and importance of NATO to the members who were prospering under its shield dominated Gruenther's time as SACEUR.[40]

Gruenther was the youngest four-star general in the US Army when he took over SHAPE, although he had never commanded anything larger than an artillery battalion. He had instead spent his career as a gifted staff officer, known for his intellect and love of card games. Eisenhower once quipped that he chose Gruenther as his deputy at SHAPE because he was a better bridge player than Walter Bedell Smith.[41] Despite the obvious jest, there was an unintentional relevance to Eisenhower's comment. Bridge is a game of calculated risk that depends on close communication between partners and the ability to synthesize information. One must remain mindful of details without losing focus on the bigger picture. All were qualities for which Gruenther was renowned.

Gruenther brought this outlook to SHAPE, especially when addressing the strategic imbalance between deterrence and defense, NATO's most pressing demand.[42] A number of factors affected NATO strategy at the time, including economic and financial constraints of fielding a large conventional force, distaste for conscription across the alliance, and varied political aims and ambitions that had little to do with the Soviet threat.[43] While Gruenther settled into his new role, the Eisenhower administration grappled with how to maintain readiness levels as it took into account spiraling budgets and a lack of political will to increase the size of conventional forces. This led to the New Look's emphasis on the deterrent effect of nuclear weapons.[44] NATO and American planners had come to the same conclusion that deterrence in Western Europe had to be built on the determination to use massive retaliatory power if the area was attacked.[45] Ridgway had initiated the first examination of how to integrate nuclear weapons into NATO strategy in July 1953, presenting a dead letter to the alliance when he came to the controversial conclusion that potential high casualty rates meant force levels would have to be increased.[46]

Gruenther established a "New Approach Group" at SHAPE in August 1953. Out of the staff's work came the transformative force-planning document MC/48 in December 1954, which emphasized nuclear weapons for the defense of Europe. The significance of the document was that it signaled a change in assumptions. Since the inception of the alliance, planners had believed nuclear weapons would play some role in defense, but they had not made those weapons a formal part of their plans. Now they argued that the West could only prevent the Soviets from overrunning Europe with an immediate and overwhelming atomic and thermonuclear response at the outset of hostilities.[47] NATO's forward defense strategy assumed that the Soviets could be held in Germany if deterrence failed using only a small force—a "shield," as Gruenther put it—backed with a larger reserve force that relied on the "spear" of nuclear weapons. Whether this policy was more necessity than a natural progression in military policy is debatable, but Gruenther had to rely on American nuclear capabilities and European conventional forces.[48] This required him to plead with the allies to increase their military spending for conventional forces while the United States, the alliance's preeminent power, refused to do so.

Building such forces was difficult in a climate of resistance to the idea of expensive armies. The alliance had groaned under the weight of the 1952 Lisbon force goals, as it was financially and politically impractical for member states to raise ninety-six active and reserve divisions by 1954. Despite Ridgway's and Gruenther's attempts, the Lisbon goals were "dead as a dodo," as Ismay put it.[49] Gruenther adopted Eisenhower's original solution, a reliance on West German manpower. Though he believed he could bring the French around to accepting Germans into the EDC, he was unable to overcome the political fight over rearmament, which climaxed in August 1954 when the French National Assembly refused to ratify the treaty establishing the EDC.[50] With the idea for a European army now dead, so too passed Eisenhower's hope that military integration would beget political integration in Europe.[51] The saga of the EDC was a critical lesson for the multinational coalition with future implications since it illustrated that smaller powers could wield significant influence in the postwar international system.[52]

The British were relieved that the "EDC tomfoolery," as Prime Minister Winston Churchill characterized it, was over. Showing how the great powers retained their influence, they orchestrated a conference that terminated allied occupation of the Federal Republic of Germany, brought West Germany and Italy into the Brussels Treaty, and invited the Federal Republic to join NATO.[53] In this new arrangement, NATO gave the allies an effective framework to deal with the German problem, ensuring that Bonn could not be militarily independent. Gruenther played a pivotal role in this arrangement, meeting with the French, British, and American foreign ministers (Pierre Mendès France, Anthony Eden, and John Foster Dulles) and convincing them that it was possible to corral West German power within the confines of NATO.[54] In prescribing how SHAPE machinery could be used for logistical and operational control of West German forces, Gruenther functioned as a NATO diplomat who argued there was a military solution to a political problem while easing French apprehensions about admitting the Germans into the alliance.[55] On May 6, 1955, the West Germans took their seat at the table, which prompted the Soviet Union to establish the Warsaw Pact, the Eastern Bloc's own collective defense organization.[56]

Events outside of Europe further strained relations within NATO. France increasingly turned to its allies to solve difficulties in Indochina. Since 1950, French officials had endeavored to convince the alliance that European and Asian defense problems were linked, even going to the extent in 1953 and 1954 of ransoming their support for the EDC for American aid in Indochina.[57] France's expectation that its allies should come to its aid annoyed Gruenther, who rejected Paris's assertion that to save Indochina was to save NATO and indeed Europe. This bickering about solidarity within NATO went to the heart of the alliance's existence. Was it a transatlantic alliance created to defend itself from Soviet aggression in Europe, or was it a collection of like-minded states concerned about the survival of the West, even to the point of becoming involved in conflicts on the other side of the world?[58] The Suez Crisis in October 1956 brought to the fore this political issue, and the effects on the alliance became obvious when one month later the Soviets exploited Western disunity over the Middle East to suppress the Hungarian Revolution.[59] The crisis resulted in a push within NATO for increased consultation to mitigate friction and avoid Soviet opportunism. Coincidentally, members were already addressing such questions with a report from the Committee on Non-Military Cooperation that appeared in December 1956.

Gruenther would not be around for those discussions, having retired three weeks after the Soviet intervention in Hungary. The man whom Ismay regarded as "the greatest soldier-statesman I have ever known" navigated a turbulent period that included a reappraisal of NATO strategy and the Federal Republic's inclusion in the alliance.[60] This took considerable skill and required his intellect and charm. Vitally, he repaired civil-military relations, leading one European to remark that Gruenther was "one soldier who doesn't have to be reminded that even generals are servants of the people. We've watched that man for quite a while now and—well, he's never yet talked to us ignorant civilians as if we were a bunch of nitwits."[61] Those qualities had shown just how far a willing SACEUR could go melding the politico-military aspects of his position, something his successor would find out soon enough.

NORSTAD (NOVEMBER 20, 1956–JANUARY 1, 1963)

Lauris Norstad faced an alliance in disarray. The Suez Crisis had made the need for increased political consultation within NATO obvious. There were more systemic problems, however. Twice in Norstad's tenure as SACEUR—first in 1956–57 and again in 1962–63—NATO threatened to disintegrate when the European allies argued that there was little value in Atlantic institutions in the absence of joint policies and common interests. This reevaluation of NATO's effectiveness was a product of the nuclear age, which emphasized political considerations in the use of military force and upended transatlantic assumptions on everything from strategy and diplomacy to geopolitical vision.[62] Norstad was at the center of these discussions and on equal terms with diplomats, shepherding an alliance that had to prepare for new threats from the outside while fighting potential decay from within.

Like Gruenther, Norstad was an acolyte of Eisenhower. The two had first met in late December 1941, when Norstad worked for commanding general of the Army Air Forces Henry "Hap" Arnold. When Eisenhower was chief of staff of the army, he made Norstad director of plans and operations in the War Department. Norstad then went to Europe, where he would stay for the next fifteen years, first as commander of United States Air Force Europe and then as the head of Allied Air Forces Central Europe in April 1951 and as air deputy to the SACEUR in July 1953.[63]

Norstad possessed the same political sensibility as his predecessor. "Everything Norstad does in NATO," according to Chairman of the JCS Nathan Twining, "he equates in the political atmosphere. His job is more diplomatic than anything else."[64] Norstad used this to great effect early into his tenure when he blocked a cash-strapped Britain from reducing its Army of the Rhine (BAOR). Ordinarily, the secretary-general would have taken the lead for NATO on negotiating British troops to remain in Europe, but Ismay, who had already announced his retirement and preferred not to comment on his own country's policies, declined. Norstad stepped into the void. He remained for the duration of his tenure a public figurehead of NATO, which European leaders supported even as they installed a more influential secretary-general. Paul-Henri Spaak, formerly the Belgian foreign minister, replaced Ismay in May 1957.[65] In an attempt to increase political consultation within the alliance, Spaak was made chairman of the NAC. A new body was created, the Committee of Political Advisors, as a forum for disagreements. As a result, the SACEUR had to adjust to the secretary-general's increased political authority, but he still maintained room to maneuver on a variety of issues.

The issue that dominated Norstad's tenure was the nuclearization of NATO. The decision under Gruenther that nuclear weapons would play an integral part in NATO strategy had created pressing questions. Norstad had to contemplate whether NATO's atomic and thermonuclear proliferation would be unilateral, bilateral, or multilateral, which would require close coordination with Britain, France, and West Germany.[66] The launch of the Soviets' first *Sputnik* satellite in October 1957 changed the West's calculus and raised the stakes in the debate about multilateral nuclearization. No longer were members discussing nuclear weapons as a stand-in for conventional forces. Now they discussed the potential for an intercontinental ballistic missile attack from the Soviets and who had the authority to launch the West's response.

Norstad played a pivotal role in the debate, communicating closely with defense and foreign ministers as well as heads of state and urging the Americans to do more than just establish a NATO stockpile of tactical nuclear weapons. He suggested a three-stage reform agenda later dubbed the Norstad Plan, built on initially offering intermediate-range ballistic missiles (IRBMs) to alliance members and developing into the creation of a NATO agency for the research and production of weapons. Norstad was wary of any arrangement that would allow Paris to pursue a national deterrent and persuade the Germans to do the same. His agenda emphasized interdependence in NATO and therefore could ensure Western unity.[67] The plan appealed to Eisenhower, who was attempting to find a way to prevent nuclear war with the Soviet Union without formally abandoning US national security policy.[68] It came to nothing, however, as discussions bogged down in the European rejection of any arrangement that required US approval before launching weapons.

The nuclearization of NATO thus became a replay of the EDC. It was already clear by 1958 that President Charles de Gaulle was offering Europe an alternative to American hegemony, forcing Washington to adopt a more dynamic and constructive approach to the alliance.[69] As a consequence, the French president became Norstad's bête noire. In fall 1958, de Gaulle proposed his three-power "Directorate" to insert France between Britain and the United States. He then vetoed the US plan to use the NATO infrastructure budget to pay for new IRBM sites in Europe. In spring 1959, he went to the extraordinary length of removing one-third of the French Mediterranean fleet from NATO command, even though the ships were American but French-flagged for NATO purposes. In June 1959, he made clear that France required involvement in any decision to use nuclear weapons and disallowed US nuclear warheads on French soil until the Americans agreed. Six months later, the French effectively scrapped the NATO plan to integrate tactical fighter forces under the SACEUR by arguing that they should have control of the nuclear weapons the aircraft would carry.[70]

To block de Gaulle's repeated attempts to improve France's standing in the alliance, Norstad tried to convince Eisenhower and others to make NATO a fourth nuclear power, with the SACEUR vested with authority to use the weapons. In December 1960, the NAC approved the Multilateral Force (MLF) instead, which was an adaptation of the Norstad Plan that the namesake did not favor. The MLF centered on Polaris submarines manned with multinational crews from at least three NATO member-states. Warheads would remain in American control, but European countries would be involved in the strategic nuclear defense. The real objective of the MLF was ensuring the Germans' involvement in NATO nuclear decisions without giving them control of the weapons, which was a part of the larger American program to cultivate a fruitful Bonn-Washington relationship for the benefit of both capitals. Such initiatives had to be conducted within a multinational body, however.[71]

Norstad's plans ran headlong into the new John F. Kennedy administration, which sought nonproliferation and centralized control of weapons. Extrapolating their belief in a strategy of flexible response, Kennedy and his advisers saw the creation of a nuclear force as an option of last resort, and they sought to reduce NATO's reliance on nuclear weapons. Kennedy's belief that the alliance's role was to deter limited aggression rather than general war stood at odds with Norstad's reading of the Soviet threat, and it undermined the SACEUR's ultimate goal: to ensure allied cohesion through interdependence. He therefore took the change in policy as a personal rebuke.[72]

Norstad's relationship with Kennedy soured further over Berlin, which had been simmering since November 1958. Soviet premier Nikita Khrushchev's ultimatum to the Western occupying powers—the United States, Britain, and France—to leave West Berlin within six months lest Moscow sign a separate peace with the German Democratic Republic had resulted in two years of dead-end negotiations. In the interim, Norstad created a secret planning group for Berlin contingencies within SHAPE with the code name LIVE OAK.[73] Planners in the Pentagon, however, had their own ideas. For all of 1961, the administration attempted to sell Norstad and the NAC on the idea of applying flexible response in Berlin, which made alliance members believe Washington was informing NATO, not consulting it.[74] When the Americans unveiled their four-stage plan to incrementally apply force over the city, Norstad spoke frankly. He told Kennedy that the instructions were "poorly drafted, ambiguous, and contradictory," as well as "replete with clichés and jargon."[75]

Kennedy's aversion to using nuclear weapons then took the debate about the nuclearization of the alliance and turned it into a referendum on NATO strategy. From the perspective of European officials, a conventional war was no more acceptable than a nuclear war. They still held that nuclear weapons would deter any conflict on the continent, not just an all-out enemy attack.[76] The debate entered a new phase at the NAC ministerial meeting in Athens in May 1962, when Secretary of Defense Robert McNamara could not impose a shift to flexible response. It reached a crescendo in 1962–63 when the Kennedy administration continued in its quest to have NATO strategy document MC 14/2 replaced with the plan

McNamara had outlined in Athens. This pushed the West Germans further into the arms of the French, which the Franco-German friendship treaty later demonstrated.

Despite Norstad's efforts for over five years to keep proliferation confined to NATO, the allies pursued national nuclear forces. For his part, Kennedy could never reconcile US policy with NATO strategy. He recognized that Norstad wore two hats, but he misinterpreted Norstad's positions as remnant of the Eisenhower era, not the representative views of NATO.[77] With no chance of reconciliation, Kennedy and McNamara forced Norstad to retire in July 1962, to the chagrin of the allies.

LEMNITZER (JANUARY 1, 1963–JULY 1, 1969)

Norstad's retirement made alliance leaders wonder if Washington believed the position of SACEUR had become too European, which might portend a more assertive United States when it came to NATO issues.[78] This perception affected Norstad's successor, Gen. Lyman Lemnitzer, US Army, as did his coming from the Pentagon as chairman of the JCS. It took the NAC five days to confirm his appointment because of de Gaulle, who made clear that NATO would not simply rubber-stamp US decisions.[79] "First they sent us a tranquil ambassador and a restless general," he quipped the day before Lemnitzer took over at SHAPE. Now "they've sent us a restless ambassador and a tranquil general."[80]

Lemnitzer's demeanor might have been more sedate than his predecessor's, but he did have a wide breadth of experience from his variety of combat and staff positions. Compared to Gruenther and Norstad, who had both spent time in SHAPE headquarters, Lemnitzer's experience with NATO was from the other side of the Atlantic. In 1949, he became the first director of the Defense Department's Office of Military Assistance. In the Korean War, he commanded the Seventh Infantry Division and then took over the Eighth Army in 1955. In 1960, he had made it to army chief of staff before serving as JCS chairman from 1960 to 1962.[81]

The battle over flexible response was not finished when Lemnitzer arrived at SHAPE, nor was the Kennedy administration's attempt to treat the SACEUR as an American first and the head of a supranational military second. Lemnitzer resisted political pressure from the administration to reorganize SHAPE into nuclear and conventional sections, citing a study he had conducted while chairman that argued the two were inseparable. Moreover, he told McNamara that he would only take such an order from the NAC, which would then have to find a new SACEUR. McNamara also unsuccessfully pressured Lemnitzer to reorganize the SHAPE staff as a means of showing American support for allies, telling the SACEUR that Land Forces Southeast should have as many Greeks and Turks as Americans, regardless of officers' abilities.[82] Due to temperament and professional experience, Lemnitzer preferred to remain in a more military realm than the arena of politics that characterized Norstad's tenure, resembling Ridgway more than his other predecessors.

France ended its participation in NATO's joint military command structure in March 1966 but did so without renouncing the NATO treaty.[83] The withdrawal of French troops was more de Gaulle's comment on the alliance's organization and the stationing of allied forces on French territory than on France's role in NATO. Before the announcement, Lemnitzer, as the military chief of an international alliance, had stood astride the schism in Franco-American relations. He understood that many US officials interpreted de Gaulle's moves as anti-American, particularly as the US commitment to Southeast Asia deepened, and he had tried to disabuse them of that notion.[84] Such friction, he argued, was damaging to the interests of both countries as well as NATO. Even though he considered de Gaulle's decision an eviction of all alliance and non-French military activities in France, he would spend the remainder of his three years as SACEUR guiding NATO through the complications of an ally's exit.[85]

NATO political leaders reacted to the French withdrawal with resolve and unity. They formed groups that took up questions de Gaulle had routinely blocked and altered the organizational structure of the alliance to reflect the political, strategic, and technological changes that had occurred in the previous two decades.[86] The Nuclear Planning Group—made up of Americans, British, West Germans, and Italians and with two seats on rotation—worked in union with the Nuclear Defense Affairs Committee to select targets, allocate warheads, and coordinate command.[87] The French exit also necessitated constitutional amendments. The Defense Planning Committee, which had been born in May 1963 out of the allied tensions regarding strategy and policy consultation, moved up to the same level of authority as the NAC, given that France could no longer participate in discussions on military topics within that supreme body.[88]

All of this would have to take place in a new location. Lemnitzer moved his headquarters to Casteau, fifty kilometers from Brussels. Over the winter of 1966–67, Belgium spent $500 million in new infrastructure, including an updated road system to the capital. Lemnitzer opened his new headquarters on March 31, 1967, completing the transfer in six months, one day ahead of the French deadline and without losing command and control.[89] This large outlay of cash occurred at a time when Anglo-American-German relations were strained over how to pay for allied forces stationed in the Federal Republic. Bonn resented the British and American demands for a German purchase of arms to offset the annual cost of the BAOR and the Seventh Army. These discussions annoyed Lemnitzer, though they did not involve him directly, for their ability to make the financial tail wag the security dog.[90] Lemnitzer asked the North Atlantic Parliamentary Assembly in November 1967 how deterrence would work when NATO members were cutting back on military budgets, reducing terms of military service, and redeploying troops to the United States, all while the Warsaw Pact was increasing its capabilities. There was also the thorny issue of how to make up for the loss of French units at the center of the alliance's front. As Lemnitzer saw it, NATO had two options: thin out Central Command to shore up other areas, or deploy more forces overall. The former was dangerous, and the latter unlikely, so he called into question flexible response and argued that the alliance would have to rely on nuclear weapons earlier than it expected.[91]

This debate resulted in MC 14/3, NATO's strategic concept for defense, which the Defense Planning Committee adopted in December 1967. It advanced three types of actions: symmetrical response, deliberate escalation, and general nuclear response. To NATO's reliance on nuclear deterrence, therefore, planners added the possibility for conventional and incremental responses, though the alliance had already been using flexible response since the Berlin Crisis.[92] Optimists claimed that it was a compromise document that merged the Americans' flexible response with the Europeans' reliance on the deterrent value of massive retaliation, but pessimists countered that no one had conceded anything—the allies had simply adopted everyone's agenda.[93]

Substantial change in NATO came the same month as MC 14/3, however, with the *Report of the Council on the Future Tasks of the Alliance.* Also known as the Harmel Report, it was significant for its attempt to improve allied cohesion, particularly through a Franco-American rapprochement. To bridge a divide between two distinct camps in the alliance, the report stated that NATO's politico-military functions made it capable of simultaneously seeking security and détente.[94] Taken together, MC 14/3 and the Harmel Report closed NATO's first era.[95] The challenge for leaders was to understand how conventional forces, tactical nuclear weapons, and strategic nuclear forces would determine force postures now that deterrence and not defense was the priority.[96] Lemnitzer oversaw the transition to this new period and retired in July 1969 after six and a half years as SACEUR. While he lacked Gruenther's intellect and Norstad's dynamism, his attention to detail and calmness was crucial in keeping together the alliance through the French military withdrawal.[97]

NATO's first two decades were an era distinct from what followed for the alliance, owing mostly to the impact of the five SACEURs who served from 1951 to 1967. Through their leadership, they transformed SHAPE from a group of planning committees to a multinational alliance capable of a range of missions, due in large part to their ability to meld military and political authority when necessary. At pivotal times, the military chiefs steered the alliance with the skill of statesmen: Eisenhower's convincing NATO members that a defense of Europe was possible, Ridgway's brokering cooperation between erstwhile enemies, Gruenther's vision when drafting a strategy for the nuclear age, Norstad's diplomacy during the Berlin Crisis, and Lemnitzer's leadership during the French schism.

What accounted for the SACEURs' ability to navigate political waters even after the allies created the position of secretary-general in 1952? The biggest reason was preponderant US military and economic power and the other members' lack of either. An American as the military chief of NATO had several cascading effects on the alliance. Given that US power underwrote NATO, American leadership in SHAPE was important to make the alliance a credible deterrent to Soviet encroachment. A NATO military chief wearing an American uniform improved the potential use of that power and therefore assured members of a continued US presence in Europe. Crucially, that pledge impressed upon Europeans that a defense of the continent was possible. Therein lay a paradox, however. Alliance members desired a continued American presence, and they often interpreted the SACEUR's words and actions as US policy, but they did not want SHAPE to become a multinational command for American use. The members need not have worried—the common virtue of the first SACEURs was that none was an American partisan. That was perhaps their greatest impact upon the alliance. Yet given that the SACEUR was at once NATO military chief and commander of US forces in Europe, it was often difficult for allies to disentangle the two.

There is particular irony that the members' perception of the position changed from 1951 to 1967 from European skepticism that the SACEUR would be too American to an American belief that the SACEUR was too European. That change was based in shifts in the postwar liberal order and their particular effect on NATO: the series of crises in the early 1960s, France's maneuvering for power and influence, the deepening American involvement in Southeast Asia, the German economic rise coinciding with the British decline, and the promise of détente. The stability that Western leaders desired after World War II did indeed underwrite the economic and political recovery of Europe by the mid-1960s. This restoration of Europe, while not making NATO egalitarian by any means, did have the effect of balancing the alliance, thereby tempering American supremacy. Crucial for SHAPE, these geopolitical, geostrategic, and global economic changes had the culminating effect of empowering NATO's political mechanisms. Now more than a body that debated deterrence, NATO developed into a forum of political consultation that debated Europe's future political order.[98] The result was a siphoning off of political influence from the SACEUR.

That bygone influence was seen most clear in the SACEURs' power to steer policymaking, which is what makes 1951 to 1967 a period distinct from what followed. The first five SACEURs held considerable sway because of the alliance's strategy toward the Soviet Union. Deterrence is inherently a politico-military endeavor, as it wages political warfare to avoid an actual war. Once NATO adopted the dual-track strategy of deterrence and détente in the wake of the Harmel Report, the alliance's highest military authority saw his stature as statesman diminish. The diplomats in both the NAC and the member nations' foreign ministries, in their quest for negotiating détente with Moscow and the Warsaw Pact, undertook a political initiative that was built on decreasing NATO military power to ease tension in Europe. Naturally, this reduced the political prestige that the SACEUR once enjoyed.

One only needs to look at the issues that dominated the first five SACEURs' tenures to understand the degree to which the West struggled with national aspirations, mistrusts, and resentments when constructing the postwar liberal order. The NATO military chief often stood astride those divisions, as they interfered with decisions regarding force posture, nuclear strategy, and burden-sharing. Despite the instances of tension, NATO, as the security cornerstone of the postwar liberal order, showed itself remarkably flexible, owing mostly to like-minded partners whose compatible political cultures and strategy outlook reinforced their desire for security and prosperity.[99] Yet a large part of why NATO was capable of overcoming those periods of tension when balancing national with rational interests was that there existed in the alliance a mediator who at once had access to allied leaders, was impartial to national aims, and had the heady responsibility of ensuring the security of the West.

NOTES

The opinions expressed in this article are the author's own and do not reflect the view of the United States Marine Corps or the Marine Corps History Division.

1 Lawrence S. Kaplan, *The United States and NATO: The Formative Years* (Lexington: University Press of Kentucky, 1984).
2 Robert Endicott Osgood, *NATO: The Entangling Alliance* (Chicago: University of Chicago Press, 1962), 349.
3 For that vision, see Lawrence S. Kaplan, *NATO 1948: The Birth of the Transatlantic Alliance* (Lanham, MD: Rowman & Littlefield, 2007).
4 Eisenhower to William Edward Robertson, letter, October 31, 1951, in *The Papers of Dwight David Eisenhower,* ed. Louis Galambos et al., vol. 12, *NATO and the Campaign of 1952* (Baltimore: Johns Hopkins University Press, 1989), 672 (hereafter *Eisenhower Papers).*
5 Walter Lafeber, "NATO and the Korean War: A Context," *Diplomatic History* 13, no. 4 (October 1989): 461–77.
6 SHAPE Historical Section, *SHAPE History: Origin and Development of SHAPE,* vol. 1 (1953): 13, http://archives.nato.int/shape-history-volume-i.
7 Lauris Norstad, interview by Thomas Soapes, November 11, 1976, OH-#385, transcript, Dwight D. Eisenhower Presidential Library, Abilene, KS, 7–8.
8 Eisenhower to William Averell Harriman, letter, March 14, 1951, *Eisenhower Papers,* doc. 81, 127–29.
9 "NATO: The Shield," *Time,* February 6, 1956, 26–33.
10 SHAPE Historical Section, *SHAPE History,* 13–14.
11 Galambos et al., *Eisenhower Papers,* xv.
12 Gregory W. Pedlow, "The Politics of NATO Command, 1950–1962," in *U.S. Military Forces in Europe: The Early Years, 1945–1970,* ed. Simon W. Duke and Wolfgang Krieger (Boulder, CO: Westview, 1993), 15–42.

13 Stephen E. Ambrose with Morris Honick, "Eisenhower: Rekindling the Spirit of the West," in *Generals in International Politics: NATO's Supreme Allied Commander, Europe,* ed. Robert S. Jordan (Lexington: University Press of Kentucky, 1987), 12–13.

14 Alessandro Brogi, *Confronting America: The Cold War between the United States and Communists in France and Italy* (Chapel Hill: University of North Carolina Press, 2011).

15 Timothy Andrews Sayle, *Enduring Alliance: A History of NATO and the Postwar Global Order* (Ithaca, NY: Cornell University Press, 2019).

16 Robert S. Jordan, "Gruenther: Attempts to Retain NATO Solidarity," in Jordan, *Generals in International Politics,* 54–55.

17 Ambrose, "Eisenhower," 11–12.

18 John Lewis Gaddis, *Strategies of Containment: A Critical Appraisal of American National Security Policy during the Cold War* (Oxford: Oxford University Press, 2005), 53–86.

19 David Clay Large, *Germans to the Front: West German Rearmament in the Adenauer Era* (Chapel Hill: University of North Carolina Press, 1996). See also William Stueck, *Rethinking the Korean War: A New Diplomatic and Strategic History* (Princeton, NJ: Princeton University Press, 2004).

20 Galambos et al., *Eisenhower Papers,* 77 (italics in original).

21 Edward Fursdon, *The European Defence Community: A History* (New York: Palgrave, 1980).

22 Kevin Ruane, *The Rise and Fall of the European Defense Community: Anglo-American Relations and the Crisis of European Defence, 1950–55* (New York: St. Martin's, 2000).

23 See Thomas M. Sisk, "Forging the Weapon: Eisenhower as NATO's Supreme Allied Commander, Europe, 1950–1952," in *Eisenhower: A Centenary Assessment,* ed. Günter Bischof and Stephen E. Ambrose (Baton Rouge: Louisiana State University Press, 1995), 64–86.

24 Bonbright to Dulles, memorandum, May 21, 1952, in *Foreign Relations of the United States* (hereafter *FRUS*), 1952–54, Western European Security, vol. 5, part 1, ed. John A. Bernbaum, Lisle A. Rose, and Charles S. Sampson (Washington, DC: Government Printing Office, 1983), doc. 162, 298–301.

25 George Eugene Pelletier, "Ridgway: Trying to Make Good on the Promises," in Jordan, *Generals in International Politics,* 34.

26 Robert S. Jordan with Michael W. Bloome, *Political Leadership in NATO: A Study in Multinational Diplomacy* (Boulder, CO: Westview, 1979), 23–54.

27 George C. Mitchell, *Matthew B. Ridgway: Soldier, Statesman, Scholar, Citizen* (Mechanicsburg, PA: Stackpole, 2002), 108.

28 Pelletier, "Ridgway," 38.

29 Dionysios Chourchoulis, *The Southern Flank of NATO, 1951–1959: Military Strategy or Political Stabilization* (Lanham, MD: Lexington Books, 2015).

30 Derek Leebaert, *Grand Improvisation: America Confronts the British Superpower, 1945–1957* (New York: Farrar, Straus and Giroux, 2018).
31 Sean M. Maloney, *Securing Command of the Sea: NATO Naval Planning, 1948–1954* (Annapolis, MD: Naval Institute Press, 1995), 170–96.
32 Matthew B. Ridgway, *Soldier: The Memoirs of Matthew B. Ridgway* (Westport, CT: Greenwood, 1974), 238.
33 Ridgway, *Soldier,* 236–37.
34 Ridgway, 237–39; Mitchell, *Matthew B. Ridgway,* 114–15.
35 Pelletier, "Ridgway," 32.
36 William I. Hitchcock, *France Restored: Cold War Diplomacy and the Quest for Leadership in Europe, 1944–1954* (Chapel Hill: University of North Carolina Press, 1998).
37 Ridgway, *Soldier,* 239.
38 Mitchell, *Matthew B. Ridgway,* 123.
39 "NATO: The Shield," 26–33.
40 John S. Duffield, *Power Rules: The Evolution of NATO's Conventional Force Posture* (Stanford, CA: Stanford University Press, 1995), 75–111.
41 Ernest O. Hauser, "The Army's Biggest Brain," *Saturday Evening Post,* October 31, 1953, 33.
42 Jordan, "Gruenther," 53–72.
43 Beatrice Heuser, "The Development of NATO's Nuclear Strategy," *Contemporary European History* 4, no. 1 (March 1995): 37–66.
44 Saki Dockrill, *Eisenhower's New-Look National Security Policy, 1953–61* (New York: St. Martin's, 1996).
45 NSC 162/2, October 30, 1953, *FRUS,* 1952–54, National Security Affairs, vol. 2, part 2, ed. Lisle A. Rose and Neal H. Petersen (Washington, DC: Government Printing Office, 1984), doc. 101, 585–86, 593.
46 Robert Wampler, "NATO Strategic Planning and Nuclear Weapons," Nuclear History Program Occasional Paper 6 (College Park: Center for International Security Studies, School of Public Affairs, University of Maryland, 1990), 9.
47 Marc Trachtenberg, *A Constructed Peace: The Making of the European Settlement, 1945–1963* (Princeton, NJ: Princeton University Press, 1999), 158–59.
48 For the former argument, see Jordan, "Gruenther," 61. For the latter, see Marc Trachtenberg, *History and Strategy* (Princeton, NJ: Princeton University Press, 1991), 153–68.
49 "NATO: The Shield," 26–33.
50 Kevin Ruane, "Agonizing Reappraisals: Anthony Eden, John Foster Dulles and the Crisis of European Defence, 1953–1954," *Diplomacy and Statecraft* 13, no. 4 (December 2002): 151–85.
51 Trachtenberg, *Constructed Peace,* 122.
52 Michael Creswell, *A Question of Balance: How France and the United States Created Cold War Europe* (Cambridge, MA: Harvard University Press, 2006).

53 Dulles to Eisenhower, telegram, September 18, 1954, *FRUS,* 1952–54, Western European Security, vol. 5, part 2, ed. John A. Bernbaum, Lisle A. Rose, and Charles S. Sampson (Washington, DC: Government Printing Office), 1227–28.
54 Trachtenberg, *Constructed Peace,* 127.
55 See, e.g, Dillon to Conant, cable, September 16, 1954, *FRUS,* 1952–54, vol. 5, part 2, 1198–99; Gruenther to Dulles, cable, September 16, 1954, *FRUS,* 1952–54, vol. 5, part 2, 1200–1201.
56 See Mary Ann Heiss and S. Victor Papacosma, eds., *NATO and the Warsaw Pact: Intrabloc Conflicts* (Kent, OH: Kent State University Press, 2008).
57 Kathryn C. Statler, *Replacing France: The Origins of American Intervention in Vietnam* (Lexington: University Press of Kentucky, 2007).
58 Jordan, "Gruenther," 64–66.
59 Lucile Eznack, *Crises in the Atlantic Alliance: Affect and Relations among NATO Members* (New York: Palgrave Macmillan, 2012), 47–68.
60 "NATO: The Shield," 26–33.
61 Hauser, "Army's Biggest Brain," 166.
62 Ralph Dietl, "In Defence of the West: General Lauris Norstad, NATO Nuclear Forces and Transatlantic Relations, 1956–1963," *Diplomacy and Statecraft* 17 (2006): 347–51.
63 Norstad, interview, 9.
64 "NATO: The View at the Summit," *Time,* December 16, 1957, 21–25.
65 Jordan and Bloome, *Political Leadership in NATO,* 55–102.
66 Robert S. Jordan, *Norstad: Cold War NATO Supreme Commander; Airman, Strategist, Diplomat* (New York: St. Martin's, 2000), 103.
67 Dietl, "In Defence of the West," 355–56.
68 Campbell Craig, *Destroying the Village: Eisenhower and Thermonuclear War* (New York: Columbia University Press, 1998). For military planning, see Edward Kaplan, *To Kill Nations: American Strategy in the Air-Atomic Age and the Rise of Mutually Assured Destruction* (Ithaca, NY: Cornell University Press, 2015).
69 Frédéric Bozo, *Two Strategies for Europe: De Gaulle, the United States, and the Atlantic Alliance* (Lanham, MD: Rowman & Littlefield, 2001).
70 Jordan, "Norstad," in Jordan, *Generals in International Politics,* 87–88.
71 Steven J. Brady, *Eisenhower and Adenauer: Alliance Management under Pressure, 1953–1960* (Lanham, MD: Rowman & Littlefield, 2010).
72 Jordan, "Norstad," 89; Dietl, "In Defence of the West," 371–72.
73 Gregory W. Pedlow, "Allied Crisis Management for Berlin: The LIVE OAK Organization, 1959–1963," in *International Cold War Military Records and History: Proceedings of the International Conference,* ed. William W. Epley (Washington, DC: Office of the Secretary of Defense, 1996).
74 Frank Costigliola, "Kennedy, the European Allies, and the Failure to Consult," *Political Science Quarterly* 110, no. 1 (Spring 1995): 105–23.

75 Kennedy and Norstad, memorandum of conversation, November 9, 1961, in *FRUS,* 1961–63, vol. 14, Berlin Crisis, 1961–62, part 1, ed. Charles S. Sampson (Washington, DC: Government Printing Office, 1993), 559; Kennedy to Norstad, letter, October 20, 1961, folder "NATO—Norstad Correspondence 3/61–3/62," box 103, subjects file, President's Office File, John F. Kennedy Presidential Library, Boston.

76 Beatrice Heuser, *NATO, Britain, France and the FRG: Nuclear Strategies and Forces for Europe, 1949–2000* (New York: St. Martin's, 1997), 46–47.

77 Ingo Trauschweizer, *Cold War U.S. Army: Building Deterrence for Limited War* (Lawrence: University Press of Kansas, 2008), 125. See also Gregory W. Pedlow, "Three Hats for Berlin: General Lauris Norstad and the Second Berlin Crisis, 1958–62," in *The Berlin Wall Crisis: Perspectives on Cold War Alliances, 1945–62,* ed. J.P. Gearson and Kori Schake (New York: Palgrave, 2002), 175–98.

78 Dietl, "In Defence of the West," 377.

79 Lawrence S. Kaplan and Kathleen A. Kellner, "Lemnitzer: Surviving the French Military Withdrawal," in Jordan, *Generals in International Politics,* 94–95.

80 *U.S. News & World Report,* December 31, 1962, 2.

81 Kaplan and Kellner, "Lemnitzer," 92–93.

82 L. James Binder, *Lemnitzer: A Soldier for His Time* (Washington, DC: Brassey's, 1997), 318–19.

83 Frédéric Bozo, "The NATO Crisis of 1966–1967: A French Point of View," in *The Strategic Triangle: France, Germany, and the United States in the Shaping of the New Europe,* ed. Helga Haftendorn et al. (Baltimore: Johns Hopkins University Press, 2006), 103–26.

84 For those views, see Thomas Alan Schwartz, *Lyndon Johnson and Europe: In the Shadow of Vietnam* (Cambridge, MA: Harvard University Press, 2003), 92–139.

85 Kaplan and Kellner, "Lemnitzer," 104, 117.

86 Andreas Wenger, "The Politics of Military Planning: Evolution of NATO's Strategy," in *War Plans and Alliances in the Cold War: Threat Perceptions in the East and West,* ed. Vojtech Mastny, Sven G. Holtsmark, and Andreas Wenger (New York: Routledge, 2006), 165–92.

87 Binder, *Lemnitzer,* 321.

88 Sayle, *Enduring Alliance,* 127.

89 Kaplan and Kellner, "Lemnitzer," 114–17.

90 Sayle, *Enduring Alliance,* 131–34. See also Hubert Zimmerman, *Money and Security: Troops, Monetary Policy, and West Germany's Relations with the United States and Britain, 1950–1971* (Cambridge: Cambridge University Press, 2002).

91 Kaplan and Kellner, "Lemnitzer," 120–21.

92 Sean M. Maloney, "Berlin Contingency Planning: Prelude to Flexible Response, 1958–63," *Journal of Strategic Studies* 25, no. 1 (March 2002): 99–134.

93 Michael O. Wheeler, "NATO Nuclear Strategy, 1949–1990," in *A History of NATO: The First Fifty Years,* ed. Gustav Schmidt (New York: Palgrave, 2001), 130.

94 Helga Haftendorn, *NATO and the Nuclear Revolution: A Crisis of Credibility, 1966–1967* (Oxford: Clarendon Press, 1996), 320–85. See also Helga Haftendorn, "The Adaptation of the NATO Alliance to a Period of Détente: The 1967 Harmel Report," in *Crises and Promises: The European Project, 1963–1969,* ed. Wilfried Loth (Baden-Baden: Nomos, 2001), 285–322.

95 Lawrence S. Kaplan, "NATO: The Second Generation," in *NATO After Thirty Years,* ed. Lawrence S. Kaplan and Robert W. Clawson (Wilmington, DE: Scholarly Resources, 1981).

96 Robert Thomas Davis II, "The Dilemma of NATO Strategy, 1949–1968" (PhD diss., Ohio University, 2008).

97 Lawrence S. Kaplan, "General Lyman L. Lemnitzer and NATO, 1948–69: A Deferential Leader," *Cold War History* 19, no. 3 (August 2019): 323–41.

98 Andreas Wenger, Christian Nuenlist, and Anna Locher, "New Perspectives on NATO History," in *Transforming NATO in the Cold War: Challenges beyond Deterrence in the 1960s,* ed. Andreas Wenger, Christian Nuenlist, and Anna Locher (New York: Routledge, 2007), 3–12.

99 Ingo Trauschweizer, "Adapt and Survive: NATO in the Cold War," in *Grand Strategy and Military Alliances,* ed. Peter R. Mansoor and Williamson Murray (New York: Cambridge University Press, 2016), 166–96. See also Seth A. Johnston, *How NATO Adapts: Strategy and Organization in the Atlantic Alliance since 1950* (Baltimore: Johns Hopkins University Press, 2017).

CHAPTER 3

Forgotten Institution

The Role of the OEEC in European Post–World War II Reconstruction and Integration

ARMIN GRÜNBACHER

When talking about postwar European reconstruction within the framework of transatlantic relations, almost everybody thinks first of the European Recovery Program (ERP), better known as the Marshall Plan. How dominant the program has been is best demonstrated by two facts. First, Gerd Hardach has highlighted that already by 1953, about five thousand books, articles, and newspaper articles had been written on it, showing what an impact the program had at the time—and subsequently—on people's imaginations.[1] While this astonishingly high number came about not least due to an insistence on publicity by the Economic Cooperation Administration (ECA, the US body that ran the Marshall Plan), it helped to create the second element about the Marshall Plan: even today hardly any large-scale disaster, man-made or natural, occurs without politicians calling for "a new Marshall Plan," irrespective of the fact that they probably do not know how the ERP had actually operated. This lack of knowledge is even more striking when it comes to the activities and importance of the Organization for European Economic Cooperation (OEEC). This organization was not only vital for the functioning of the Marshall Plan but also for European reconstruction in areas beyond US aid and thus ultimately proved to be a decisive factor in the emerging process of European integration. The OEEC's history can tell us a great deal about transatlantic relations.

The OEEC developed out of the Committee for European Economic Cooperation (CEEC). The CEEC had been set up by the European countries that would participate in the Marshall Plan in order to coordinate Europe's requests for aid. After the passing of the passing of the Economic Assistance Act by the US Congress, the "conference" was then transformed into "organization" and tasked not only with the running of the Marshall Plan on the European side but also with the much wider task of promoting European economic reconstruction and political cooperation and integration. This chapter will revisit economic historians' views on the OEEC, highlight some significant gaps in research, and provide a different perspective on why the organization was so important to early European integration. It argues that the full impact and importance of the OEEC has, particularly in anglophone historiography, not been fully appreciated. This case will be made by looking first at the role intended for the organization and why it failed in its most prominent (though not necessarily most important) task, the allocation of Marshall aid; second, at its role in European currency convertibility and trade liberalization; and, finally, briefly at its role in raising European productivity. It will begin, however, with a look at the historiography on the organization.

In a 1983 article about the challenges of the process of European integration to contemporary historians, Hans-Peter Schwarz pointed out that while there was a plethora of studies on European integration and in particular on the European Coal and Steel Community (ECSC) and the creation of the European Economic Community (EEC), there were hardly any studies on the other multinational bodies that had appeared in the late 1940s and early 1950s. He explicitly mentioned the North Atlantic Treaty Organization, the General Agreement on Tariffs and Trade, and the International Monetary Fund and their transnational history.[2] If multinational organizations were investigated, he argued, it was usually from a national perspective—for example, "Country X and its role in / relations with . . ." The exception to this trend is investigations into the Marshall Plan proper.[3] By the sheer nature of the topic, in particular the power relationship between the United States and any participating country, it had always been necessary to look at least at the relations between that country and the United States.[4] This focus on the Marshall Plan, however, kept the view away from the OEEC's tasks, which went beyond the narrow confines for the aid program. Immanuel Wexler, Michael Hogan, and Gerd Hardach are the typical representatives of this group that mentions the OEEC only within the ERP context. Alan Milward in a very strong way confirms Schwarz's claim of neglect of international bodies in regard to the OEEC when he states that "there is no history of the OEEC, only descriptions of its function and judicial guides to its labyrinthine structures."[5] Nevertheless (or because of this fact), he is the one historian who, in his *The Reconstruction of Western Europe 1945–1951,* has dedicated as much as two chapters to the OEEC and its predecessor, the CEEC. Nonetheless, he is also the organization's fiercest critic, even speaking of "the collapse of the OEEC" in 1949–50.[6] By so doing, Milward limits the work of the OEEC to a mere economic policy tool of the Marshall Plan, and he reduces the organization and its work even further, as he limits his argument around US intentions and wishes of making the OEEC (in its pure organizational form) into an instrument for European political integration.[7] This is a rather myopic view that disregards the organization's other tasks and its (sometimes indirect) achievements, which had a very significant impact on European economic and political development in the 1950s.

Since Schwarz wrote his article, there have been a significant number of new studies on some of the more prominent multinational organizations. The institution that has received most scholarly attention, and one very important within the history of the OEEC, is the European Payments Union (EPU).[8] While some of this attention arose not least in the wake of the collapse of the communist regimes in Eastern Europe in the early 1990s and the need to rebuild economic links between the Soviet Union's successor states,[9] the EPU was, apart from the ECSC, Europe's most important institution in the 1950s. Its significance will be discussed shortly and in some detail. Werner Bührer's monograph *Westdeutschland in der OEEC* is an excellent study in its own right and essential for anyone researching the OEEC's history, but it nevertheless also reinforces the point made by Schwarz about the focus of single-nation studies.[10] Richard T. Griffiths's edited volume *Exploration in OEEC History* suffers to a good degree from the same one-state approach. Apart from the very mixed quality of the contributions on aspects of the OEEC's history, half of the eighteen chapters have a country name in their title, reconfirming again the still very nation-based nature of the research into the OEEC so far.[11] Nevertheless, it is Griffiths himself who points out that the OEEC had more roles to play than simply supporting or administering the Marshall Plan on the European side of the Atlantic. Since the plan could only alleviate the symptoms but not tackle the underlying European economic problems, the OEEC was also tasked with the crucial task of raising European productivity; making, in line with the Bretton Woods agreements, the European currencies convertible; and helping liberalize intra-European trade.[12]

While the OEEC may not have been a direct result of the Cold War, it was at least one of its by-products due to the organization's link to the Marshall Plan. It is, therefore, striking that nowhere in the literature a link is made between the OEEC and the East-West conflict or how it influenced East-West relations. It can, for example, only be speculated how far the OEEC's internal conflicts eased after 1950 because the United States had finally laid down the ground rules or because the outbreak of the Korean War helped to focus European minds. But so far, the research on the organization remains a purely inner-European and transatlantic affair and neglects the wider East-West relations and the global Cold War.

THE OEEC'S INTENDED ROLE

When Secretary of State George C. Marshall outlined his plan for European reconstruction in a speech at Harvard University on June 5, 1947, he expected and emphasized that the initiative for the program had to come from the Europeans.[13] All historians who have looked at the OEEC performance in administering the Marshall Plan agree that this process did not, to understate the mater, run smoothly. While the British and French foreign ministers took up the call and managed to organize the first meeting of the CEEC to take place in Paris on July 12, 1947, just six weeks after Marshall's speech had publicized the idea of the venture, this was as far as they could agree.[14] Milward argues that right after the committee's constitution, the United States had to apply significant pressure on the Europeans to advance their idea of the body becoming a springboard for European economic and political integration.[15] At the same time, the Americans saw themselves confronted with rather unrealistic demands for aid from the Europeans: the initial CEEC request was for $29 billion, twice the amount the United States had already spent on aid to Europe through various agencies, including the United Nations Relief and Rehabilitation Administration.[16] Just how unrealistic European aid requests were becomes obvious when looking at the size of the funds Congress would eventually grant—just over $14 billion. The huge figure the Europeans had requested highlighted a belief in unlimited US resources, but it also seemed to express a sense of entitlement, at least on the part of some countries. When Washington rejected the first European aid request, a Norwegian CEEC delegate wrote back to Oslo, stating that "the American demand means we should write a new report at American dictation." The British, for their part, convinced of their special status among European countries, demanded 40 percent of all aid allocated in 1949–50.[17]

There were also significant "hard" political obstacles the Americans had to overcome after the CEEC had been converted into the OEEC. The organization's founding act took place on April 16, 1948, just two weeks after Congress had passed the Marshall Plan bill. In the process of creating the OEEC, the Americans had once again put significant pressure on the Europeans but were not able to get all their ideas accepted.[18] In this context, it was the French who resisted American demands to have any German representatives, or even mere "observers," present at the opening ceremony, despite the fact that there had been an agreement reached among the three occupying powers on March 2 that their respective zones of occupation would be included in the Marshall Plan.[19] A German presence at the CEEC founding ceremony in 1947 had been out of the question so shortly after the war. However, the French refusal even in 1948 to allow any German representatives (i.e., not just political representatives but also diplomats and economic experts), who were supposed to work at the OEEC, to attend the opening ceremony was heavily criticized by the Americans and seen as a personal snub to the US military governor, Gen. Lucius D. Clay.[20] Nevertheless, the United States had to accept the French rejection in order to avoid further antagonism, irrespective of the March agreement.

As this shows, the German case had been a particular bugbear for the French. Based on their experience of invasion and occupation in 1870–71, 1914–18, and 1940–45, they had very little interest in supporting German reconstruction and obstructed American plans in this direction as long as they could. This French desire stood in stark contrast to the interests of Germany's smaller neighbors the Netherlands, Belgium, Luxemburg, Austria, Denmark, and Norway, which, because of their traditional trade links, all needed Germany, either as a market or as a supplier.[21] Even Britain supported the revival of the German economy, as it would help to reduce British occupation costs.[22] In November 1949, the newly founded Federal Republic of Germany (FRG) took up full membership in the OEEC. For the Germans, this meant their first step onto the international scene, at a time when the country was still under occupation rule and the Allies were formally conducting the country's foreign policy. Prior to the formal German accession, the three occupation zones had officially been represented by the respective Allied military governors, though, since 1948, German "experts" had been allowed to join the military governors' delegation. For obvious reasons, the choice of those delegates was politically very sensitive. There were not many former diplomats available who were not tainted by their associations with the Nazis, and businessmen who had enough diplomatic skills and international experience were scarce. Some suitable candidates (e.g., Karl Blessing) were not willing to take the position, and others were for political reasons unacceptable to the French, as in the case of Hermann Josef Abs, whom the French had refused just weeks earlier for a leading job at the newly established central bank, the Bank deutscher Länder.[23] The man eventually chosen to head the German delegation proved in the event to be inspired. Hans Karl von Mangold, a Munich banker, turned out to be an excellent ambassador for his country who was able to quickly gain the trust and confidence of his European counterparts and thus helped to reintegrate the FRG into the Western fold. Perhaps the best sign of Mangold's diplomatic skill and personal integrity can be seen in the fact that Jacob J. Kaplan and Günther Schleiminger dedicated their book on the EPU to his memory.[24]

THE OEEC'S FAILURE IN ALLOCATING MARSHALL AID

The United States had intended to establish the OEEC with a strong general secretariat and majority voting in the council in order to create a European body able to fulfill US expectations of European integration and to allocate the Marshall aid. The smaller European countries would have welcomed such a structure as it would have given them some protection against the overwhelming political power of the two big countries, Britain and France.[25] However, it was British opposition that prevented such a structure as it was thought to be contrary to UK interests.

Doubtless there was strong and widespread European resistance to all forms, real or perceived, of US meddling in national affairs or the imposition of US ideas on the future OEEC countries.[26] Especially for the British, a strong OEEC central body, in particular one that had political powers and was intending to pursue political aims of European political integration, as the United States had intended, was not acceptable. It would have reduced the United Kingdom to the role of one player among many, putting it into the same league as, say, the Netherlands or Norway (or, for that matter, Luxembourg). For a country that saw itself as a victor of World War II and third only to the United States and the Soviet Union, this prospect was not acceptable, not least because it would have undermined the British claim to great-power status. Perhaps even more important, it would have seriously damaged the myth of the "special relationship" with the United States. Thus, British politicians and diplomats fought doggedly and skillfully against this American proposal and were able to water it down to a level that did not pose such a threat.[27]

In an attempt to counter the more nationalistic individual European approaches and to make the Europeans work together, the ECA decided that it would be up to the OEEC to agree and allocate to the participating countries the ERP aid budget. The unmitigated disaster this decision turned out to be is well known and documented.[28] By early September 1948 and once more under considerable US pressure, the OEEC had finalized the allocation for the aid year 1948–49, but to call the process a tumultuous affair would be a massive understatement.[29] The American military governor, General Clay, had to personally intervene on behalf of the UK-US occupation zones in order to bring their share of the aid to a reasonable level, which in turn did not raise the standing of the German OEEC representatives because the other nations had the feeling that too much aid had been given to them because of Clay's intervention.[30] If the Americans had hoped that things would get better over time, they were to be disappointed. The aid allocation for 1949–50 was even more acrimonious, with Britain asking for as much as 40 percent of the total aid allocated.[31] A complete collapse of the negotiations could only be prevented through the intervention of Robert Marjolin and Baron Jean-Charles Snoy, the OEEC's secretary and council chairman, respectively, who came up with what became known as the Marjolin-Snoy compromise. However, this satisfied no one, not even the Americans, as the compromise overdrew the available funds by $150 million and the Europeans accepted it only with "resentful acrimony."[32] This meeting in August 1949 had demonstrated to the United States that European national interests, and in particular Britain's claim for "special treatment," were far stronger than the will to cooperate in European reconstruction; national interests had not only threatened the meeting but also had brought the OEEC itself close to collapse. Such a failure would have threatened the Marshall Plan as a whole and with it America's anticommunist policy in Europe. Therefore, the ECA decided, in agreement with the OEEC council, to allocate any future aid tranches themselves. Significantly, though, the allocation would be carried out based on the formula developed by Marjolin and Snoy.[33]

It is clear from these events that the OEEC's attempts to allocate the Marshall Plan funds were an outright disaster and without a doubt the OEEC's biggest failure, and yet it may have been the turning point for European cooperation. Bührer cites Ernst van der Beugel, a Dutch delegation member who argued that being confronted with the reconstruction plans of the other countries forced the participants to agree, at least nominally, to a common reconstruction plan, and out of this forced toleration they eventually developed real cooperation.[34] Of course, this argument can be called idealistic and thus dismissed outright, as Milward did when he claimed the OEEC's utter collapse.[35] However, Milward's view does not match up with the continuing existence of the organization and its definitive successes (albeit, again, not without difficulty) in its three other areas of operation.

THE OEEC'S ROLE IN ACHIEVING EUROPEAN CURRENCY CONVERTIBILITY AND TRADE LIBERALIZATION

Europe's postwar economic recovery was closely linked with, if not outright dependent on, trade liberalization and currency convertibility, and both issues themselves were closely intertwined. The era of relative free trade in Europe had ended in 1914 with the outbreak of World War I. The failure in the interwar years to reestablish free trade and a stable international currency system was a key contributor to the Great Depression and the subsequent rise of the Nazis in Germany. The absence of a free-trade system for more than thirty years had helped to entrench in European minds the idea that bilateralism provided economic safety and security for a national economy, in particular if a country could dominate smaller trading partners. Weimar Germany and even more so the Nazi economic policy under Reichsbank president and economics minister Hjalmar Schacht are only the most infamous examples of this thinking. After World War II, lack of dollars hampered intra-European trade, but this shortage of, and need for, dollars was simply a reaction to a nonexisting system of currency convertibility or a proper payments-clearing system.

How desperately a solution to this system was needed became obvious in the 1947 sterling crisis. A response to this was attempted by the ERP with what was called "the little Marshall Plan." From October 1948 onward, Marshall Plan countries that had a trade surplus with other European countries had to grant so-called drawing rights to countries with a trade deficit. In essence, the ECA told the surplus countries to allocate a small share of their Marshall aid allocations to the deficit countries to reduce their trade deficit. The system, known as "conditional aid," had significant shortfalls and was even criticized as "Monte Carlo roulette" due to a level of unpredictability, and at the end of its lifetime by mid-1950, 15 percent of allocated funds had not been used.[36] Overall, Barry Eichengreen's criticism is not totally unjustified but too strong. Kaplan and Schleiminger have pointed out that in just the first six months of the little Marshall Plan, $200 million were used for intra-European trade and claim that this broke the existing logjam of intra-European payments.[37] Nevertheless, the ECA realized that a more powerful system was needed to really get intra-European trade going. Consequently, on December 9, 1949, the agency proposed to the OEEC a European payment union.[38] Once again, the Europeans were still stuck in the entrenched nationalist mentality they had adopted over the last thirty-five years and had displayed during the OEEC's attempts to allocate Marshall aid. Volker Hentschel goes so far as to question whether the Europeans on their own would have set up a payments union at all because this would have meant to join a "*Solidargemeinschaft*"—a community based on shared principles of mutuality—which would have run counter to egotistic national interests. So, it was once more the ECA that had to apply pressure and threaten an end to further US aid before, in mid-June 1950, the OEEC agreed to the ECA proposals. The outbreak of the Korean War one week later seems to have focused minds: at its meeting on July 6–7, the OEEC council formally adopted the proposal, so that the EPU was officially created on September 19, although it had started its operations already on July 1.[39]

The workings of the EPU have been well described in literature before, and it is seen as one of the success stories of the OEEC.[40] Yet the overall impact and significance of the EPU is not fully appreciated, in particular in the English-speaking world, which becomes clear when looking at the EPU's first crisis less than six months into its existence. Eichengreen's study of the EPU is a case in point. He mentions the "German trade expansion," but while he rightly attributes this to the EPU, he fails altogether to explain the scale of the crisis this expansion caused and how it was the EPU that solved it.[41] Perhaps more than the other big industrialized countries in Europe, West Germany had been dependent on Marshall aid to sustain its economic recovery. But despite imports of $1.6 billion under the GARIOA (Government Appropriations for Relief in Occupied Areas) aid program (mainly food, fuel, feed, and medicines) and $1.4 billion under Marshall aid, Germany's balance of payments had remained negative throughout the late 1940s. Up to late 1949, when the economics minister, Ludwig Erhard, liberalized foreign trade restrictions in order to boost his version of the "Social Market Economy," German imports and exports had amounted to about $72 million per month in each direction. From November 1949 to June 1950, average monthly imports increased to $120 million, compared with $95 million of exports. The outbreak of the Korean War and the almost simultaneous creation of the EPU accelerated this trend significantly. While EPU rules allowed the FRG to import even more raw materials and the Economics Ministry issued more and more import licenses and requested ever more foreign currencies from the central bank for the purpose, the Korean War had two simultaneous impacts: world raw material prices rose by about 25 percent, and the terms of payment changed, with exporters now demanding much faster payment.[42] Consequently, West Germany's trade and balance-of-payments deficit increased significantly, and foreign currency deposits fell even faster. On December 13, 1950, West Germany had to approach the EPU to ask for a special line of credit of $180 million in order to avoid insolvency. Both Hentschel and Bührer agree that this loan has to be seen as an act of European solidarity of the other EPU member states.[43] This is despite the fact that the decision to grant the special line of credit was made only after controversial discussion among the OEEC countries, which expressed their significant displeasure about German import policy. Of course, willingness to support the FRG at this stage was not driven by sheer idealism. Almost all European countries needed West Germany as a trading partner, either because they imported German goods or as a market for their own. This situation shows the strong economic (and thus political) position West Germany was actually in: the country was needed both as market and as supplier, which partly explains the extra credits provided.[44]

In December 1950, it appeared for a short time as if the German balance-of-payments crisis began to ease, but despite economic warnings from the Central Bank and despite political warnings from Mangold in Paris, the Economics Ministry encouraged continued and increased imports. This caused international and domestic upset. Other OEEC members accused the FRG of a new form of "beggar-thy-neighbor" policy as the special line of credit was used to purchase scarce raw materials on the world market, and Wilhelm Vocke, the chairman of the Central Bank, was warning that if things did not change, West Germany's trade liberalization would have to be suspended due to lack of funds.[45] The writing was on the wall, and unsurprisingly the situation deteriorated very fast. By January 1951, the deficit had reached its highest level and in the first two weeks of February alone surpassed the size of the January deficit. The suspension of liberalized imports had become unavoidable, and they had eventually to be deferred on February 21, 1951. This signified, as did some other events in Germany (in particular the *Investitionshilfe Gesetz* [Auxiliary Investment Law], which was passed in 1952), a failure of Erhard's brand of "social market economy."[46]

It would be an understatement to say that the other OEEC members were "not pleased" about the suspension of Germany's import liberalization, and there were suggestions that Germany should be excluded from the organization. After all, Erhard had used most of the special line of credit, which was supposed to run until April 1951, not to improve the balance-of-payments situation but to acquire more raw materials. Had the FRG been thrown out of the EPU, it would have lost all remaining international credit, which would have terminally devastated its economic situation.[47] Seen from this angle, it is highly likely that Konrad Adenauer's letter to the Allied High Commission of March 6, 1951, in which he acknowledged German pre- and postwar foreign debt, was just an attempt to allay Western anger over Germany's irresponsible economic policy.[48] Indeed, the suspension of import liberalization had no immediate effect; in the two weeks following the suspension, the deficit got worse.

The turnaround that followed after the second week in March is both remarkable and as yet not fully explained.[49] By the end of March, Germany's trade deficit had fallen to the lowest level since the creation of the EPU; at the end of the second quarter of 1951, the country had achieved a quarterly trade surplus of $183 million and a payments surplus of $173 million. By the end of November 1951, the FRG had turned from a debtor nation to a creditor, or from "problem case into troublemaker," as the surplus would steadily grow. In January 1952, trade liberalizations were restored.[50]

Eichengreen's assessment of the EPU as "a special arrangement designed to respond to the challenges and opportunities facing Western Europe after World War Two" is absolutely accurate.[51] He points out that while there had indeed been alternatives to the EPU, the union, imperfect as it was, was essential for the reconstruction of Western Europe because the alternatives available were politically not palatable (or outright unacceptable) at the time.[52] Thus, Eichengreen's speculation about alternatives to the EPU in the setting of 1949–50 is to a large extent an issue of economic theory versus political reality and therefore a bit artificial. The fact that he does not mention at all the German payments crisis (and the EPU's role in it), despite the existential danger it posed for Western Europe at the time, confirms the hypothetical nature of some of his arguments.

The introduction of currency convertibility in 1958 made the EPU superfluous and allowed its dissolution.[53] But before this happened, the EPU had to help resolve other situations. The most important was arguably the French economic crisis in the second half of the 1950s. While the German payments crisis had the potential to halt and reverse European reconstruction altogether, the French case might not have been as devastating, but it would have caused significant negative economic effects to its European neighbors. Paul M. Pitman argues that it was EPU loans and the upcoming end of the EPU itself that helped (and forced) the French to turn their economy around by strengthening the need for economic reform and trade liberalization. He admits that while the overall influence of the EPU was waning, it was this declining influence that made the French seek further integration into "the Lotharingian core of the European continent."[54]

Despite all the arguing and problems among its members, the EPU has to be seen as a success in stimulating intra-European trade. However, as Eichengreen's statistics show, while trade did indeed grow because of the EPU's clearing system, the scheme could expand trade only up to a certain level.[55] Trade restrictions, both tariffs and import quotas, which the European countries had introduced in the interwar period, remained a stumbling block. Milward points out that since 1929, almost all German and Italian imports had quotas imposed, while France and Switzerland had quantitative limits on about 50 percent of their imports.[56] The ECA's plans for increased European trade could only succeed if those trade barriers were removed, and once again the OEEC was the organization that was to bring about these changes. The eventual success of this trade liberalization, Monika Dickhaus argues, was only possible because of the EPU agreement.[57] Considering how important European trade was for the continent's reconstruction, it is surprising that the OEEC's role in the process has not been studied in more detail. It certainly deserves closer scholarly attention.

Some European countries clung to the restrictive patterns they had learned and internalized since World War I more than others. Only bilateral trade deals, they thought, would bring benefits to their country's economy or maintain political influence. One of the firmest opponents of European trade liberalization was Britain, which continued to favor bilateral agreements since in this way it expected to keep more political and economic leverage over its European trading partners. ECA administrator Paul Hoffman accused Britain of "a long-run[ning] policy of nationalism" and eventually had to apply very strong pressure for the country to agree to trade liberalization.[58] Other countries' actions were not much better. Once British obstinacy had become clear, France had tried to introduce a system of a small European customs union of France, Italy, Netherlands, Belgium, and Luxemburg (FINeBeL). Negotiations about the scheme went on throughout 1948–49, but they had significant shortfalls. The French ideas to open up trade were limited from the outset—for example, they refused to consider expanding the scheme to include West Germany, something that was unacceptable to the Netherlands. As a result, although the United States saw customs unions initially as a first step forward, they were not enough to receive full American backing and thus went nowhere.[59] By the end of 1949, the French had all but given up on the FINeBeL idea. This was when another attempt to create a small customs union, the so-called UNISCAN, was developed by Britain and Norway in their combined anti-Europeanism.[60] Miward's criticism of this scheme, and in particular of the myopic outlook with which Britain approached it, is justified. UNISCAN can be seen as a precursor to the equally doomed British attempt to establish a European Free Trade Association (EFTA) in 1960 in response to the creation of the European Economic Community.[61]

Considering the difficult birth of the OEEC and the lengthy negotiations about the EPU, trade liberalization was not easy either, and on closer inspection, many narratives created about national "champions of liberalization" turned out to be nothing more than myths. This is particularly true in the West German case. The ECA had to recognize that by early 1950, the two big European powers, Britain and France, were trying very much to pursue their own narrow national interests, and the United States had to realize that even threats of withholding Marshall aid could only go so far.[62] It was therefore hoped that the leading role in trade liberalization would be taken up by West Germany, the continent's potentially strongest economy. However, here they found strong resistance against trade liberalization as well, in particular from Ludwig Erhard, who only later on styled himself as the free-trader-in-chief.[63] The German position was expressed by the country's chief economist at the OEEC, Otmar Emminger, who suggested that the FRG should sign or extend as many bilateral trade agreements as possible before a 50 percent trade liberalization the OEEC had painfully negotiated came into force on October 1, 1949. These new agreements were then to be presented as Germany's contribution to trade liberalization.[64] When West Germany presented a first draft of its liberalization plans on October 10, 1949 (even before it had officially joined the OEEC), the numbers suggested that the country would liberalize 74.9 percent of its OEEC area imports, although a closer look showed that in fact only 37.4 percent of commodities were really free, the rest being statistical window dressing. Almost half (47.9 percent) of these imports were raw materials, and a further 28.5 percent were foodstuffs. Still, Bührer points out that even the actual percentage of liberalized imports put the FRG ahead of most other OEEC countries, as their average liberalization was just 30 percent.[65]

Once again, it was US intervention that moved things forward. During the OEEC's meeting on October 30–31, 1949, ECA administrator Paul Hoffman was able to persuade the Europeans to agree a 50 percent liberalization from January 1, 1950, onward. There were renewed US hopes that Germany would become the pacemaker for extended liberalization by promising further unilateral liberalization without reciprocity from other OEEC countries. This was out of the question because West Germany was struggling to reach the 50 percent target in the first place. It only managed to do so due to an ambiguity in the OEEC agreement text that did not specify whether the 50 percent liberalization had to be achieved in all three areas—raw materials (69 percent), foodstuffs (29 percent), and finished products (33 percent)—in order to qualify or the total of imports applied.[66]

The OEEC continued its pressure for trade liberalization and reached a further step with the creation of the EPU, wherein the participating member states agreed to expand trade liberalization to 60 percent. However, West Germany could not be the pacemaker the United States had hoped for. There were political pressures at home on the Adenauer government, with large parts of industry calling for a slower pace in the liberalization. These calls emanated not only from the usual suspects, such as the textile and steel industry, but also from more export-driven sectors such as chemicals. Economically, West Germany was even more unsuited to take the leading—and especially unilateral—role. It lacked the necessary currency reserves and had a growing balance-of-payments deficit.[67] While the latter had been mainly due to the country's own decisions, the suspension of trade liberalization altogether in February 1951 demonstrated the German weakness in this area.

There were other fronts on which the OEEC continued to fight for free trade. By the middle of the 1950s, it had taken up the fight against national export subsidies, and this time West Germany was at the forefront of the campaign. However, total trade liberalization was still not achieved as several countries, most notably France, were very keen to protect their agricultural sectors from opening up their markets. It is at this point (and similarly to the development of the ECSC) that West Germany prioritized the political rapprochement with France over further trade liberalization, even to its own detriment: West Germany would have benefited more from cheaper non-OEEC farm imports. Instead, Adenauer, contrary to OEEC attempts, supported the French line on agricultural protectionism.[68] It was only at a very late stage and in combination with the French balance-of-payments crisis in 1957–58 that the OEEC was finally able to overcome French resistances to the liberalization of agricultural imports.[69]

The overall effectiveness of French liberalization can be questioned, as the newly founded EEC would have taken over at least parts of the protective measures. Nevertheless, in the face of differing national interests and significant national egotisms, the OEEC's labors to increase unfettered intra-European trade at a time when the general mind-set was still steeped in protectionism has to be seen as a success. Of course, the process took a very long time and, as already seen in the case of the EPU, it needed compromises by all sides involved—European as well as American. The fact that from the 1960s onward most European politicians, businessmen, and ordinary citizens saw trade liberalization and free trade in general as the best way forward for the European economies is the clearest sign that the OEEC fulfilled its task in this field. It may have done so in an imperfect way, but that is the nature of compromise.

THE OEEC'S ROLE IN EUROPEAN PRODUCTIVITY IMPROVEMENTS

The OEEC's program for expanding European productivity is by far the least researched of the organization's three major aims. Bührer covers this part of the organization's activities in two and a half pages. He highlights the OEEC's very ambitious target of raising European productivity by 25 percent over a five-year period, from mid-1951 to 1956.[70] The short chapter on the European Productivity Agency (EPA) by Bent Boel in Griffiths's volume confirms the lack of secondary literature; all his references are to archival material or OEEC reports.[71] Right at the beginning of the ERP, the Americans had identified Europe's lack of productivity as the key obstacle to economic recovery. In order to alleviate the problem, they had initiated the United States Technical Assistance Program (USTAP) as part of the Marshall Plan, a scheme that also included training European management in American business methods.[72] It is therefore not surprising that already in 1949 the OEEC had set up a Committee for Productivity, although apparently due to British requests this was soon divided into two committees.[73] When in 1952 the Mutual Security Agency (MSA), the successor body to the ECA, proposed a new European productivity agency, there was little European enthusiasm, although the MSA was to provide $100 million from ERP counterpart funds. The strongest opposition came, once again, from Britain, whose representatives spoke of a "distasteful proposal."[74] Despite British resistance, in March 1953, the OEEC decided to establish the EPA, which took up operations in May. It is not surprising that the new body was founded as a semiautonomous agency of the OEEC, as the organization's general secretary, Robert Marjolin, was of the firm opinion that European increases in productivity could solve all of the OEEC's big problems: balance of payments, currency convertibility, and trade liberalization.[75] It can only be speculated why the British were opposed to European cooperation. They possibly saw American tutelage as humiliating to the country that had sparked the Industrial Revolution and had prided itself on having been "the workshop of the world." Or, more deviously, it was a British attempt to keep their productivity advantage over their European competitors. In any case, considering what happened to British industry from the 1960s onward and how much the British fell behind their European rivals, their decision was mistaken.

While it appears that in its early years the EPA was "simply the continuation of the technical assistance project," Boel argues that from 1956 onward, when the Europeans had to carry the costs of the agency themselves, it began to transform into a "Europeanized" organization with increased OEEC-internal cooperation.[76] Although he speaks of the EPA's "relative success" in raising productivity, Boel claims that it is impossible to estimate, let alone precisely measure, its real impact.[77] What is clear is that European productivity did significantly increase during the 1950s, with France, Germany, and Italy seeing productivity increases of 5.0, 5.2, and 5.5 percent, respectively, for the period 1953 to 1961. The only exception to these significant improvements was Britain, where productivity growth was only 2 percent.[78] In a recent study on the West German "economic miracle," Tamás Vonyó argues that in the German case actual increases in productivity due to increased mechanization and rationalization happened only from the mid-1950s onward. Until then, any rise in output was merely the result of increased input factors, in particular a growing labor force, which could utilize production capacity that had been expanded under the Nazis.[79]

There were certainly other factors at play that contributed to Europe's growth in productivity. The creation of the ECSC in 1951–53 prevented, or at least reduced, competing investments in basic industries. Growing labor shortages almost everywhere in Western Europe forced companies to rationalize and take the first steps into automation. The growing boom in world trade and exports from the mid-1950s onward had a significant effect, if only by encouraging companies to modernize. From all this it is clear that large parts of the productivity increases are subsumed under growth factors other than the OEEC's productivity program. Nevertheless, one should not underestimate the fact that in too many cases the OEEC's role was deliberately and conveniently "forgotten" in favor of national *Heldensagen* (heroic sagas) of how the reconstruction was achieved by a country on its own and by its own means and institutions, including national productivity agencies. The West German "economic miracle" is a case in point. Even in the 1990s, some German economists called for a return to the economic policy principles of the 1950s to revive the economy, which had been flagging in the wake of German unification.[80]

It is obvious that the OEEC was a product of its time. Its creation but perhaps even more so its end and subsequent transformation into the OECD are testaments to this. There are several interlocking and overlapping reasons why the OEEC has been all but forgotten as an institution. In the first instance, it was the Marshall Plan itself that caught people's attention—that of scholars and laypersons alike—so much more. It is nigh impossible for an administrative agency to compete with the famous Marshall Plan, which was supposed to have saved Europe. As historians, we have to accept the fact that some topics are just "sexier" than others. There are, of course, other less obvious reasons why the OEEC is not so popular in either American or European memory. For one, the organization reminds the Europeans that it was the Americans who had to drag them kicking and screaming into the OEEC and into the various multinational agreements that the organization created. Having to rely on an international body and international cooperation for their reconstruction was in direct conflict with national self-perception and pride.

What the OEEC is mainly remembered for is the failure of its member countries to agree upon the allocation of the Marshall Plan funds. This can be seen as a failure of European willingness to cooperate, which shows the Europeans as following their own national egotisms, something that is in contrast to the idea of European unity peddled so much in the 1950s. The early history of the OEEC also highlights the inability of the Americans to push through their ideas in face of European opposition. Not even the supposedly all-powerful United States was able to implement its ideas of the OEEC as the active starting point for European political integration. The various European national (and nationalist) interests were too strong to allow this. Regardless of this clear early failure of US intentions and the Europeans' failure willingly to compromise, the OEEC was crucial for European reconstruction and integration. It made the Europeans—at least those on the continent—realize that they would have to cooperate and compromise if they wanted to reconstruct their countries. For the smaller countries, the OEEC apparatus and procedures allowed some protection from the power and influence of the two big countries, Britain and France, and their respective policies. For this reason alone, they learned to appreciate the organization, despite strong grumblings early on, as the Norwegian case has shown.[81] For West Germany, the OEEC was the first tentative step back onto the international stage and an exercise in creating trust among its neighbors. It was in regard to Germany that the OEEC's subsidiary body, the EPU, took what can be seen as the most crucial step—namely, providing the extra line of credit for Germany, despite the fact that at the time the FRG acted egotistically. The extra line of credit should be understood as politically vital for future European integration for a simple reason: while Germany's political integration in the OEEC context was important for Chancellor Adenauer's policy of *Westintegration* (integration into the West), economic historians agree that had the FRG crashed out of the EPU, the consequences would have been dire not only for Germany. The 1920s had shown what a negative impact the absence of Germany within the European trading bloc could have. If the OEEC countries had lost West Germany in 1951 as provider and as a market, the economic consequences for European reconstruction would have been devastating. In the light of initial European obstinacy, it is doubtful whether the United States would have had provided additional funds to the Marshall Plan to prop up a failing Europe even further. The OEEC's role in saving the Germans from themselves thus should be seen as the organization's single biggest achievement, and for this achievement alone it has to be seen—contrary to Milward's view—as an astounding success.

NOTES

1 Gerd Hardach, *Der Marshall Plan: Auslandshilfe und Wiederaufbau in Westdeutschland 1948–1952* (Munich: dtv Wissenschaft, 1994), 13.
2 Hans-Peter Schwarz, "Die europäische Integration als Aufgabe der Zeitgeschichtsforschung: Forschungsstand und Perspektiven," *Vierteljahrshefte für Zeitgeschichte* 31, no. 4 (October 1983): 555–72, 556.
3 Schwarz, "Integration."
4 Good examples for this approach are Michael Hogan, *The Marshall Plan: America, Britain and the Reconstruction of Western Europe, 1947–1952* (Cambridge: Cambridge University Press, 1987); Chiarella Esposito, *America's Feeble Weapon: Funding the Marshall Plan in France and Italy, 1948–1950* (Westport, CT: Greenwood, 1994); and Alan Milward, *The Reconstruction of Western Europe 1945–1951* (London: Routledge, 1984).
5 Milward, *Reconstruction,* 168.
6 Milward, 69–89, 168–211, here 195.
7 Milward, 89, 195.

8 Jacob J. Kaplan and Günther Schleiminger, *The European Payments Union: Financial Diplomacy in the 1950s* (Oxford: Clarendon, 1989); Volker Hentschel, "Die Europäische Zahlungsunion und die deutsche Devisenkrise 1950/51," *Vierteljahrshefte für Zeitgeschichte* 37, no. 4 (October 1989): 715–58; Barry Eichengreen, *Reconstructing Europe's Trade and Payments: The European Payment Union* (Manchester: Manchester University Press, 1993).

9 Eichengreen, *Reconstructing Europe's Trade.*

10 Werner Bührer, *Westdeutschland in der OEEC: Eingliederung, Krise, Bewährung 1947–1961* (Munich: Oldenbourg, 1997).

11 Richard T. Griffiths, ed., *Explorations in OEEC History* (Paris: OECD, 1997).

12 Wendy Askbeek Brusse and Richard T. Griffiths, "Exploring the OEEC's Past and Sources," in Griffiths, *Explorations,* 15–32, 17.

13 Harvard Speech, in *Foreign Relations of the United States,* 1947, The British Commonwealth, Europe, vol. 3, ed. S. Everett Gleason, Fredrick Aandahl, Ralph E. Goodwin, Marvin W. Kranz, David H. Stauffer, Howard M. Smyth, and Owen Sappington (Washington, DC: Government Printing Office, 1972), 237–39.

14 Kaplan and Schleiminger, *European Payments Union,* 16.

15 Milward, *Reconstruction,* 70–89.

16 Milward, 80.

17 Milward, 85, 203–4.

18 Hentschel, "Zahlungsunion," 718.

19 Bührer, *Westdeutschland,* 68–69.

20 Bührer, 51; Milward, *Reconstruction,* 178.

21 Bührer, *Westdeutschland,* 58–59.

22 Bührer, 68–71.

23 On Abs's rejection for the Bank deutscher Länder, see Armin Grünbacher, *Reconstruction and Cold War in Germany: The Kreditanstalt für Wiederaufbau 1948–1961* (Aldershot, UK: Ashgate, 2004), 30–31.

24 Kaplan and Schleiminger, *European Payments Union,* dedication.

25 Milward, *Reconstruction,* 171.

26 Milward, 174–80.

27 Milward, 184.

28 See, among others, Bührer, *Westdeutschland;* Hardach, *Marshall Plan;* Hogan, *Marshall Plan;* Imanuel Wexler, *The Marshall Plan Revisited: The European Recovery Programme in Economic Perspective* (London: Greenwood, 1983).

29 Milward, *Reconstruction,* 189.

30 Bührer, *Westdeutschland,* 104–8.

31 Milward, *Reconstruction,* 85, 203–4.

32 Kaplan and Schleiminger, *European Payments Union,* 19; Bührer, *Westdeutschland,* 120; Milward, *Reconstruction,* 206.

33 Bührer, *Westdeutschland,* 123; Milward, *Reconstruction,* 207.

34 Ernst van der Beugel, *From Marshall Aid to Atlantic Partnership: European Integration as a Concern of American Foreign Policy* (Amsterdam: Elsevier, 1966), 147, cited in Bührer, *Westdeutschland,* 114.
35 Milward, *Reconstruction,* 69–89, 168–211.
36 Eichengreen, *Reconstructing,* 21–25.
37 Kaplan and Schleiminger, *European Payments Union,* 24.
38 Hentschel, "Zahlungsunion," 725.
39 Hentschel, 727, 731.
40 For details, see the already mentioned works by Schleiminger and Kaplan, Hentschel, Eichengreen, and Bührer, which also provide ample further reading on the topic.
41 Eichenrgeen, *Reconstructing,* 32.
42 Hentschel, "Zahlungsunion," 731, 734, 747–48.
43 Hentschel, 746; Bührer, *Westdeutschland,* 214.
44 Bührer, *Westdeutschland,* 221.
45 Bührer, 209, 219.
46 Hentschel, "Zahlungsunion," 749, 751. For the Investitionshilfe Gesetz, see Grünbacher, *Reconstruction,* 94–106. The Investitionshilfe Gesetz raised DM 1 billion from all commercial businesses in support of basic industries (coal, iron, steel, and electricity) after the Korean War had exposed them as bottleneck sectors due to lack of investment, which now prevented further output expansion. In addition, the bill granted the sectors significant tax depreciation, totaling DM 3.2 billion, on new investments.
47 Hentschel, "Zahlungsunion," 745, 752–53.
48 The National Archives, Kew, UK, Public Record Office, FO 371 93728.
49 Hentschel, "Zahlungsunion," 754.
50 Hentschel, 754–56.
51 Eichengreen, *Reconstructing,* ix.
52 Eichengreen, 81–84, 94.
53 Richard T. Griffiths, "'An Act of Creative Leadership': The End of the OEEC and the Birth of the OECD," in Griffiths, *Explorations,* 235–56, 235.
54 Paul M. Pitman, "The French Crisis and the Dissolution of the European Payments Union, 1956–1958," in Griffiths, *Explorations,* 219–27 *passim.*
55 Eichengreen, *Reconstructing,* 27, 29.
56 Milward, *Reconstruction,* 299.
57 Monika Dickhaus, "'It's Only the Provisional That Lasts': The European Payments Union," in Griffiths, *Explorations,* 183–200, 185–86.
58 Dickhaus, "'Only the Provisional,'" 187.
59 Milward, *Reconstruction,* 300–303.
60 Milward, 316–19.
61 The members of the 1960s EFTA were Britain, Austria, Switzerland, Sweden, and Portugal, with a combined population of 89 million (51 million of whom were British)—compared to the EEC's 170 million. The size of the internal

market explains in part why, from 1957 to 1961, European GDP grew by 27 percent compared to Britain's 14 percent. See Martin Dedman, *The Origins and Development of the European Union 1945–1995* (London: Routledge, 1996), 111–12.

62 See Esposito, *America's Feeble Weapon.*

63 Bührer, *Westdeutschland,* 140–44. For Erhard's claims of being an early adopter of free trade, see Ludwig Erhard, *Deutschlands Rückkehr zum Weltmarkt* (Dusseldorf: Econ-Verlag, 1954), also available as *Germany's Comeback in the World Markets* (London: Allen & Unwin, 1954).

64 Bührer, *Westdeutschland,* 179–80.

65 Bührer, 181–88.

66 Bührer, 184–85.

67 Bührer, 183, 198.

68 Bührer, 329–39.

69 Pitman, "French Crisis," 224.

70 Bührer, *Westdeutschland,* 232–34.

71 Bent Boel, "The European Productivity Agency, 1953–1961," in Griffiths, *Explorations,* 113–22.

72 See Jacqueline McGlade, "The United States Technical Assistance Programme: From Reform Programme to Production Drive," in *The Americanisation of European Business,* ed. Matthias Kipping and Ove Bjarner (London: Routledge, 1998), 18–34.

73 Boel, "European Productivity Agency," 114.

74 Boel, 114.

75 Boel, 113.

76 Boel, 116–17.

77 Boel, 118.

78 See, e.g., Andrea Boltho, "Growth," in *The European Economy. Growth and Crisis,* ed. Andrea Boltho (Oxford: Oxford University Press, 1982), 9–37, 22.

79 Tamás Vonyó, *The Economic Consequences of the War: West Germany's Growth Miracle after 1945* (Cambridge: Cambridge University Press, 2018), 87–128.

80 See, e.g., Herbert Giersch, Karl-Heinz Paque, and Holger Schmieding, *The Fading Miracle: Four Decades of Market Economy in Germany* (Cambridge: Cambridge University Press, 1994).

81 Milward, *Reconstruction,* 85, 203–4.

CHAPTER 4

Shaping Australia into a Neighborhood Power

Decolonization, Vulnerability, and the Cold War

LAURA M. SEDDELMEYER

When one thinks about the Cold War, the first thought might not be of Australia, due to its isolation from centers of conflict. However, Australia's experiences during the Cold War era were relevant, varied, and transformative. As a nation of Western heritage located "on the edge of Asia," Australia has an outlook and experiences that extend beyond its national borders.[1] Events unraveling on Australia's doorstep from the 1960s through the 1970s, such as British decolonization, postcolonial uncertainty in the Asia-Pacific region, and US policy changes toward Asia, linked Australian interests with broader global changes. Australia could not ignore the potential instability created by regional events or the fading visibility of traditional allies in the region. The concerns of the global Cold War became peripheral to the more immediate need to stabilize and secure the Asia-Pacific region in the wake of British decolonization. While officials in Canberra understood the value of considering all of the Asia-Pacific as an area of concern, they understood that Australia's immediate "neighborhood"—Indonesia, Papua New Guinea, the Southwest Pacific, the maritime approaches to Australia, and Antarctica—required particular attention. Consequently, Canberra reevaluated its strategic outlook and asserted Australia's distinct national interests within its neighborhood to achieve stability and security. Over time, this strategy ultimately strengthened Australia's position as a regional ally within a broad Western alliance during the Cold War.[2]

The focus of scholarship about Australia's postwar relations often looks in one of three directions. The first examines Australia's developing relationship with the United States, which included a surge of scholarship about Australia's decision to join the United States in the Vietnam War.[3] The second direction reevaluates the Anglo-Australian relationship within the context of post–World War II changes.[4] A third direction includes scholarship that examines Australia's engagement in Southeast Asian conflicts.[5] While these directions are not mutually exclusive and often overlap, the scholarly conversations often end in the 1960s with questions about the 1970s left unanswered or underdeveloped due, in part, to limited sources. Respected scholars, such as Coral Bell, have attributed Australian motives for engagement to its relationship with its "great and powerful friends"—Britain and the United States. However, in doing so, Australia's independent motives have been dismissed and its consistent interest in regional affairs minimized. Alliances mattered to Australia, especially postwar formal and informal alliances with Britain and the United States, but Australia could be both a good ally and capable of making decisions that were right for its own national interests at the same time. In fact, prioritizing regional alliances and development had the potential to strengthen Australia's position as a valuable Western ally in the Southern Hemisphere.

Recently declassified documents provide an opportunity for fuller assessment of Australia's Cold War experiences during the late 1960s and 1970s. The changes that Australia experienced during these decades followed a pattern of ongoing shifts in the relationship between Britain and its empire throughout the twentieth century. For Britain, a relationship built on imperial preference at the beginning of the century transitioned into a period of decolonization after World War II. For many Pacific colonies, decolonization gave way to independence and uncertainty in the 1960s and 1970s.[6] For Australia, a century that began with federation and reliance on British defense support developed into a postwar period of increasing responsibility in the Asia-Pacific due, in large part, to decolonization.[7] In 1967, Australian prime minister Harold Holt acknowledged that "some of the greatest dangers and some of the greatest opportunities exist in this part of the world [Asia] today."[8] His words could not have been more accurate in characterizing the decade ahead for Australia. The perceived dangers created by the Cold War and decolonization provided the opportunities Canberra needed to develop an independent long-term strategy. Australia's actions in the late 1960s and 1970s reflected both its emerging independent strategy to develop into a neighborhood power and its efforts to strengthen its position as a key Western ally in the Asia-Pacific.

Twenty years after British decolonization began with the partition of India in 1947, it expanded east of the Suez Canal—or "east of Suez"—and served as a catalyst for Australia's search for regional stability during a period of uncertainty. By July 1967, the rumblings of British decolonization in the Asia-Pacific region came to fruition with British prime minister Harold Wilson's announcement of Britain's withdrawal of defense forces and facilities from east of Suez. The official press release outlined plans in Asia for a 50 percent reduction of troops from Malaysia and Singapore by 1970–71. In addition to the progressive withdrawal of forty thousand troops from the region over the next few years, Britain planned to provide economic aid to Malaysia and Singapore to compensate for the tremendous economic losses resulting from the abandonment of dockyards and airstrips. While the official text omitted the exact date of withdrawal, it mentioned complete withdrawal by the mid-1970s.[9] The decision was not a surprise to government officials in Australia, New Zealand, Malaysia, or Singapore; all had been informed through official visits about the likelihood of withdrawal in April of that year. Still, Prime Minister Holt publicly remarked that Britain's new defense policy came as a "shock to the system" and denounced proposals for the reduction of troops by half in the region. He also worked in conjunction with his contemporaries in the United States, New Zealand, Singapore, and Malaysia to influence the terms of withdrawal.[10] Officials in Canberra objected to Britain's departure because they viewed it as a threat to the stability and security of Southeast Asia in the face of a global communist threat. Additionally, the withdrawal of forces and abandonment of facilities in Southeast Asia created a vacuum that left Australian borders vulnerable and South Pacific security compromised. In response to increasing concerns, officials in Canberra began to reassess Australian strategy with the goal of stabilizing Southeast Asia and securing the dependencies in the South Pacific from external threats.

Concerns in Canberra increased when the United States delivered a perceived second blow to security in the Asia-Pacific region. President

Richard Nixon's remarks in July 1969 during a press conference in Guam, later known as the Nixon Doctrine, acknowledged that the United States planned to reassess its policy in the region after the Vietnam War ended. Nixon explained that the United States would expect Asian nations to become increasingly responsible for their own internal and external defense, unless the nation faced a nuclear attack.[11] In response to questions from the press, Nixon expanded on his views of US-Asian relations and the expectations after Vietnam with three points. First, the United States planned to uphold its treaty commitments. Second, military and internal security issues became the primary responsibility of Asian governments rather than the United States. Finally, collective security with the potential for US support provided a long-term solution for regional security.[12] Some officials in Canberra questioned how Australia fit into the changes Nixon proposed and how a reduced American presence might change the regional dynamic.[13] Within the span of two years, it appeared as though Australia's two English-speaking allies wanted to leave a region that remained critical to Australian security, leaving Canberra struggling to compensate for the losses in the midst of the Cold War.

The beginning of the 1970s offered more clarity in Canberra about the motives behind British and American decisions, as well as their impact on Australian defense planning. Britain had already unveiled its intention to withdraw military forces from east of the Suez Canal in 1967, and the fulfillment of the plans reinforced the importance placed on the relationship with Europe. The United States, through the expression of the Nixon Doctrine, clarified its own position toward Asia by emphasizing self-reliance and a contraction of US power in Asia. Britain's decision resulted from economic problems, which influenced political and military decisions in Southeast Asia. For the United States, the public outcry resulting from the Vietnam War created an environment in which the United States could no longer serve as the primary guarantor of security in mainland Asia. Though British and American officials reassured Australians of their ongoing commitments to the security of the Asia-Pacific, the Australian defense establishment undertook back-to-back reviews to identify potential risks and build the capacity to respond to such threats without the regional presence of its great and powerful friends. By the end of the decade, Canberra not only recognized the need to reevaluate the core of Australia's defense outlook in response to the changes but also identified the importance of shaping itself into what officials would eventually call a neighborhood power to ensure stability in a vulnerable region.

The 1970s began a transitional period, which left Canberra considering how to reconcile Australia's limitations with its long-term interests in becoming a neighborhood power. Instead of viewing Australia's isolation from its Western allies as a disadvantage, Canberra began to acknowledge the advantages. Distance from centers of global conflict offered the stability necessary to develop an independent approach to defense that could guide Australia's strategic outlook in the decades ahead.[14] As part of an overall reevaluation of Australian strategy, a 1970 report from the National Intelligence Committee (NIC), a group that reported to the larger Defence Committee, determined that the "great and powerful friends of yesteryear can no longer be relied upon to work to produce situations which will go most of the way towards solving Australia's problems."[15] In the same report, the NIC identified Australia's regional problems as the move toward independence in Papua New Guinea and the Southwest Pacific (two areas in the neighborhood), an increase in Soviet activity, and Chinese-initiated insurgency and subversion. With so many changes and challenges happening on Australia's doorstep, the NIC determined that the oceans and airspace, areas where defense officials had previously expressed concern, were now even more vulnerable to potential disruptions of air and sea communications due to decolonization and Cold War tension.[16]

The 1970 NIC report influenced Australian defense planning in the neighborhood; Australia focused on the Southwest Pacific to preserve lines of communication and address potential vulnerability. Independence, remote location, general lack of resources, and small population made the Southwest Pacific islands less relevant for US Cold War concerns, but the islands remained critical to Australia. Canberra wanted to preserve communication lines, maritime interests, and access to strategically important facilities, allowing Australian air and naval patrols to combat such issues as smuggling, gun running, and "intrusions" into Australian areas of interest.[17] Due to geography and relative isolation from its allies, Australia depended on the protection of sea and air lines for defense and trade, which made the security of communication lines and, by extension, the areas near those lines of communication an important strategic interest.[18] Additionally, Canberra understood that British decolonization meant independence and the end of internal security and defense responsibilities for Britain in its Pacific dependencies, including Fiji, the British Solomon Islands, the Gilbert and Ellice Islands, and the Pitcairn Islands.[19] These concerns of communication security and independence overlapped. For example, communication lines in Papua New Guinea connected Australia to Southeast Asia, Japan, and other areas to the north. Farther away in Fiji, communication lines connected Australia to the United States and beyond. As a result, Australia had to closely monitor the developments in the neighborhood to avoid potential internal instability that could draw the attention of hostile external powers. Time would help to determine what specific needs the neighborhood had and what ability, if any, Australia had in meeting those needs. For the purpose of strategic defense planning, the Department of Defence determined that Australia must preserve the security of its neighbors in the Southwest Pacific to secure these varied interests, which could become vulnerable due to instability.[20]

The identification of vulnerable areas affected by British decolonization allowed officials to anticipate and reinforce these areas with the aim of achieving the stability and security Australia desired. The Department of Defence acknowledged that Australia's proximity to Asia and "reputation as an independent, non-imperialist nation with special interests in the security of Southeast Asia have given it a special position, which should enable it to exercise influence somewhat disproportionate to its power."[21] Canberra hoped to exercise that power close to home in the Southwest Pacific—an area facing uncertainty as a result of British decolonization—and anticipated that the newly independent islands might pursue a regional identity separate from Asia.[22] Canberra related to the need for the expression of a separate identity, so this perspective opened the opportunity for Australia to adopt a leadership role in the neighborhood by providing economic, technical, and political support that allowed the island governments to achieve their goals.

While encouraging the development of a regional identity formed the core of Australia's approach toward the Southwest Pacific, Canberra also paid close attention to potential disruptions in the neighborhood. Fiji, in particular, caught Canberra's attention after it gained independence from Britain in 1970. Internal instability caused by racial tensions between indigenous Fijians and Indian Fijians had the potential to make Fiji a target for communist insurgency, which would create widespread challenges for Australia.[23] In addition to internal conflicts in Fiji, the Joint Intelligence

Committee warned that Canberra should pay special attention to larger island groups because a change in one location could lead to changes in the whole group. For example, Australia administered the islands of Buka and Bougainville in the Solomon Islands as part of the Territory of Papua and New Guinea. As a result, the committee anticipated that Australian relations with Papua New Guinea, and by extension Buka and Bougainville, could influence developments in the British Solomon Islands Protectorate.[24] Still, Australia wanted to avoid direct military intervention in the Southwest Pacific in an effort to "win the confidence of the peoples and governments" and maintain friendly relations with an area recognized for its strategic importance.[25]

Rather than responding with direct military intervention, Australia decided to adopt a leadership role by providing economic, technical, and political support to locations identified as vulnerable. By working in conjunction with New Zealand, Australia could provide aid and civil defense as key components for areas in the Southwest Pacific most at risk from external influence, thus fostering a regional sense of strategic community. Because the states in the area were so small, traditional defense aid would be difficult. Instead, Australia and New Zealand could assist in the organization of local security forces, train the military and police, and provide aid in the form of surveillance, patrol, and construction. From the perspective of the Department of Defence, Australia's attempt to build itself into a neighborhood power provided a longer-term opportunity to support American efforts against Soviet expansion. One report expressed the opportunity to "make a significant contribution to the alliance relationship and to the US global effort. The US looks to Australia to carry this responsibility."[26] The Defence Committee suspected that the visibility of Western support in the Southwest Pacific would limit the extent of Soviet overtures to the region. By maintaining a close, positive relationship with Britain's former Pacific dependencies, Australia might be in a position, along with New Zealand, to reduce island vulnerability. However, the Defence Committee worried that Britain's withdrawal left the small, newly independent islands of the Southwest Pacific with little capacity to fend off larger, predatory powers such as the Soviet Union and China.[27]

The Soviets had already proven to be troublesome in Southeast Asia. Singapore's Prime Minister Lee Kuan Yew used Australian concerns to his advantage when he visited the Soviet Union in 1970 and extended an invitation for use of the soon-to-be abandoned British dockyards to the Soviet Navy. Lee hoped to use his offer as leverage, forcing Australia and New Zealand to make a definitive commitment toward Singapore at a time when Britain and the United States seemed to be withdrawing from the area.[28] Soviet activity also extended into the neighborhood, specifically to the South Pacific, by 1976. The Soviet Union approached New Zealand, Tonga, and Western Samoa for access to fishery-support facilities, offered aid to Papua New Guinea, and expressed a general interest in maritime research in the area. The increase in Soviet requests for contacts in the region posed enough of a concern for the Defence Committee to suggest that Australia should work to prevent the Soviet presence, which could jeopardize Australian lines of communication to the United States.[29] Canberra would have to find ways to limit Soviet influence and presence in the neighborhood in an effort both to preserve Australia's long-term interests and prevent the erosion of Western influence in the region. As the new decade began, Australia focused on the advantages of its isolation from centers of global conflict, which offered the time and space necessary to ensure regional stability and security as a neighborhood power.

As the 1970s continued, Australia's strategic outlook continued to shift. Rather than acting in conjunction with its great and powerful friends, Australia seized the absence of those friends to transition into a neighborhood power. Canberra's focus toward stabilizing vulnerable areas in the Southwest Pacific by means beyond direct military intervention did not negate the need for defense planning within the wider Asia-Pacific region. Ultimately, Australian objectives had to match the country's defense capabilities. Australia's military capacity would not be strong enough to address the internal and external threats to all of the countries in the neighborhood and Southeast Asia independently, but Australian support could help build a foundation that would encourage both regional and neighborhood defense responses. Australia's show of support achieved two objectives. First, by supporting local governments, Canberra increased its influence in the Pacific—a move that supported Australia's strategy of shaping itself into a neighborhood power. Second, Australia's growing regional influence and efforts to act independently in the region provided a way to attract great-power support for initiatives that could increase Australia's diplomatic profile within the Asia-Pacific region.[30] Both objectives allowed the Australians to be a stronger and more appealing ally to

Western powers, which might help in the event of a large-scale conflict during the Cold War.

Although Canberra anticipated that building itself into a neighborhood power could facilitate its acceptance as a strong Western ally in the Asia-Pacific region, the government had to overcome one major hurdle to gain support at home for this global position. Australia housed American facilities that functioned in different capacities. For example, the Australian Department of Supply operated one facility—a complex of tracking stations—at Honeysuckle Creek outside of Canberra on behalf of NASA. This station played a fundamental role in Project Apollo—the US program to land an astronaut on the moon. When Apollo 11 landed on the moon in July 1969, the Honeysuckle Creek station received the first images of that landing before transmitting them to the United States.[31] Other facilities communicated with nuclear submarines in the Pacific and Indian oceans and monitored Soviet and Chinese activities for intelligence and defense purposes. The intelligence- and defense-related facilities remained more secretive and also more problematic for Australians and Americans alike.

In addition to building a strategy to make itself into a stronger ally in the region, Australian geography and the presence of US defense installations in Australia suggested that Australia already served an important role in the broader Western Cold War strategy. However, collective security arrangements provided a layer of security after the British and American presences in the Asia-Pacific declined. In addition to the Canberra Pact from 1944, Australia actively participated in a multitude of organizations from global ones, such as the United Nations, to regional ones, such as the Southeast Asia Treaty Organization (SEATO).[32] The Australia, New Zealand, United States Security Treaty (ANZUS Treaty) became the most valuable collective-security arrangement for Australia after its creation in 1951 because it fulfilled Canberra's postwar objective of moving toward the United States and served as the foundation for Australia's postwar strategic outlook through the 1960s.[33] The early 1950s marked a period when Australia welcomed regional collective-security arrangements in response to the perception that communism would invade a weak Southeast Asia, thus potentially threatening Australian borders and interests. The ANZUS Treaty provided a loose framework that allowed for cooperation and consultation between the three nations on a scale not experienced before the war.

In this way, Canberra viewed the agreement as a shield against potential communist expansion.[34]

The presence of US facilities in Australia reinforced the close relationship that the ANZUS countries shared with their other English-speaking allies—Canada and Britain—but nothing suggested trust quite like sharing a critical, intertwined intelligence network that would help identify global security risks. However, in 1970s Australia, US intelligence activities came under attack for the uncertainty surrounding American installations in Australia and for the concern that Australia had become more susceptible to an attack by the Soviet Union because of these installations. The two most controversial intelligence-related facilities included Pine Gap and Nurrungar. According to Sir Arthur Tange, permanent head of the Department of Defence, programs conducted at the Joint Defence Space Research Facility at Pine Gap and the Joint Defence Space Communications Facility at Nurrungar "had the highest significance in the nuclear standoff between the United States and the Soviet Union."[35] Thus, Tange viewed Australia as a critical component of Western strategy. However, others in politics, who did not have similar access to information, did not share his appreciation for their importance during the Cold War.

Concerns came to a head when the polarizing Gough Whitlam became prime minister in 1972. Whitlam brought the Labor Party to power after twenty-three years, but dissent within the party contributed to tension that extended to Australia's relationship with the United States. The Labor Party's left wing posed the greatest internal challenge to Whitlam's party leadership, and the best example of this divide centered on the hot-button issue of American installations in Australia. According to Tange, suspicion about the activities at Pine Gap and Nurrungar grew within the Labor Party before they won the majority because previous coalition governments had denied access to the information and refused to justify their secrecy over the joint facilities.[36]

With the start of a new government, Tange became responsible for informing Prime Minister Whitlam and Defence Minister Lance Barnard about the joint facilities. He visited both sites in his official capacity and shared the functions of each facility with the two men, but Whitlam and Barnard chose to limit knowledge of high security matters to a "need-to-know" basis, thus alienating those in the Labor Party who remained suspicious of the activities. This decision, although a longstanding practice in government, led some of his ministers to demand equal access to information. Tange attributed some of this frustration to the inexperience of new ministry members who "never had the responsibility of preserving the confidence of allies." In his capacity as permanent head of the Department of Defence, Tange had to preserve secrecy and maintain positive relations with the allies on the point of these facilities, so he focused on preventing leaks and security breaches. He mentioned that the former became difficult when the new government included people who openly challenged security-related decisions they attributed to dated coalition government policies. Because security and the preservation of it retained a high priority for Tange, he chose to bypass existing procedures in place and deliver any intelligence-related information himself, which created friction among his peers.[37]

The government's inability and unwillingness to share information about the intelligence facilities and functions led some on the left of the Labor Party to argue that the presence of US facilities in Australia constituted too much American influence. While they attempted to rally public support for their perspective, Barnard faced calls for assurance from Washington that Labor Party challenges would not jeopardize the agreements that both parties signed. After all, the release of information through any means could provide the Soviet Union access to US intelligence information, jeopardizing Western Cold War strategy. Meanwhile, Whitlam faced added pressure from his party when they accused him of reneging on another policy that would bring all overseas Australian forces home. Whitlam did, in fact, recall Australian advisers and forces from Southeast Asia soon after Labor's victory in 1972, but he kept a token force of six hundred troops in Singapore.[38] Whitlam's attempt to pacify his party and Barnard's attempts to pacify the United States left Tange in a difficult position.

As a peripheral power, Australia could not risk jeopardizing its relationship with the United States, but according to Tange, Whitlam's public explanation about Singapore breached security. Whitlam's report admitted the existence of a previously "unacknowledged signals intelligence unit" that could not be immediately relocated elsewhere. The Defence Signals Division unit in Singapore monitored military and civilian radio traffic in Asia as part of a wider intelligence network with the United States, Britain, New Zealand, and Canada.[39] When details about the unit's presence in Singapore reached the media, Tange argued that "there was an added reason for

Australia's intelligence partners to be concerned as they watched for signs in the new Government of a slackening of protection of the information they entrusted to Australia." Tange recalled that the anxiety expressed by the United States about leaked information also included operational information and information about weapons, and he became responsible for allaying Washington's concerns, which he indicated were "not always unfounded."[40] If Canberra hoped to build itself into a valuable ally, revealing intelligence information would undermine that goal and the relationship with its intelligence partners.

In an attempt to control the damage, Defence Minister Barnard addressed questions from Labor Party members, the media, and the public in a statement to Parliament in February 1973, while conversations to address concerns in the United States occurred privately. In his public statement, Barnard aimed to remove some of the mystery behind the functions of the joint US-Australian facilities. He began by elaborating on the use of defense installations across Australia. According to him, the US Air Force measured atmospheric disturbances at Amberley in Queensland, while the Joint Geological and Geophysical Research Station at Alice Springs (Northern Territory) conducted studies to detect any man-made tremors caused by nuclear testing underground. Both locations aided in monitoring nuclear disarmament. As a result, he used his statement to assure people that the facilities were just as important to Australia as the United States, and Canberra received access to assessments from these facilities. Barnard also used the opportunity to reject public and political calls to end the ANZUS Treaty, which underpinned the motivation for allowing such facilities into Australia in the first place.[41]

In the portion of his statement aimed directly toward dissenters in the Labor Party, Barnard turned his attention to the two joint installations at Pine Gap and Nurrungar, which he acknowledged had "long been matters of concern and debate in Parliament." He explained that, as common practice, the leader of the Opposition was excluded from receiving information about these installations, which meant that the Labor Party had to wait until an election victory to determine its policy toward them. Despite the calls from within the party for access to information gathered from these joint facilities, Barnard reiterated the importance of preserving the confidence of the original arrangements. He added that the "Government will respect all classified information shared between us and the United States, as well as with Britain, New Zealand and other powers, including our friends in Asia. Defence cooperation cannot be conducted on any other basis." He revealed that Australia had access to the installations, Australian civilians and servicemen participated in the joint management of both facilities, the United States and Australia had access to all of the data collected, and the facilities could be used to address the individual interests of either government. Barnard reassured Parliament that he planned a review to determine whether or not the agreements coincided with current national security interests, and he pacified some of the other complaints by offering limited parliamentary access to the facilities.[42] The information Barnard shared in his statement about four of the facilities and the promise to discuss existing arrangements with Washington reduced the momentum of those in Australia calling for the end of American facilities in Australia. However, dissenters continued to protest US control over facilities in Australia.

Unlike the US facilities such as Pine Gap and Nurrungar, whose arrangements with the United States remained as part of a broader Western strategy, other facilities were targeted due to their importance for Australian strategy. One such facility was the US naval communication station at the North West Cape in Western Australia, which began through a formal agreement between the United States and Australia in 1963. This agreement gave Australia "title and sovereignty" over the land and provided Australian authorities access to the station. The terms also required the Australian government to consent to the use of the facilities for anything other than defense matters with an agreement to consult occasionally on matters related to the station at the request of either government.[43] When the North West Cape facility was commissioned on September 16, 1967, Britain's Royal Navy still patrolled the Indian Ocean. As a result, US activities at the cape focused on the Pacific Ocean first and the Indian Ocean second. Initially established as a very-low-frequency communications station to channel messages to and from American submarines in the Indian and western Pacific oceans, the station added more than forty high-frequency transmitters within its first year. When Prime Minister John Gorton renamed the station the Harold E. Holt Naval Communications Station in September 1968, he acknowledged that it would increase in strategic importance after the Royal Navy ceased its operations in the Indian Ocean. From Gorton's perspective, the station "will enhance the military capacity not only of the United States but also of our own nation."[44] However, by the 1970s, questions arose over the potential vulnerability caused by the American presence at the station.

On the heels of the Yom Kippur War in 1973, the Labor Party's concerns about US presence in the North West Cape escalated as they had done with other American facilities in Australia. Although the North West Cape facilities did not run counter to Australian security and allowed Australian communication with its own submarines, questions arose about whether the mere existence of the station could result in Australia becoming a target for a nuclear attack by the Soviet Union. Additionally, concerns increased due to the view that the agreement "did not carry with it any degree of control of the Station or of its use."[45] This latter concern came to a head during the Yom Kippur War when the United States moved American forces to the North West Cape on an emergency alert without first notifying Canberra of the decision.[46] Many in Canberra argued that Australia should have been notified first since the facilities were located on Australian soil and could impact Australian security. According to their platform, the Labor Party was "opposed to the existence of foreign-owned, -controlled or -operated bases and facilities in Australian territory, especially if such bases involve a derogation of Australian sovereignty."[47] The party viewed American actions during the war as a breach of Australian sovereignty, though Tange questioned that interpretation.[48]

Defence Minister Barnard attempted to placate party uproar by renegotiating the terms of the original North West Cape agreement to reflect greater Australian involvement in and awareness of the activities taking place at the cape. During Barnard's visit to the United States in January 1974, US defense secretary James Schlesinger agreed to make the North West Cape a joint installation similar to Pine Gap and Nurrungar. Additionally, the new agreement reduced US-controlled property to one communications building and allowed for more Australian personnel at the cape, along with the appointment of an Australian deputy commander.[49] Barnard's success in revising the agreement pacified concerns from some Labor Party members, but other party members from the notoriously radical Victorian branch openly supported an anti-American protest at the cape in May 1974.[50] These protests, paired with additional discontent from Labor Party and Liberal Party members, helped to undermine Whitlam's government. By the time Whitlam's government began to break, Australia had achieved some success in advocating for national security interests as they related to joint installations rather than simply falling in line as a compliant Western ally.

Malcolm Fraser's arrival as prime minister in 1975, after Gough Whitlam's controversial dismissal, brought more long-term solutions to the American installations question and solidified Australia's commitment to its role in Cold War planning. Unlike Whitlam's, Fraser's government, a coalition of the Liberal and Country parties, openly acknowledged the benefits of American installations for Western strategy and supported the presence of those installations in Australia because it was viewed as part of the Western World's collective defense. Still, this explanation was not a complete departure from the Whitlam government. The Fraser government supported US installations as an extension of Australian security, but much like the Whitlam government it preferred Australian control of the facilities and only agreed to US operation of those facilities if Australians received access to the information.[51]

Fraser's government had the benefit of inheriting relative security and stability in the region, which meant that Canberra could shift its focus toward developing its position within the broader context of the Cold War as part of a Western strategy. Under Fraser's government, a decade's worth of questions and strategic reviews that stemmed from British withdrawal from east of Suez gained clarity. A review accepted by Fraser's cabinet in November 1976 revealed the order in which Australia would address the layers of concern the nation faced on the road to its version of independence. First, Australia's primary concern must be its own security and ability to act independently in low-level engagements. Second, Canberra must pursue policies that encouraged stability in Australia's region of interest, making Australia a neighborhood power. Finally, as a neighborhood power, Australia contributed to the broader alliance relationship that it had with the United States and others in the Western community.[52] The changes iterated in the review voiced measures adopted after 1967. Australia had already started its path toward becoming a neighborhood power by identifying the support it could provide to newly independent Pacific islands after Britain's departure. Officials in Canberra already understood the connection between its role as a neighborhood power and Western strategy and fought to maintain US installations in Australia as part of that strategy. Ultimately, by continuing to work on parts two and three of the review, Australia could achieve the first objective centered upon national security and independent action.

As Harold Holt suggested, the 1960s represented a time of great danger and great opportunities in the Asia-Pacific region, but the 1970s allowed for the time to distinguish between the two and respond accordingly. The complexities of Australia's strategic position became apparent once Britain formally announced its withdrawal from east of Suez in 1967. That decision, though not a surprise, triggered officials in Canberra to consider the consequences of withdrawal upon Australia's position as a Western nation on the edge of Asia in the midst of an ever-changing Cold War environment. Examining Australia's relationships through the 1960s is helpful in establishing a foundation, but pushing the research into the 1970s exposes the reach of global changes into an area of the world that was seemingly isolated. In the case of Australia, the withdrawal of British troops and facilities from east of Suez and the drawback of American forces from Asia during the final years of the Vietnam War exposed potential vulnerabilities and led Canberra to reevaluate its strategic outlook into the 1970s. When planning for the decade ahead in a changing global environment, Canberra considered Australia's role as part of the Western community on the global level, its regional position as a developing neighborhood power, and its domestic environment as it related to alliance vulnerability. While the Cold War remained the overarching global danger, Australia's focus turned to the opportunity of building the nation into a neighborhood power in an effort to strengthen its regional position before playing its part within the broader Western Alliance.

NOTES

1 Sir Keith Waller, the Australian ambassador to the United States, suggested that British withdrawal from east of Suez required Australia to place increasing importance on its relationship with the United States since British withdrawal left Australia "more isolated than ever on the edge of Asia." "Anzus Treaty Is Still Our Best Shield," *Canberra Times,* July 24, 1969, A1945, 16/2/2, National Archives of Australia (hereafter NAA).

2 "Draft—Strategic Basis of Australian Defence 1973," May 1973, A1838, 677/3, annex B, NAA.

3 As a starting point, see Henry Albinski, *The Australian-American Security Relationship* (St. Lucia, QLD: University of Queensland Press, 1982); Coral Bell, *Dependent Ally: A Study in Australian Foreign Policy* (Melbourne: Oxford University Press, 1988); W. David McIntyre, *Background to the Anzus Pact* (New York: St. Martin's, 1995); and Carl Bridge's *Munich to Vietnam* (Carlton, VIC: Melbourne University Press, 1996).

4 See Lorna Arnold, *A Very Special Relationship: British Atomic Weapon Trials in Australia* (London: Her Majesty's Stationery Office, 1987); Andrea Benvenuti, *Anglo-Australian Relations and the "Turn to Europe," 1961–1972* (Woodbridge, UK: Royal Historical Society and Boydell Press, 2008); David Goldsworthy, *Losing the Blanket: Australia and the End of Britain's Empire* (Carlton South, VIC: Melbourne University Press, 2002); R. F. Holland's *Britain and the Commonwealth Alliance, 1918–1939* (London: Macmillan, 1981); Ritchie Ovendale, *The English-Speaking Alliance: Britain, the United States, the Dominions, and the Cold War 1945–1951* (London: Allen & Unwin, 1985); Jeffrey Pickering, *Britain's Withdrawal from East of Suez* (New York: St. Martin's, 1998); Wayne Reynolds, *Australia's Bid for the Atomic Bomb* (Carlton South, VIC: Melbourne University Press, 2000); and Stuart Ward, *Australia and the British Embrace: The Demise of the Imperial Ideal* (Carlton South, VIC: Melbourne University Press, 2001).

5 See Peter Dennis and Jeffrey Grey, *Emergency and Confrontation: Australian Military Operations in Malaya and Borneo, 1950–1966* (St. Leonards, NSW: Allen & Unwin in association with the Australian War Memorial, 1996); Peter Edwards and Gregory Pemberton, *Crises and Commitments: The Politics of Diplomacy of Australia's Involvement in Southeast Asian Conflicts, 1948–1965* (Sydney: Allen & Unwin in association with the Australian War Memorial, 1992); Peter Edwards and David Goldsworthy, eds., *Facing North: A Century of Australian Engagement with Asia*, vols. 1 and 2 (Carlton South, VIC: Melbourne University Press with the Department of Foreign Affairs and Trade, 2003); and Peter Edwards, *A Nation at War: Australian Politics, Society and Diplomacy during the Vietnam War, 1965–1975* (Sydney: Allen & Unwin in association with the Australian War Memorial, 1997).

6 W. David McIntyre evaluated the process of British decolonization in the Pacific in *Winding up the British Empire in the Pacific Islands* (Oxford: Oxford University Press, 2014). For a broad understanding of South Pacific relations, see Donald Denoon and Philippa Mein-Smith with Marivic Wyndham, *A History of Australia, New Zealand, and the Pacific* (Oxford: Blackwell, 2000).

7 See Donald Gordon, *The Dominion Partnership in Imperial Defense, 1870–1914* (Baltimore: Johns Hopkins University Press, 1965); John Eddy and Deryck Schreuder, eds., *The Rise of Colonial Nationalism: Australia, New Zealand, Canada and South Africa First Assert Their Nationalities, 1880–1914* (Sydney: Allen & Unwin, 1988); Holland, *Britain and the Commonwealth Alliance;* Ovendale, *English-Speaking Alliance;* and Francine McKenzie, *Redefining the Bonds of Commonwealth, 1939–1948: The Politics of Preference* (New York: Palgrave Macmillan, 2002).

8 "Mr. Rusk Regrets British Defence Cuts," July 19, 1967, M1002, 122, NAA.

9 "White Paper on Defence (Outside Europe Section)," July 18, 1967, AWM121, 31/C/2, NAA.

10 "Conference at No. 10 Downing Street," June 13, 1967, M1003, East of Suez Talks London, NAA.

11 Richard Nixon, "Informal Remarks in Guam with Newsmen," July 25, 1969, Gerhard Peters and John T. Woolley, American Presidency Project, http://www.presidency.ucsb.edu/ws/?pid=2140.

12 Nixon, "Informal Remarks in Guam."
13 "President Nixon's Policy towards Asia," July 29, 1969, A5882, CO818, NAA.
14 "International Developments and Their Implications for Australia up to 1980," n.d., A1838, 683/70/1, part 3, NAA.
15 "International Developments and Their Implications for Australia up to 1980," August 13, 1970, A1838, 683/70/1, part 1, NAA.
16 "International Developments," August 13, 1970.
17 "Draft—Strategic Basis of Australian Defence 1973."
18 "Strategic Basis of Australian Defence Policy, 1971," A452, 1971/910, NAA.
19 "British Responsibilities and Commitments East of Suez," May 8, 1967, A1838, TS691/1/1, part 1, NAA.
20 "Strategic Basis of Australian Defence Policy, 1971."
21 "Strategic Basis of Australian Defence Policy (1971)," in Stephan Frühling, *A History of Australian Strategic Policy since 1945* (Canberra, ACT: Defence Publishing Service, Department of Defence, 2009), 391–434.
22 "Strategic Basis of Australian Defence Policy (1971)," 391–434; "Strategic Basis of Australian Defence Policy, 1971."
23 Indian Fijians outnumbered ethnic Fijians but were often considered subordinate to them as descendants of indentured Indian laborers who worked in the sugar industry. Tension continued into the 1960s and impeded discussions about the creation of a multiethnic constitution. Denoon and Mein-Smith, *History of Australia, New Zealand, and the Pacific,* 33, 110, 198, 390.
24 Australian Brief for Quadripartite Talks," April 1967, A8738, 33, NAA.
25 "Strategic Basis of Australian Defence Policy, 1971."
26 It is also worth noting that a Soviet presence already existed south of Australia in Antarctica. The Antarctic Treaty signed in 1959 provided a level of security to ensure no military activity in the southern approaches to Australia. The Defence Committee noted that United States and the USSR refused to recognize Australian claims in Antarctica, which led to three Soviet stations located on Australian territory. However, Canberra expressed little interest in challenging this presence. "Australian Strategic Analysis and Defence Policy Objectives," 1976, A12389, D67, NAA.
27 "Australian Strategic Analysis and Defence Policy Objectives," 1976.
28 "Strategic Basis of Australian Defence Policy (1971)," 391–434.
29 "Australian Strategic Analysis and Defence Policy Objectives," 1976. For more on Australia's relationship with the Southwest Pacific during this period, including Soviet interest in the region, see R. A. Herr, "Australia and the Southwest Pacific," in *Independence and Alliance: Australia in World Affairs, 1976–80,* ed. P. J. Boyce and J. R. Angel (Sydney: Allen & Unwin, 1983), 279–92.
30 "Strategic Basis of Australian Defence Policy (1971)," 391–434.
31 "Research—Space—Honeysuckle Creek—ANIB [Australian News and Information Bureau]," B4498, 124D6, NAA.
32 See Leszek Buszynski, *S.E.A.T.O.: The Failure of an Alliance Strategy* (Kent Ridge, Singapore: Singapore University Press, 1983).

33 McIntyre, *Background to the Anzus Pact,* 2.

34 "Strategic Basis of Australian Defence Policy—1967," March 1967, A8738, 33, NAA.

35 Arthur Tange, *Defence Policy-Making: A Close-Up View, 1950–1980; A Personal Memoir,* ed. Peter Edwards (Canberra: Australian National University Press, 2008), 69. Henry Albinski argued that Whitlam's own call for reform provided fuel for the arguments from radical elements of the party in society at large. Albinski, *Australian External Policy under Labor* (Vancouver: University of British Columbia Press, 1977), 71–76, 260–61.

36 Tange, *Defence Policy-Making,* 69–70.

37 Tange, 69–75; E. Gough Whitlam, *The Whitlam Government, 1972–1975* (Ringwood, VIC: Penguin Books Australia, 1981), 689.

38 Tange, *Defence Policy-Making,* 70.

39 Albinski, *Australian External Policy,* 9, 51.

40 Tange, *Defence Policy-Making,* 70.

41 Lance Barnard, "United States Defence Installations in Australia—Speech," February 28, 1973, Commonwealth of Australia, Parliamentary Debates, House of Representatives, http://parlinfo.aph.gov.au.

42 Barnard, "United States Defence Installations." Tange noted that US ambassador Walter Rice questioned this idea of parliamentary access because it was unclear what this access actually meant. Tange recalled that politicians showed little interest in visiting sites when the opportunity became available. Tange, *Defence Policy-Making,* 75.

43 Barnard, "United States Defense Installations."

44 Peter Robinson, "Growth of US-Australian Partnership in ANZUS—N.W. Cape Spotlights Indian Ocean Role," *Australian Financial Review,* September 23, 1968, A1838, 250/9/11, part 1, NAA. By 1968, the number of base personnel ballooned from an initial projection of four hundred to twenty-five hundred, including both Americans and Australians.

45 Tange, *Defence Policy-Making,* 76–77.

46 Whitlam, *Whitlam Government,* 48; Albinski, *Australian External Policy,* 262; Neville Meaney, "The United States," in *Australia in World Affairs, 1971–1975,* ed. W. J. Hudson (Sydney: Allen & Unwin and the Australian Institute of International Affairs, 1980), 192.

47 Quoted in Albinski, *Australian External Policy,* 256.

48 Tange, *Defence Policy-Making,* 76–77.

49 Tange, 84; Meaney, "United States," 192–93.

50 Albinski, *Australian External Policy,* 263; Meaney, "United States," 195; Barnard, "United States Defence Installations."

51 Dr. Forbes, "Opposition Defence Policy," April 24, 1974, A1838, 67/1/3, part 11, NAA.

52 "Strategic Basis of Australian Defence Policy 1975," n.d., A7942, D94, part 10, NAA.

CHAPTER 5

A "Controlled Revolution"

The UN during the Congo Crisis as Public Stage, Actor, and Incubator for Ideas

ALANNA O'MALLEY

This chapter argues that the United Nations (UN) can be viewed as having three distinct dimensions through which it can set the international agenda and shape normative behavior. The UN has long been construed in one-dimensional terms based on the misconception that the organization has no tangible role in structuring the interaction between states, thereby effecting the development of international norms. Here, through an examination of the role of the UN during the Congo Crisis, three distinct dimensions are revealed: public stage, socializing space, and actor. Exposing these dimensions through the Congo Crisis from 1960 to 1964, which was a critical moment in the development of the functions and capacity for agency of the UN, shows how the various dimensions of the organization can be identified clearly during this crisis, which itself had multiple political, social, and economic levels. Here the UN represented a public stage and a socializing space for states to negotiate policy, played a role as an actor on the ground in the Congo, and served as an incubator for ideas about how to manage decolonization and accelerate the end of empire. Taking these three dimensions together demonstrates how the UN facilitated the agency of Global South actors who sought to remake the global order.

"We continued—and still continue to redefine and re-enlarge the meaning of self-determination in an ever-widening arc of freedom moving from politics, to the social structure, to the educational structure, to the economic structure, to our rights and duties in the family of nations."[1] When Adlai Stevenson, the US ambassador to the UN, penned this statement in 1961 for a speech to be delivered in the General Assembly in response to a Nigerian-sponsored resolution on colonialism, he was all too aware of the shifting international environment at the UN. Mounting pressure from the Afro-Asian bloc on colonial questions threatened to fracture Western unity, particularly important at a moment of escalating tensions in the Cold War.[2] Stevenson revealed his awareness of the role of the UN in moderating these challenges and in particular the agency of the organization in leading what he termed a "controlled revolution of political independence or self-government."[3] While he highlighted this aspect of the UN as one of the areas of greatest potential, it was also clear that as part of this process the UN was changing how principles of sovereignty and statehood were understood in the context of decolonization. The role of the UN during the Congo Crisis as an incubator for ideas has remained a neglected aspect of the organization's role, with most of the literature focused on the peacekeeping mission and its consequences. While some valuable contributions later highlighted how UN ideas shaped the world, little attention has been paid to how the organization functioned in this regard during the crisis.[4] As the UN became a driver of normative change, it is possible to trace this process by examining the role of the organization in managing the conflict through three distinct dimensions: in its function as a public stage, as a socializing space for state and non-state actors, and as an actor on the ground in the Congo and in the UN Secretariat in New York.

First, the UN functioned as a public stage on which countries openly debated their different visions and approaches to the Congo problem. The open nature of debates in the General Assembly in particular exposed former colonial powers such as Belgium, Britain, and France to severe attack from newly decolonized nations. These burgeoning states exploded onto the world stage from 1958 to 1960, forming the African group, the Asia and Pacific group, the combined Afro-Asian bloc, and later the Group of

77 (G77), which would spearhead many initiatives to accelerate political and economic decolonization generally and shape UN Congo policy more specifically. The public nature of UN diplomacy was repeatedly utilized as a platform for propaganda by the USSR as the battle for influence between raged under the Cold War veil that colored the superpowers' vision of the crisis. Crucially, however, Secretary-General Dag Hammarskjöld seized upon the public nature of UN debates in directing the attention of the world to the Congo in June 1960. Invoking, for the first time ever, the powers of the secretary-general under Article 99 of the UN Charter, Hammarskjöld introduced the Congo Crisis as an issue of serious international importance, effectively internationalizing what might otherwise have been a bloody war of independence. By raising it to public attention, he succeeded in securing support for the peacekeeping mission from anticolonial states such as Argentina, India, Ghana, and the Philippines. His publicizing of the mission in this way also opened up the debate about how decolonization should unfold and what the role of the UN should be in managing the process and ordering the decolonized world.

The second dimension of the UN refers to its role as an actor in the Congo through ONUC (Opération de Nations Unies au Congo), the UN mission to the Congo from 1960 to 1964. Much has been written on the UN's military operation in the Congo, given the precedents that it set for later peacekeeping missions and also the debatable success of the UN in preventing a full-blown civil war.[5] ONUC, however, also had an important political function in shaping the development of the Congolese state and in creating new committees that brought together a wide array of actors participating in the mission, often without the presence of the permanent five members of the UN Security Council.[6] In this way the organization also developed its own agency to shape events, particularly due to the personal influence of Hammarskjöld, who initiated this process by creating the "Congo Club" in the Secretariat as a deliberative forum for leading UN Congo policy away from the direct influence of the superpowers. Crucially, some of the military actions taken by ONUC had the effect of drawing the ire of the Americans, the Belgians, and the British, representing the extent to which the organization at moments proceeded contrary to the aims of Western powers in the Congo. In this way, as an actor, the UN shaped Congo policy as a response in particular to African demands, rather than acting as a vehicle for Western interests.

Third, as briefly mentioned above, the UN served as an incubator for shaping new ideas and interpretations of sovereignty and statehood as actors socialized together in its various spaces. Simultaneously undergoing a dramatic change in its membership due to the emergence of dozens of newly decolonized nations, the debates that took place in the committees, corridors, and in particular the General Assembly, helped to universalize ideas of sovereignty and statehood in the decolonized world. The process of proliferating, disseminating, adapting, and adopting these ideas into various resolutions on the Congo is reflective of the role of the UN in legitimizing the end of empire in various guises. In the process, the UN fostered the development of a postimperial internationalism, which in many ways challenged, rather than served, Western interests.

The longer history of the UN has been blighted by the misconception that it has no agency and therefore no part to play in structuring the international order.[7] On the contrary, here it is argued that from the outset the UN had a clear role as both the facilitator and the agent of normative transformation with regard to decolonization in the Congo. This is a departure from the conventional perspective focused on states and bipolar Cold War power balancing, which tends to neglect both the increasing importance of the UN and newly decolonized countries. This chapter contests Mark Mazower and Paul Kennedy's view of the UN (among others) as a "parliament of man" that simply reflects the whims of its members.[8] In particular, it will engage some of the arguments of Mazower's *Governing the World: The History of an Idea,* by expanding on the concept of the UN as a site for changing forms of internationalism. While Mazower does concede that the UN played a role in the dismantling of old European empires, this chapter will flesh out precisely how the UN facilitated a revision of ideas about empire through this multidimensional perspective. It will thus challenge the basic assumption that the organization was a passive entity in international relations and in fact point to the agency of the UN in this process of normative transformation.

This multidimensional image of the UN was exposed for the first time during the Congo Crisis. The crisis was a turning point in international relations that propelled certain trends, such as the recognition of the right to self-determination and changing notions of empire, and foreclosed others, such as traditional colonial rule, by encouraging an array of actors to adapt their views on imperialism and its relationship to internationalism. This process of adaptation was advanced primarily at the UN where these ideas were public debated, propelled by the actions of the UN in the Congo, and subsequently transformed into resolutions that embodied these principles and envisioned an international order in which sovereignty and statehood were universal.

AN INTRACTABLE CRISIS

The Congo Crisis erupted a week after the country secured independence from Belgium on June 30, 1960. Congolese soldiers of the Force Publique gendarmie mutinied against their Belgian officers, leading to chaos on the streets of the capital, Léopoldville. In response, the Belgians sent paratroopers to their former colony, ostensibly to protect the remaining European community, an act that was interpreted by the Congolese as a signal that Belgium would try to regain control of the Congo. The newly elected prime minister, Patrice Lumumba, appealed to the UN to intervene in order to defend the sovereignty of the Congo from an act of Belgian imperialism. Hammarskjöld's decision to intervene was momentous; it was the first time the UN had acted in defense of the sovereignty of one of its soon-to-be members. The crisis was a revealing episode for the UN, for the first time exposing both the scope and the limits of what the organization could achieve as it sought to moderate the parallel challenges of the Cold War and decolonization.

It is important to note that the Congo Crisis from the outset was far more than another struggle of decolonization and had a threefold importance internationally. First, it was viewed by other African states as a test case for decolonization. From the beginning of the crisis, a host of states, including Ghana, the United Arab Republic (until 1961 and then Egypt and Syria afterward), and Guinea viewed their fate as newly independent anticolonial nations hanging in the balance. As the crisis progressed, they became increasingly irate and vociferous at the UN about the perceived advance of neocolonialism in the country. In part this was in response to the efforts of the Belgians and the British who consistently sought to protect their extensive economic and political interests in the region. The secession of the southeastern province of Katanga on July 11, 1960, under a puppet regime led by Moïse Tshombe exacerbated the predicament of the Congo, as the entire country relied on Katangan resources such as copper, cobalt, and diamonds. These strategic materials were largely controlled by the Belgian company Union Minière du Haut-Katanga (UMHK) and its partner benefactor the British Tanganyika Concessions group.[9] This was the second aspect of why the crisis was so important: it directly affected the flow of revenue from the region to British and Belgian shareholders and associated financial groups. In addition, for the British, instability in the Congo threatened their remaining colonial regimes in Rhodesia, Nyasaland, and Uganda.

Third, the unstable political situation in the Congo represented a power vacuum in the heart of Africa that seemed to invite Cold War rivalry. For the United States, the country was strategically important in the global struggle against communism, and Washington's policy throughout the crisis was to ensure the Congo was governed by a West-friendly regime. In addition, Katanga was a source of important materials, not least of which was uranium that had been used for the production of American nuclear weapons. The USSR also viewed the Congo as a potentially important ally. Moscow had already established friendly relations with Ghana and Guinea, helping these newly independent states to create economic regimes in the Soviet image.[10] Moreover, the Soviets used the Congo Crisis as a platform for propaganda at the UN where they launched scathing attacks on the actions of Western members and the secretary-general and attempted to court the more radical members of the Afro-Asian bloc.

Considering the explosive potential of a crisis that contained all of these elements, it is perhaps not surprising that the Congo also became a revealing episode for the UN itself. The first reason is that this episode took place at a moment when the composition and structure of the UN changed fundamentally. The process of decolonization had led to the emergence of a multitude of actors from the Global South who found sonorous expression through the UN. By 1960, a quarter of UN membership was composed of former colonies, a formidable influence they used to drive their agenda for change. As Bernard Firestone has said, "The newly independent states of African and Asia were determined to wrest control of the UN's agenda from its founders and to refocus global attention and resources on issues such as poverty, dependency, imperialism and post-colonialism."[11] The advent of these new nations on the world stage brought with it a changed set of ideals that challenged traditional Western ideas about sovereignty and statehood. In particular, the universalization of the idea of self-determination for all peoples was accelerated, and the old patriarchal, colonial system was gradually delegitimized. While the eminent position of the principle of self-determination in the charter indicated that from 1945 the UN would seek its realization across the colonial world, it was mainly through successive discussions and efforts of the Afro-Asian group, in cooperation with its Latin American counterparts in the General Assembly, that this was pursued. Questions of respect for sovereignty and self-determination were inherent in debates about the Congo, which served to accelerate this longer process of universalization.

Second, the personal vision of Dag Hammarskjöld as secretary-general of the UN as an organization that should advance decolonization was a crucial component and came to the fore during the early years of the crisis. Hammarskjöld's emphasis on bolstering the position of weaker countries within the international system granted further precedence to the Afro-Asian bloc. The organization portrayed itself as the defender of Congolese sovereignty, in the process echoing the Afro-Asian demands for the acceleration of decolonization and calls for the respect of the sovereignty of all colonial nations. Hammarskjöld himself indicated his position explicitly, pointing out that the UN would be the instrument that would safeguard the peace and independence of Africa and that this could be achieved through the cooperation of the African member states.[12] Ove Bring describes his approach to the charter as upholding tenets of international law while applying innovative procedures to reshape international norms.[13] Given the context of escalating danger to international peace posed by deteriorating stability in the heart of Africa, the notion of a moral guardian for the world held particular attraction for newly independent nations, who soon began to look to Hammarskjöld as the custodian of their independence and a counterweight to the world powers, many of which they viewed as former colonial oppressors. As described by one UN official who served as his special representative in Katanga, "Hammarskjöld . . . had given the United Nations a focus of moral authority which could attract an international loyalty and use it in the cause of peace and justice."[14]

The growing empathy with these ideals and the responsibility of the General Assembly to execute them led to a sense of brotherhood between the secretary-general and the smaller nations of the UN. The significance of this bolstering of the position of the Afro-Asian members was manifest in their influence over UN Congo policy. Hammarskjöld's vision for the role of the UN in guaranteeing the sovereignty of all nations, his dynamic interpretation of the charter, and his innovative techniques also proved politically important for the nature of the institution that he fostered. Under his leadership during the crisis, the UN served to advance the process of universalizing the idea of respect for the sovereignty of all nations by basing General Assembly and Security Council resolutions on this principle. By doing so, the organization developed the normative agenda for decolonization and established the UN as having the capability to reinterpret and legitimize the formal end of empire.

Finally, the Cold War had a detrimental effect on the UN and its efforts to bring about a resolution of the Congo Crisis. The struggle for the hearts and minds of cold warriors at the UN proved no less taxing in the debate chambers in New York than anywhere else. The Cold War hampered the UN's efforts in the Congo in many regards. First, the dichotomous impact of the conflict rendered the institution hamstrung in many instances where escalating tensions between the two superpowers often spilled over into rhetorical combat. The Congo was an issue that particularly exposed the rift between the superpowers as they both viewed it as a direct threat to their relative geopolitical positions. Not only did this serve to exacerbate the overall sense of polarity, but it also prevented the institution from functioning efficiently. In many cases where the conflict was directly exposed, it even halted proceedings altogether. One example of such a "Cold War exchange" took place following the presentation of the *First Report from the Secretary-General on Assistance to the Republic of the Congo,* on July 18, 1960, between Ambassador Henry Cabot Lodge of the United States and Vasily V. Kuznetsov, first deputy foreign minister of the USSR. Kuznetsov introduced a draft resolution that called for the withdrawal of Belgian troops in three days. In the course of a speech denouncing Western "colonialism," he said that if "the aggression" continued, more effective measures would be necessary, both by the UN and by the "peace-loving states" that sympathized with the Congo as "a cause."[15] Lodge replied by pointing out that the United States had demonstrated its full support for ONUC, not only in words but by such practical assistance as providing the airlift for most of the UN troops and large quantities of equipment, supplies, and food as well. He then warned, "With the other United Nations members we will do whatever may be necessary to prevent the intrusion of any military forces not requested by the United Nations."

Not only did this rhetorical combat hold up the proceedings, but it also reflected the mounting tensions between the two superpowers and generated an atmosphere of hostility. Moreover, it unwittingly entrenched the Cold War proportions of the crisis, leading in one particularly acrimonious incident on September 17, 1960, to the suspension of Security Council negotiations because the lack "of unanimity among its members . . . has prevented it from exercising its primary responsibility for the maintenance of international peace and security."[16]

However, this division of the chambers also created the opportunity for smaller nations to form a bloc opposed to those of the two superpowers. In the polarity of the moment, the formation of a third bloc carried considerably more appeal and influence than it may otherwise have done. The consolidation of the Afro-Asian bloc not only served to unite the voices of opposing factions within that group, but it also provided a means by which these nations brought their limited influence to bear. The sharp division of the General Assembly between two powerful blocs meant that there was a power vacuum into which the Afro-Asian bloc moved and from where their dissenting voices and concerns about neocolonialism carried most weight. The bipolarity of the international system at this stage offered developing nations the chance to advance their agenda as they attempted to play the superpowers off each other. In addition, the traditional power base of the West and its control of the General Assembly was numerically undercut by the rise of the African and Asian actors. The United States in particular could no longer "abuse the Assembly as a revivalist meeting-hall to rally the West."[17] The General Assembly was now controlled by the Afro-Asian bloc for which it became an "anvil upon which power and privilege are to be browbeaten into their images of right and justice."[18]

As a result of this altered power balance, Afro-Asian demands to end colonialism were treated as a foil by the superpowers. For their own Cold War reasons, both the Americans and the Soviets attempted to court favor with the Afro-Asians, in the process advancing the cause of decolonization and accepting Afro-Asian interpretations of sovereignty and statehood. Formalizing their ideas through the UN, these actors used Hammarskjöld's interpretation of the charter, his innovative vision for the UN, and the adjusted power structure within the organization to change the normative agenda of decolonization during the Congo Crisis. The three dimensions of the

UN through which these changes took place are evident in key moments during the crisis that serve to illustrate how the UN facilitated this shift in the international order.

THE UN AS A PUBLIC STAGE

It is important to expand on the first dimension of the UN as a public stage and reflect on how Hammarskjöld in particular sought to utilize this aspect of the organization in order to bring about a resolution to the crisis. As mentioned above, following the outbreak of violence in the Congo, Lumumba appealed to the UN to intervene in order to defend the sovereignty of the Congo from Belgian imperialism.[19] Hammarskjöld was not caught off guard by the request, having already dispatched undersecretary Ralph Bunche to oversee the independence ceremony amid fears that civil war would break out. Moreover it may be argued that the secretary-general viewed the request for intervention as an opportunity to demonstrate the peacekeeping capacity of the UN.[20] The objective was the containment of the Congo Crisis, in particular by ensuring that all aid and support came through the official channels of that organization, thereby preventing any one power from gaining a foothold in the country and drawing it into the Cold War.[21] This view was shared by the Afro-Asian bloc, which, led by Ghana, urged for the "Africanization" of the crisis by "forestalling all *non-African* and in particular imperialist and neo-colonial intervention."[22]

In responding to Lumumba's appeal of July 13, 1960, Hammarskjöld defined the tenor of his office and his "hands-on" approach. Crucially, he formally evoked Article 99 of the UN Charter by bringing the question of intervention to the immediate attention of the Security Council, thereby inscribing it on the global security agenda.[23] In his opening statement to the council, he recommended that the UN accede to Lumumba's request for military assistance in defending Congolese independence following the dispatch of Belgian troops to the Congo,[24] which was in response to the mutiny in the Force Publique on July 8.[25] The UN's action was, as described by *The Economist,* "a task that has no precedent."[26] Never before had the UN been asked to intervene in a sovereign country to protect its independence. By invoking his powers under Article 99, Hammarskjöld reflected his determination to take an innovative approach, activating the various channels of the organization in response to the crisis. As Norman Bentwich and Andrew Martin describe the situation, "it is for the Secretary-General to determine at his discretion which is a proper case for the use of his *exceptional powers* under this article."[27] The permissive nature of Article 99 and Hammarskjöld's decision to invoke it reflected his effort to bring the Congo to the attention of the international public. In doing so, Hammarskjöld put the Congo question directly in the spotlight, urging the parties to the conflict to publicly negotiate at the UN.

The response to Hammarskjöld's initial actions was mixed. On the one hand, the unanimous agreement of the members of the Security Council to create ONUC was extraordinary because it superseded the usual division between the West and the communists.[28] On the other hand, however, Hammarskjöld's action of "sweep[ing] away all before him at the outset of the crisis" was met with not a little consternation, among Western powers in particular.[29] This level of activism and direct investment of the secretary-general was unprecedented and, as Alan James describes, "states tend to be unenthusiastic about the prospect of an international organization's top official building up a quasi-independent power base."[30] In particular, the condemnation of Belgian actions drew the ire of other colonial states such as Britain and France, which were sympathetic to Belgian arguments that they had to maintain a presence in the country to guarantee the safety of the European community there. In addition, the former colonial powers were skeptical about what they viewed as UN interference in colonial policy.[31]

Although they had abstained rather than voted against the first Security Council resolution, Britain and France had acquiesced to the UN's censure of Belgian actions in the Congo. The resolution unambiguously called upon Belgium to withdraw its troops.[32] This was viewed by the Western nations—including France, Britain, the United States, and Italy—as an indirect condemnation of Belgian actions, which, in their view, were justified to protect European lives in the Congo. These growing tensions in New York were sharpened by the bad faith behavior of the Belgian government. Although Belgium was unequivocal to the rest of the world in its nonrecognition of Katanga as an independent state, simultaneously it promised support and recognition to Tshombe. In order to protect its substantial investments there by the Société General financial group and the big mining conglomerate UMHK, Brussels not only supplied troops for the defense of the new "state" but also installed political advisers in the Tshombe government.[33] Instead of withdrawing its forces from the Congo as promised, Belgium proceeded to relocate them in Tshombe's "independent" Katanga. The duplicitous Belgian approach toward Katanga exacerbated UN efforts to bring about a resolution. The exposition of these tensions among Western states about how the UN should proceed in the Congo revealed the broader debate about the role of the organization in managing decolonization. Their public discussions on the matter served to dispel the myth of Western unity on the issue and thereby opened up the process to the influence of African and Asian nations.

This rupture in the Western position was an important moment for engagement with members of the Afro-Asian bloc on this question. As mentioned earlier, Hammarskjöld's view of the Congo Crisis was close to that of the African states which advocated the removal of all foreign powers from the country. This effort to "Africanize" the UN force was linked to the visions of African leaders such as Kwame Nkrumah of Ghana and Gamal Abdel Nasser of Egypt, who led the charge in the General Assembly against the neocolonial actions of Belgium and the West. Nkrumah viewed Belgian actions as reflective of a larger process of neocolonialism that was taking place in the Congo, and he repeatedly called for the elimination of all elements that were attempting to "sabotage the independence" of the country.[34] Beyond the critiques of Western actions as neocolonial was a broader debate about the balance between the demands of the Afro-Asian bloc and the security fears of the West in the process of decolonization. The United States in particular sought to expand its influence with African leaders, as reflected by a close engagement when drafting resolutions at the UN. The public nature of General Assembly debate served to reveal the depth of disagreement on core questions of how decolonization would take place and brought the anxieties of the West to the surface.

What became evident as the crisis progressed was the increasing movement of the West toward the African position on the Congo. The collapse of the Western consensus on how the UN should proceed deepened the divide between the United States and its European allies as the crisis accelerated. By the inauguration of President John F. Kennedy in January 1961, the United States actively sought to negotiate resolutions on the Congo with the Afro-Asian bloc. Crucially, on two occasions, in February and November 1961, the United States was forced to capitulate to African demands, having failed to secure amendments to increasingly radical African resolutions. Resolution 161 passed in the Security Council on February 21, authorizing

UN peacekeepers for the first time ever to use force in self-defense. The resolution came on the back of the breakdown of law and order in the Congo following the announcement of the murder of Lumumba.[35] News of the assassination had been met with widespread outrage, with the Soviets publicly charging that the UN had failed to protect the besieged prime minister.[36] It also served to radicalize some African states, which demanded ONUC take firmer action to bring about a resolution.

The African states now pressed for the implementation of Resolution 161. Although the sanctioning of peacekeepers' use of force in self-defense went further than the revisions to the ONUC mandate that Ambassador Stevenson had introduced in a speech on January 15, historian Lise Namikas has argued that for their own Cold War reasons, and the hope that further empowerment of the UN force would ease the conflict, Kennedy opted to support the Afro-Asian position. Central to this decision were the efforts of the State Department to thwart Soviet influence by winning-over the Afro-Asian bloc.[37] As Stevenson reflected, supporting the Afro-Asian bloc without securing American amendments to moderate the use of force and to remove the call for the immediate withdrawal of all Belgian military personnel was important in order to avoid alienating moderate elements within it. The reaction to the resolution by Britain and Belgium was predictably hostile. While the British had voted for it, chief UN representative Patrick Dean insisted that force could only be used to prevent civil war, not to end the secession of Katanga. The Belgians were "shocked" by the open condemnation of their policy. Despite their unease, however, the United States, Belgium, and Britain were even more marginalized when the Afro-Asians presented a follow-up on November 24 to strengthen Resolution 161.

By early November 1961, the situation in the Congo had deteriorated dramatically. Despite the installation in August of a Western-friendly regime in Léopoldville under a new prime minister, Cyrille Adoula, the fighting between UN troops and the Katanga rebels had intensified. In August and September, ONUC had launched two military initiatives against the province in order to arrest Tshombe and end the secession. The second one ended in disaster, with the UN sustaining losses and one Irish contingent besieged in Jadotville. In addition, on his way to negotiate a ceasefire, Hammarskjöld had been killed when his plane crashed in mysterious circumstances on September 18 in Northern Rhodesia. His successor, U Thant, similarly supported the positions of the Afro-Asians, taking an "unexpectedly strong stand," by ordering his representative to take "every possible measure" to restore law and order in the Congo.[38] This was in response to the threat of secession of another province in northern Congo, led by Antoine Gizenga, leader of the pro-Lumumba Stanleyville group, who had been advancing his influence in eastern Congo in the wake of the UN military operations.[39] As Gizenga was considered by the State Department to have communist leanings, Washington felt it imperative to further empower ONUC and try again to bring about a resolution.

On November 16, the execution and dismemberment of sixteen Italian airmen serving with the UN force by Congolese militiamen under Gizenga served to divide Afro-Asian opinion. On November 13, the Ethiopian delegate on the Security Council introduced a resolution that would strengthen the existing mandate for ONUC and authorize the secretary-general to use force to evict mercenaries from Katanga. Britain and Belgium had immediately objected to the resolution, viewing it as an extreme use of force. Initially, the United States had backed their position, and the Security Council was adjourned for forty-eight hours in order to work out an agreement. The Americans sought to add an amendment to the resolution that prevented ONUC from using force to end the secession and another to ensure it could be equally applied to Gizenga, both of which failed. Supported by the Soviets, the Afro-Asians held firm to the belief that the UN needed a stronger hand to formally end the secession. In response, the United States conceded defeat, and Stevenson voted for the draft on November 24 "with great reluctance."[40] The British abstained, viewing the new resolution as a direct conflict with their position on the use of force. Now, armed with a new mandate that authorized the secretary-general to "take vigorous action, including the use of the requisite measure of force . . . for the immediate apprehension, detention . . . and/or deportation of all foreign military and paramilitary personnel and political advisors not under United Nations command," the UN actively sought to end the secession of Katanga, which it finally succeeded in doing by December 1962.[41]

Hammarskjöld's initial positioning of the Congo question at the Security Council was important in immediately bringing the issue to the attention of the international public but also in encouraging public discussion of the Congo at the UN. While the West and the USSR attempted in many incidences to hijack the Congo to further their own aims, whether they were Cold War objectives or neocolonial desires, the discussion of these issues in the General Assembly was important for two reasons. First, as described above, it led to direct engagement with the Afro-Asian bloc to the extent that African leaders succeeded in charting the course for UN Congo policy in line with their own aims. Second, the public discussions with Afro-Asian leaders about the Congo opened up the dialogue with the United States in particular about how decolonization should be managed. The American acceptance of the Afro-Asian position on the role of the UN reflected the wider recognition of the Afro-Asian bloc's interpretations of sovereignty and statehood in the Congo. As Steven Metz describes it, the Congo Crisis was a moment of realization for the Americans that "decolonization is not merely an exchange of flags, but is a transformation of both attitudes and actions."[42] This transformation was brought about in no small part by the exposition of the fragility of Western unity on issues of decolonization in the public debates. The public dimension was essential in opening dialogue, but it was the second dimension of role of the UN as an actor that helped manifest this normative transformation.

THE UN AS AN ACTOR

The active capacity of the UN to shape the dynamic of the Congo Crisis is interpreted here not in the military actions of the peacekeeping mission but rather in the operationalizing of existing UN structures to create Congo policy at the Secretariat level. In particular, the decision of Hammarskjöld in July 1960 to create the Congo Advisory Committee (CAC) was an important effort to establish a UN committee designed to deal specifically with one issue of international security. In addition, he held weekly meetings in his office over dinner with the main participating countries and his closest advisers, which affectionally became known as the Congo Club. The group met late in the evening when delegates would review the day's events in the Congo and decide on a strategy for the following day.[43] This reflected Hammarskjöld's ability to approach the Congo Crisis innovatively and his determination to activate existing structures within the UN, which had arguably been underutilized up to this point. The CAC was designed to help him gain leverage to steer the complex and controversial ONUC operation through the General Assembly. It comprised representatives from the eighteen countries that had contributed troops to the operation. The CAC became an important avenue of communication between the secretary-general and the

Afro-Asian bloc, and a crucial instrument in fleshing out proposals for the Congo outside the General Assembly and therefore away from the pervasive influence of the Cold War. Additionally, it offered the African and Asian members an opportunity to improve cohesion on their Congo policies and agree a position before presenting their views in the General Assembly.[44]

The CAC and the Congo Club had an open-door policy in order to safeguard the statements of its members and foster open and frank discussions.[45] They became increasingly important forums for the development of UN Congo policy, both in realizing the secretary-general's activist role for the UN and in discussing ideas of how to contain the crisis and its longer-term impacts. Carole L. Collins attributes the development of this aspect of the UN, as a "de facto player" in the political dynamics of the crisis, to the pivotal role of Undersecretary Andrew Cordier, one of three American UN officials who attended meetings of the committee.[46] Although Namikas argues that Cordier acted as a conduit through which the State Department influenced UN Congo policy,[47] it is evident both from the events described earlier and the work of the committee that the impact of the CAC and the Congo Club on UN Congo policy was to direct it more toward African aims rather than Western ambitions.

One such example of the manifestation of African influence on UN Congo policy was the discussions that took place in November 1960 to create a Conciliation Commission for the Congo. The Conciliation Commission was a group of African and Asian representatives who were dispatched to the Congo in January 1961 in order to assess the situation on the ground and urge the various Congolese political factions into talks in order to restore the Parliament. The commission was carefully constructed to take the views of the Congolese themselves into account from the beginning. In a speech to the CAC on November 23, President Joseph Kasavubu pressed that it was "for the Congolese to do the thinking and for the technicians to translate their wishes . . . into what we need." The success of the commission, he argued, could only come through intense cooperation with the Congolese.[48] In response to this appeal to take the views of the Congolese seriously, the CAC agreed to delay the departure of the commission for several weeks in order to allow the various factions within Léopoldville the opportunity to meet and decide how best to use the assistance offered by the commission.

As part of its investigations, the commission met with all the various leaders in the Congo to discuss how to restore a functioning government.

The efforts of the commission were effective in bringing the Léopoldville-based political groups into a constructive dialogue. On February 9, 1961, Kasavubu had replaced the Council of Commissioners-General, which had been set up by Gen. Joseph Mobutu in September 1960, with a provisional government under the leadership of Joseph Iléo. In addition, the commission's report was an important basis for the development of Resolution 161 in February 1961. The commission's findings were also considered a legitimate basis on which to devise three more resolutions on April 15, 1961, which further empowered UN troops in the Congo to implement the February resolution.[49]

The Conciliation Commission was important for reflecting the views of the Congolese government on how the crisis should be managed by the UN. While it was not a revolutionary initiative, its results reflected the emphasis on including the Congolese themselves in the shaping of UN Congo policy and also the active part played by the UN in various guises to take their opinions into account. It also points to the agency of the Congolese and the Afro-Asian bloc in shaping UN policy. Moreover, however, the close cooperation between the secretary-general and the Africans on the CAC reflected the development of the capacity of the UN to directly address the aims of newly decolonized nations. The CAC provided the UN with a form of agency that was essential in formulating strategies in the Congo for ONUC but also in influencing draft resolutions before they were presented in the General Assembly and the Security Council. In this way, the tangible role of the UN in shaping Congo policy points to the agency that the organization had through these structures. The most important aspect of the CAC was that it gave the secretary-general a source of authority, the Afro-Asians gained a forum in which to consolidate their policy and, it was a platform where ideas were presented, discussed, and often assimilated into UN policy. This is the third dimension of the UN—as an incubator for ideas in a socializing space.

THE UN AS AN INCUBATOR FOR IDEAS AND SOCIALIZING SPACE

The third dimension of the UN that is evident throughout the Congo Crisis is its role as an incubator for ideas. In reflecting on the task before him in managing the process of decolonization, Hammarskjöld noted that the UN was going through the process of "adopting, adapting, and assimilating" ideas about how the world should be ordered. As highlighted above, the Afro-Asian bloc played a major role in advancing the universalization of ideas of sovereignty and statehood. These were precisely the issues at the heart of the crisis, as the varying interpretations of Congolese sovereignty and the political organization of the new Congolese state were frequently points of contention during UN debates. Through the CAC and the General Assembly, the debates on the Congo helped to formalize Congolese interpretations of these principles in the context of the state. In activating the channels of the Secretariat such as the CAC, which allowed the Afro-Asians to consolidate their position on the Congo question before it was presented to the General Assembly, the UN provided a space where ideas were fostered, shared, debated, and legitimized. The universalization of sovereignty in the decolonized world and the gradual acceptance by Western powers that colonialism and traditional imperialism were no longer acceptable were evident in the passing of General Assembly Resolution 1514 on December 14, 1960, titled "Declaration on the Granting of Independence to Colonial Countries and Peoples."[50]

Though the process of decolonization as a whole continued to be "lengthy, painful and discontinuous" for all sides,[51] Article 1, Chapter 1, of the UN Charter was further enshrined into international law by Resolution 1514.[52] This resolution had been passed in the General Assembly by an overwhelming vote of 90–0 (with nine abstentions, including by former colonial powers Britain, Belgium, France, and Portugal and by the United States). The unanimous vote underlined the assertion behind the statement that colonialism was no longer acceptable. The resolution restated the right of all peoples to self-determination, condemned acts of violence against those struggling for independence, and called for "immediate steps" to be taken to transfer all powers to people still under colonial regimes. Essentially, the resolution presented a set of "ordering principles" based directly on the charter but interpreting the principle of self-determination in a way that more accurately reflected the reality of international society, including newly decolonized states.

Although the declaration was nonbinding, it was a critical moment in legitimizing Afro-Asian visions of world order. It opened the path toward later legislative acts such as Resolution 1515 (December 15, 1960) on the right of states to control their own wealth and resources and Resolution 1803 (December 14, 1962), which declared states' rights to permanent sovereignty over natural resources. These, alongside later efforts in the 1970s to establish a New International Economic Order, demonstrate the tangible success of the declaration. As Edward McWhinney writes, the declaration and later acts "are demonstrations of the prophetic quality of the resolution . . . in providing an inevitable legal linkage between self-determination and its goal of decolonization."[53]

Beyond acting as a reflection of the aims of the charter and a guide for the development of international law, Resolution 1514 was also a critical moment for the development of international society. The Afro-Asian bloc seized upon the crisis as a moment that demonstrated that when sovereign integrity was not maintained and sovereignty was not respected in the context of decolonization, there was potential for international conflict. The debates and lobbying that took place in the lead-up to the passing of the resolution were strategic and tactical, advancing African interpretations of sovereignty and codifying these views into international law. It is important to note that despite the nine abstentions, there was no open objection to the declaration, even though it was an open condemnation of Western colonial policies. Rather, the resolution reflected the role of the UN in acting as a legal authority that sought to implement the principles of the charter by developing international law.

The passing of the declaration, alongside later resolutions and the work of the Special Committee on Decolonization (the Committee of Twenty-Four) gradually helped speed up many colonies' transition to independence by requiring colonial powers to submit information on the progress of political and economic development. Although this agreement had been in place since Resolution 66 had been passed in 1946, the process was now reinvigorated. As part of this, Britain now began to submit additional information to the UN regarding the progression to independence of non-self-governing territories, which had been identified as "the only area of maneuverability" on British colonial policy at the UN.[54] All of these legal developments were, however, grounded in Resolution 1514. The declaration had the effect of not only formalizing the Afro-Asian consensus on issues of sovereignty and statehood but also in legitimizing these views. Crucially, UN agency in shaping, ratifying, and codifying these principles gave expression to this intellectual shift. The effect was that the pursuit of these principles, and their use as a legal basis henceforth on colonial matters, encouraged colonial powers to adapt their views on colonialism and the end of empire.

Critically, it also began a process of reconsidering how imperialism related to internationalism and how these ideas would order the decolonized world.

Such was the invigoration of the General Assembly that in 1961 the British foreign minister, Alec Douglas-Home, ruefully noted that the UN "was now run by the Afro-Asian bloc."[55] During the Congo Crisis, it is clear that the bloc succeeded in shaping UN Congo policy, in the process invigorating previously underutilized organs of the UN. Their efforts in reviving the General Assembly and using lessons from the Congo to demonstrate the consequences for international security when sovereignty was not applied universally had the effect of launching a broader debate about how decolonization was to be managed. The reinvigoration of efforts to ensure that principles of sovereignty and statehood were applied universally in the decolonized world also represented a wider review of how to order international society to reflect the realities of a world that was different from that on which the charter was based.

The UN played a crucial role in this process of managing the shift in the international order. Across the three dimensions outlined here, the institution had an active part during the Congo Crisis in advancing the universalization of sovereignty and statehood. In the first dimension, the UN acted as a public stage or multidimensional platform that put, front and center, the crisis of principles that the conflict produced. Through the General Assembly, Security Council, and the various committees, the UN fostered a public and frank dialogue between the former colonial powers and the newly decolonized nations, in the process opening up the question of how relations could be managed and organized in accordance with which principles. In focusing the attention of the world on the Congo, Secretary-General Dag Hammarskjöld in particular encouraged an array of actors on both sides to consider how violations of sovereignty in the decolonized world could be addressed and what the implications for the broader process of decolonization were.

In the second dimension, as an actor, the UN Secretariat undertook a series of initiatives to directly bring about a resolution in the Congo—namely, creating the CAC and later the Conciliation Commission. In this way, the organization sought to formulate a coherent policy toward the Congo that was decoupled from the influence of the superpowers and avoided further interference in the country from outside forces. In the process, both the CAC and the commission offered the Congolese themselves a voice in the formulation of policy and more broadly helped the Afro-Asian members consolidate their position. Moreover, these two initiatives, alongside the peacekeeping mission ONUC, offered an opportunity for members of the UN Secretariat, including the secretary-general, to influence the progress of events. In this way, the UN can be viewed as having, and realizing, a capacity for action in the Congo.

The third dimension of the UN is in its role as a socializing space and an incubator for ideas. This is of course not limited to events during the Congo Crisis, but it is argued here that the particular set of circumstances that prevailed in the UN headquarters in New York and the very active role of the Secretariat at this time had the effect of helping to universalize ideas of sovereignty and statehood in the decolonized world. In taking the events in the Congo as an example of the implications of violating sovereignty, the Afro-Asians propelled the universalization of sovereignty through Resolution 1514 and the guidelines it provided for the later development of international law along these lines. The UN provided a source of authority that codified these principles and compelled former colonial powers to take them into account thereafter. In doing so, the organization played a role in advancing and accelerating decolonization and defining its implications for how the world should be ordered.

The meaning of decolonization proved to have political effects not just for former colonies and imperial powers at the UN but also for the ways in which powers such as the United States approached issues of sovereignty and statehood in the decolonized world. It is maintained here that UN agency, across these three dimensions, was crucial in shaping, formalizing, and giving expression to this intellectual challenge, causing former colonial powers and the West to adapt their views on colonialism, imperialism, and empire. The UN would prove to be the site of normative transformation as principles of sovereignty and statehood were reinterpreted by former colonies and codified into international practice. In creating the space for this public debate, invigorating the organs of the organization in defense of these principles in the Congo, and facilitating a dialogue that led to the legitimization of Afro-Asian view of sovereignty and statehood, the UN accelerated the end of empire and fostered the development of postimperial internationalism. As the British Foreign Office reflected ruefully on the crisis, it noted: "We have recently learnt a few lessons in the Congo operations—(1) The Secretary-General of the United Nations is a post of tremendous importance which can well make or ruin the United Nations by the interpretation it makes of the Resolutions, etc. passed by the Security Council or other organs of the organisation . . . (2) 'The Secretariat is a source of ideas and not merely is it there to service the policy-making organs."[56]

NOTES

1 Draft Statement on Colonialism in Response to Nigerian Resolution A/6.357 27 October 1961, folder 1, Colonialism, box 341, series 5, United Nations, subseries 4: US Ambassador, Adlai E. Stevenson papers, Mudd Manuscript Library, Princeton University.

2 The Afro-Asian or Asian-African bloc refers to a loose and informal coalition of states from Africa, Asia, and Southeast Asia that worked together at the UN, particularly in the General Assembly and its committees.

3 Draft Statement on Colonialism.

4 Richard Jolly, Louis Emmerij, and Thomas Weiss, eds., *UN Ideas That Changed the World* (Bloomington: Indiana University Press, 2009); Thomas Weiss and Ramesh Thakur, *Global Governance and the UN: An Unfinished Journey* (Bloomington: Indiana University Press, 2010).

5 Trevor Findlay, *The Use of Force in UN Peace Operations* (Oxford: Oxford University Press, 2002); Ernest W. Lefever, *Crisis in the Congo: A United Nations Force in Action* (Washington, DC: Brookings Institution, 1965); Norrie MacQueen, *Humanitarian Intervention and the United Nations* (Edinburgh: Edinburgh University Press, 2011); George Abi-Saab, *The United Nations Operation in the Congo, 1960–1964* (Oxford: Oxford University Press, 1979).

6 Carole Collins, "The Cold War Comes to Africa: Cordier and the 1960 Congo Crisis," *Journal of International Affairs* 47, no. 1 (1993): 250.

7 Ryan M. Irwin, *Gordian Knot: Apartheid and the Unmaking of the Liberal World Order,* Oxford Studies in International History (Oxford: Oxford University Press, 2012); Samuel Moyn, *The Last Utopia: Human Rights in History* (Cambridge, MA: Harvard University Press, 2010); Erez Manela, *The Wilsonian Moment: Self-Determination and the International Origins of Anticolonial Nationalism* (Oxford: Oxford University Press, 2007); Adam Roberts and Benedict Kingsbury, "Introduction: The UN's Roles in International Society since 1945," in *United Nations, Divided World: The UN's Roles in International Relations,* ed. Adam Roberts and Benedict Kingsbury (Oxford: Clarendon, 1993); Glenda Sluga and Sunil Amrith, "New Histories of the U.N.," *Journal of World History* 19, no. 3 (September 2008): 251–74; Akira Iriye, *Global Community: The Role of International Organizations in the Making of the Contemporary World* (Berkeley: University of California Press, 2004); Ilya V. Gaiduk, *Divided Together: The United States and the Soviet*

Union in the United Nations, 1945–1965 (Stanford, CA: Stanford University Press, 2012).

8 Mark Mazower, *No Enchanted Palace: The End of Empire and the Ideological Origins of the United Nations* (Princeton, NJ: Princeton University Press, 2009); Mark Mazower, *Governing the World: The History of an Idea* (New York: Penguin, 2012); Paul M. Kennedy, *Parliament of Man: The United Nations and the Quest for World Government* (London: Penguin, 2007).

9 David N. Gibbs, *The Political Economy of Third World Intervention: Mines, Money and U.S. Policy in the Congo Crisis* (Chicago: University of Chicago Press, 1991); John Kent, *America, the UN and Decolonisation: Cold War Conflict in the Congo* (London: Routledge, 2010); Anne Sophie Gijs, "Fighting the Red Peril in the Congo: Paradoxes and Perspectives on an Equivocal Challenge to Belgium and the West (1947–1960)," *Cold War History* 16, no. 3 (2016): 273–390.

10 Gaiduk, *Divided Together;* Alessandro Iandolo, "Beyond the Shoe: Rethinking Khrushchev at the Fifteenth Session of the United Nations General Assembly," *Diplomatic History* 41, no. 1 (2017): 128–54; Sergey Mazov, *A Distant Front in the Cold War: The USSR in West Africa and the Congo, 1956–1964* (Stanford, CA: Stanford University Press, 2010).

11 Bernard J. Firestone, *The United Nations under U Thant, 1961–1971* (Lanham, MD: Scarecrow Press, 2001), vii.

12 "The strongest support we have in this great test in the instrument of the independent nations of the world—the United Nations—is the confidence and solidarity of the African Member states, acting with a common purpose, that of maintaining Africa in peace and free of all interference alien to the African world." Secretary-General to the President of the Republic of Guinea, telegram, August 7 1960, Security Council Official Records, Fifteenth Year, Supplement for July, August, September 1960, S/4417/Add.1/Rev. II., in *Public Papers of the Secretaries-General of the United Nations,* ed. Andrew W. Cordier and Wilder Foote, vol. 5, *Dag Hammarskjöld: 1960–1961* (New York: Columbia University Press, 1975), 68.

13 Ove Bring, "Dag Hammarskjöld and the Issue of Humanitarian Intervention," in *Nordic Cosmopolitanism: Essays in International Law for Martti Koskenniemi,* ed. Jarna Petman and Jan Klabbers (Leiden: Brill, 2003), 486. See also Brian Urquhart, *Hammarskjöld* (New York: Norton, 1994); Peter Heller, *The United Nations under Dag Hammarskjöld, 1953–1961* (Lanham, MD: Scarecrow Press, 2001); Roger Lipsey, *Hammarskjöld: A Life* (Ann Arbor: University of Michigan Press, 2013); and Carsten Stahn and Henning Melber, eds., *Peace Diplomacy, Global Justice and International Agency: Rethinking Human Security and Ethics in the Spirit of Dag Hammarskjöld* (Cambridge: Cambridge University Press, 2014).

14 Conor Cruise O'Brien, *To Katanga and Back: A UN Case History* (London: Hutchinson, 1962), 15.

15 First Report from the Secretary-General to the Security Council on Assistance to the Republic of the Congo, New York, July 18, 1960, Security Council Official Records, Fifteenth Year, 877th Meeting. Cordier and Foote, *Public Papers of the Secretaries-General,* 28.

16 S/4526, Resolution 157 of the Security Council, September 17, 1960, states, "The Security Council, Having considered the item on its agenda as contained in document S/Agenda/906, Taking into account the lack of unanimity of its permanent members at the 906th meeting of the Security Council has prevented it from exercising its primary responsibility for the maintenance of international peace and security, Decides to call an emergency special session of the General Assembly, as provided in General Assembly resolution 377 A(V) of 3 November 1950, in order to make appropriate recommendations."

17 Maurice Keens-Soper, "The General Assembly Reconsidered," in *Diplomacy at the UN,* ed. G. R. Berridge and A. Jennings (London: Palgrave Macmillan, 1985), 89.

18 Keens-Soper, "The General Assembly Reconsidered," 85.

19 Madeleine Kalb, *The Congo Cables: The Cold War in Africa, from Eisenhower to Kennedy* (New York: Macmillan, 1982); Lise Namikas, *Battleground Africa: Cold War in the Congo 1960–1965* (Stanford, CA: Stanford University Press, 2013); Stephen R. Weissman, *American Foreign Policy in the Congo 1960–1964* (Ithaca, NY: Cornell University Press, 1974).

20 Alanna O'Malley, *The Diplomacy of Decolonisation: America, Britain and the United Nations during the Congo Crisis 1960–1964* (Manchester: Manchester University Press, 2018).

21 Jitranda Mohan, "Ghana, Congo and the United Nations," *Journal of Modern African Studies* 7, no. 3 (1969): 602.

22 Mohan, "Ghana, Congo and the United Nations," 375.

23 Article 99 of the UN Charter grants the secretary-general the power to "bring to the attention of the Security Council, any matter which in his opinion may threaten the maintenance of international peace and security." Leland. M. Goodrich, Edvard Hambro, and Anne Patricia Simons, *Charter of the United Nations, Commentary and Documents,* 3rd rev. ed. (New York: Columbia University Press, 1969), 588.

24 Opening Statement in the Security Council, New York, July 13, 1960, Security Council Official Records, Fifteenth Year, 873rd meeting, in Cordier and Foote, *Public Papers of the Secretaries-General,* 23.

25 Colin Legum, *Congo Disaster* (London: Penguin, 1961), 106.

26 "Congo Express Derailed," *The Economist,* July 16, 1960, 16.

27 Norman Bentwich and Andrew Martin, *A Commentary on the Charter of the United Nations* (New York: Routledge & K. Paul, 1969), 173 (italics added).

28 Legum, *Congo Disaster,* 126.

29 Alan James, *Britain and the Congo Crisis, 1960–1963* (Basingstoke, UK: Palgrave Macmillan, 1996), 65.

30 James, *Britain and the Congo Crisis,* 65.

31 See Richard D. Mahoney, *JFK: Ordeal in Africa* (New York: Oxford University Press, 1983), and Crawford Young, *Politics in the Congo: Decolonization and Independence* (Princeton, NJ: Princeton University Press, 1965).
32 S/4387 Security Council Official Records, Fifteenth Year, Supplement for July August and September 1960, draft resolution, "*Calls upon* the Government of Belgium to Withdraw Its Troops from the Territory of the Republic of the Congo," in Cordier and Foote, *Public Papers of the Secretaries-General,* 25.
33 Namikas, *Battleground Africa,* 6.
34 Kevin C. Dunn, *Imagining the Congo: International Relations of Identity* (Basingstoke, UK: Palgrave Macmillan, 2003).
35 For more on Lumumba's assassination, see Namikas, *Battleground Africa.*
36 Kalb, *Congo Cables,* 228
37 Kalb, 237.
38 Kalb, 309–10.
39 See generally Mazov, *Distant Front.*
40 Kalb, *Congo Cables,* 311.
41 S/4741, UN Security Council Resolution 161, "The Congo Question," November 24, 1961, http://unscr.com/en/resolutions/169.
42 Steven Metz, "American Attitudes toward Decolonization in Africa," *Political Science Quarterly* 99, no. 3 (1984): 533.
43 Lipsey, *Hammarskjöld,* 404.
44 "The Congo Advisory Committee provided a regularly scheduled group procedure that helped to clear misunderstandings and to cope with difference that had already begun to emerge among the African members and were soon to become more serious." Note on the composition and function of the Congo Advisory Committee in Cordier and Foote, *Public Papers of the Secretaries-General,* 151.
45 Remarks from the secretary-general to the first meeting of the United Nations Congo Advisory Committee, Wednesday, August 24, 1960, Meeting No. 1, S-0849-01-00001, Records of the Congo Advisory Committee, UN Archive.
46 Collins, "Cold War Comes to Africa," 245.
47 Namikas, *Battleground Africa,* 80–81.
48 Speech of President Joseph Kasavubu to the Congo Advisory Committee, November 23, 1960, Minutes of the Congo Advisory Committee, S-0849-01-0001, UN Archives.
49 "Questions Concerning the Situation in the Republic of the Congo (Leopoldville): Political Developments," 58, http://www.un.org/depts/dhl/dag/docs/congo61.pdf.
50 General Assembly Resolution 1535 of December 15, 1960, complemented Chapter 11, Article 73, in Goodrich, Hambro, and Simons, *Charter of the United Nations,* 454.
51 Prosser Gifford and Roger W. Louis, eds., *Decolonization and African Independence: The Transfers of Power, 1960–1980* (New Haven, CT: Yale University Press, 1988), ix–xxix.

52 Article 1, Chapter 1 of the UN Charter, paragraph 2, states, "One of the purposes of the United Nations [is] to develop friendly relations among nations based on respect for the principle of equal rights and self-determination among peoples, and to take other appropriate measures to strengthen universal peace." Goodrich, Hambro, and Simons, *Charter of the United Nations,* 19.

53 Edward McWhinney, "Declaration on the Granting of Independence to Colonial Countries and Peoples," commentary, United Nations Audiovisual Library of International Law, 2008, 3, http://legal.un.org/avl/pdf/ha/dicc/dicc_e.pdf.

54 Sir Hugh Foot, UK ambassador to the UN, and Assistant Secretary of State Harlan Cleveland, memorandum of conversation, September 1, 1961, 741.00/7–1561, State Department files: Britain, National Archives and Records Administration, College Park, MD.

55 Quoted in James, *Britain and the Congo Crisis,* 73.

56 Note on the Future of the UN, Briefs—Commonwealth Prime Ministers Conference, 1961, 11/3/61–16/3/6, RG 17/1/256, National Archives Britain.

CHAPTER 6

Insurgency's Three Waves

STEVEN METZ

Insurgency has existed as long as civilization itself.[1] While the word "insurgency" is often used by scholars and analysts to describe a particular organization, it is more accurately conceptualized as a strategy, specifically one used by the weak against the strong to alter the existing power structure or policy.[2] Often it pits a nonstate entity against a state with its inherently greater economic, military, and political resources, but weak states have also used the strategy of insurgency against great powers or an existing political order.[3] An organization can adopt the strategy of insurgency in its development, refine or adjust it to better reflect the organization's ideology, objectives, and strategic setting, abandon it when it no longer suits the organization's needs or capabilities, and even readopt it at a later point.[4]

The objectives of insurgent organizations vary. Most people think first of *revolutionary* insurgencies, which seek to destroy and replace the existing power structure, thus becoming the state. Some revolutionary insurgents even have a grandiose notion of reshaping their regional or the global power system. Many scholars, analysts, and government strategists treat revolutionary insurgencies as the only type.[5] But history is filled with insurgent movements with nonrevolutionary objectives, whether forcing their own inclusion in the power system, gaining autonomy from the state within a defined geographic, economic, or political realm, or altering specific state policies. Hence, it is more accurate to think of insurgent objectives on a continuum. One pole is the revolutionary transformation of the entire global power system, the other compelling the state to change a specific policy that the insurgents find intolerable. There are many points in between. In fact, a given insurgency-based organization can shift along the continuum as conditions change.

The strategy of insurgency is dangerous to those who use it, given the greater resources of the state or power system and thus has a low probability of success. This makes it a strategy of desperation, only used by organizations too weak to attain their objectives by other means. While there have been nonviolent organizations that share some characteristics of insurgency—the American civil rights movement for instance—true insurgency always involves violence.[6] The degree to which insurgency-based organizations rely on violence varies. Again, it makes sense to think of a continuum. At one end are organizations like the Islamic State of Iraq and Syria (ISIS) that rely heavily on armed action or the threat of it; at the other end might be something like the African National Congress (ANC), which used limited and selective violence during its struggle with apartheid, instead emphasizing political action.[7]

Since an organization using insurgency cannot match the military capability of the state until or unless it adjusts the power asymmetry, insurgents usually rely on irregular or asymmetrical forms of violence such as guerrilla operations, terrorism, subversion, sabotage, and assassination.[8] Their strategic logic is what is often described as "death by a thousand small cuts." No one campaign or battle is decisive, but the accumulation of attacks gradually weakens the state or power structure.[9] Over the past seventy-five years, a few insurgency-based movements have used irregular or asymmetrical violence to set the stage for conventional war—the Chinese and North Vietnamese, for instance—but many more have been forced to rely solely on it, with mixed results.[10] Generally subversion, guerrilla attacks, and terrorism only work without conventional military operations when the will of the state is fragile (as with Fulgencio Batista in Cuba and the British occupying power in Palestine) or when these methods are primarily supplements to political action (the antiapartheid campaign led by the ANC).

Because insurgencies are weaker than the state in the conventional military realm, they seek to focus the conflict in other domains where tangible resource superiority matters less, particularly the psychological, informational, and political. Insurgents believe—often correctly—that their fight with the state or the power structure is fairer or, at least, less asymmetrical in these domains where skill and ruthlessness matter more than tangible resources or manpower. Insurgents cannot build tanks and aircraft or, in most cases, mobilize large military formations, but they can develop and weaponize narratives as effectively as the state. Moreover, insurgents almost always believe that time is on their side, assuming that the longer they can survive and function, the more the power balance shifts in their favor. When a state is unable to quell an insurgency, political pressure mounts. This can cause it to make strategic mistakes—often by overreacting or becoming brutal and repressive. For this reason, organizations using insurgency often plan for a protracted conflict, deliberately attempting to postpone decisiveness and provoke the state into errors.

At times organizations have adopted insurgency almost instinctively, particularly nomadic or warrior cultures resisting encroachment by more formally organized states or empires. For these groups, persistent conflict, irregular tactics, banditry, and raiding were normal, making it easy for them to become informal or protoinsurgents. At other times organizations have adopted insurgency after assessing their own and their enemy's strengths and weaknesses. Insurgency was a strategic choice rather than an instinctive response to incursion, repression, injustice, or some other grievance.

Because insurgents are less constrained than the state by bureaucratic processes, law, and the need to satisfy multiple constituencies, they can be more innovative. Just as a startup company has greater opportunity for innovation than a large, long-standing one, so too insurgents. Insurgent leaders or potential leaders sometimes learn about insurgencies elsewhere and can adopt their methods. Emulation is an important driver of the evolution of insurgency, even though it does not always succeed.

From a global perspective, the strategic significance of insurgency ebbs and flows. There has probably never been a time when there were no insurgencies under way anywhere in the world, but during times of direct confrontation between great powers or between great and regional powers, insurgency becomes strategic background noise and draws less attention from policymakers, strategists, intelligence analysts, and scholars. At other times, such as the 1960s and 1970s and again in the first decade of the twenty-first century, the strategic significance of insurgency increases. Then it draws more attention both from those who seek to understand it and from government officials and security services who must counter it.

This combination of innovation and shifts in its strategic significance make it possible to conceptualize modern insurgency as three waves. The first ran from beginning of the Chinese Revolution in the 1920s to end of the Cold War in the early 1990s, the second was from the rise of transnational jihadism in the late 1980s until recently, and the third is now taking shape and probably will persist for a few decades. Insurgency's incoming and receding waves, like those in the ocean, overlap, coexist, and influence each other for some period of time. Each wave has a dominant form of insurgency—a paradigm or several paradigms—but also outliers. As in the evolution of species, mutations often become extinct but in rare instances can become a new paradigm in their own or the next wave. And during this evolution, some of forms of insurgency merge while others begin similarly and then diverge, becoming more distinct and proceeding on their own evolutionary path. This chapter will elaborate the three-wave construct to trace the recent evolution of insurgency and speculate as to its future.

THE FIRST WAVE

The first wave of modern insurgency took shape when Mao Zedong and his colleagues in the Chinese Communist Party combined nationalism, the desire for modernization by China's emerging intelligentsia, and the resentment, awakening, and political mobilization of the peasantry with an effective ideology combining traditional Chinese populism and Marxism. While Mao had no military training and there were no other communist insurgencies to serve as a model, he did have genius and luck. He was fortunate to survive the dangerous first years of the Chinese Civil War, and then brutal Japanese aggression provided him an opportunity build a national united front that his Communist Party eventually dominated. The strategy Mao created, which he labeled revolutionary "people's war," eventually became the gold standard of insurgency's first wave.[11] It was refined and applied in dozens of places. Part of its brilliance was its flexibility: it could be adapted to many different political, geographic, and cultural settings.

While the ideological foundation of people's war was an adapted version of Marxism, it was more closely linked to Lenin's thinking. Lenin had created the idea of a "vanguard party" to compensate for Russia's backwardness and the limited size of its industrial proletariat. Mao's China was even more backward than Lenin's Russia, the vast majority of its people peasants. Mao's strategy was to build a base in the rural hinterlands where the government was weak using the intelligentsia-based vanguard party and later move on China's cities.[12] The driving idea was that the state was inherently weaker in the hinterlands, whether because of a lack of capacity or a lack of will, and the intense resentment of the rural peasantry against the corruption and injustice of the existing political system provided fuel for revolution. Mao harnessed the discontent of the peasantry, organizing, focusing, and disciplining it with Marxism and the promise of modernization. The peasantry was, of course, intensely interested in greater political and economic justice. Justice thus became a central component of the narrative of people's war and remained so wherever it was attempted. Mao then linked the quest for internal justice with nationalism fueled by China's weakness and the intervention of outside powers, first the Europeans then the Japanese.

This combination of Marxism and mass resentment of corruption and injustice proved viable in many modernizing nations: an awakening peasantry, an intelligentsia energized by modernization and nationalism, a corrupt, repressive, unrepresentative, or inept state, and a hinterland where the state was weak. Eventually there were Maoist-style insurgencies in places as diverse as the Philippines, Vietnam, Cambodia, Malaya, Nepal, Angola, Mozambique, Colombia, Peru, Zimbabwe, India, Guatemala, and El Salvador. In some of them, people's war merged with ethnic and racial conflict, particularly when the power distribution within a nation was based on it. Maoism was malleable enough to allow tailoring it to a specific situation. And like Mao, many of his emulators initially built a united revolutionary, anticolonial, or nationalist front and later tried to destroy or subjugate the noncommunist components. The strategic logic was to build strength by alliances or coalitions, gain control of parts of the nation that the state was unwilling or unable to fully control, and mobilize enough power to directly challenge the state, then win through a combination of conventional military means and the continuous weakening of the state through all available methods, whether political, informational, or violent.

While people's war, like all true insurgency, used violence, Mao himself considered it secondary to political activity, at least until the insurgency-based movement became strong enough to take on the state in conventional war.[13] Infiltrating the government and security forces was also important, being used to collect intelligence and subvert counterinsurgency efforts.[14] Some of Mao's emulators, though, placed greater emphasis on armed action, often because it seemed more glamorous and quicker. There were even military-centric theories of insurgency such as *focoism,* which revolutionary theorist Régis Debray derived from Che Guevara's ideas and Fidel Castro's strategy.[15] What advocates of this approach missed, though, was that focoism only worked against a particularly inept and weak state or power structure.

Until the final phase of an insurgent campaign, the psychological effects of armed action were as important as the tangible ones. The use of force by Maoist-style insurgents was often described as "armed theater." As in a play, the actors on the stage—in this case insurgents and state security forces—interact with each other with the intent to send messages to an audience. While state security forces often overlooked this and focused on the number of insurgents killed or the amount of territory gained during military operations, insurgents—at least astute ones—shaped their use of violence to the transmission of specific messages to specific audiences. The message may be that the state is weak and inept, that the state is brutal, that the insurgents are bold, that the insurgency is more widespread than believed, or that the insurgents can operate wherever they want. They key is, though, that particularly for a Maoist-style insurgent, the psychological and political domains rather than the military one are decisive.

The just and effective administration of territory that the insurgents controlled—so called "liberated zones"—was central to people's war. The thinking was that population of the liberated zones would support the communists once they saw conditions improve, then word would spread to other areas, thus shaving support away from the often corrupt, repressive, and inept state and shifting it to the communists. This was often called the "propaganda of the deed"—insurgents went out of their way to behave better than the state and its security forces. By being more just than the state, the insurgents hoped to be seen as legitimate.

In Mao's model, the ultimate objective of the insurgents was to supplant the state. After a period of weakening the existing power structure through irregular military operations and political activity and exercising state authority in the "liberated zones," insurgents might transcend insurgency, build a conventional military, and conquer the nation. Insurgency, in other words, was only a phase of the struggle and eventually segued into conventional civil war. Today's analysts and scholars sometimes forget that Mao's guerrillas and the Viet Cong did not win their conflicts: Mao's conventional military units and the People's Army of Vietnam did.[16]

During the Cold War, Maoist-style insurgency merged with anticolonial struggles in Africa and parts of Asia and became a form of proxy conflict between the West and the Soviet bloc. The anticolonial dimension made it easier for insurgents to build a united front with noncommunist nationalist groups. This gave African and Asian insurgencies a higher success rate than ones in Latin America, where the dominant elite was indigenous rather than foreign. Maoist insurgency only worked in the Americas when the state was particularly inept, as in Cuba under Batista and Nicaragua under Anastasio Somoza. The use of insurgency as proxy conflict often gave insurgents (and counterinsurgents) outside support, including weaponry, money, intelligence, and advice and sometimes physical sanctuary as well, particularly for their political component. This meant that they could focus their effort on the conflict itself rather than on funding and supply. Put differently, having external sponsors meant that insurgents did not have to become parasitic, which helped their efforts to win local support.

While Maoist-style insurgency did have a few stunning success, most notably in China and Vietnam, it often failed, particularly when insurgent leaders were impatient and unwilling or unable to continue their fight for the decades that it took Mao and Ho Chi Minh, when insurgent leaders emphasized military action rather than political and psychological efforts, when there was inadequate or no outside support, when the insurgent leaders were unable to understand and exploit the perceptions and grievances of the rural peasantry they relied on for support, or when the state was skillfully led. In broad terms, Maoist-style insurgency only worked under specific conditions—it was not an irresistible force.

A few Maoist-style insurgencies continued after the end of the Cold War, including ones in Nepal, India, the Philippines, Peru, and Colombia.[17] The two South American ones were previews of the changes coming with the Soviet Union gone and insurgency support no longer a form of great-power proxy war. Over time both devoted more effort to resource accumulation and self-funding largely by involvement in narcotrafficking, whether providing security to and taxing the drug producers or getting into the business themselves. Ideology and politics once animated them but eventually became a thin veneer for what was essentially organized crime. A similar process took place in West and Central Africa where there were insurgent groups that mouthed some political slogans, whether quasi-Marxist or simply populist, but were more warlord militias than politically based Maoist insurgents. This melding of crime and insurgency, which began when insurgent-based movements could not get external support, soon became a common characteristic of insurgency.

THE SECOND WAVE

The second wave of modern insurgency began well before the first one was over—some of its central conflicts had roots in the Cold War and decolonization struggles—but it reached full flower after the demise of the Soviet Union. One of the driving forces was the emergence of what security scholars often call "new wars." Coined by Mary Kaldor, the phrase suggested that protracted low- or medium-level violence by varying combinations of states and nonstate actors fighting for identity politics and relying on predatory or criminal activity had become both common and strategically significant in the post–Cold War period.[18] Taking place in an environment of transnational connectivity and transparency, new wars are never contained in one nation but have a web of connections across nations and often around the world. Many of the participants adopted the strategy of insurgency.

Several features defined and distinguished insurgency's second wave. One was the need for insurgents to be self-supporting since there were no longer superpowers willing to arm and fund them. This drove second-wave insurgents deep into crime, including narcotics production and trafficking (e.g., the Taliban in Afghanistan, Sendero Luminoso in Peru, the Revolutionary Armed Forces of Colombia [FARC]), smuggling and human trafficking (e.g., al-Qaeda in the Islamic Maghreb), resource extraction and theft (e.g., the Revolutionary United Front in Sierra Leone, the Casamance Movement of Democratic Forces in Senegal, the Forces Nouvelles in Ivory Coast, ISIS in Iraq, the Movement for the Emancipation of the Niger Delta in Nigeria), sale of looted antiquities (e.g., ISIS in Syria and Iraq),[19] poaching (e.g., the Lord's Resistance Army in Central Africa, al-Shabaab in East Africa), bank robbery and kidnapping (e.g., ISIS and many others),[20] and, more recently, cybercrime (e.g., ISIS). The Iraqi insurgency developed alliances with organized crime very early in its existence.[21]

The need to be self-supporting increased the extent to which insurgents extracted money from populations they could tax or extort. This made it more difficult to follow Mao's notion of winning voluntary popular support. If the insurgent administration was just as or more parasitic than the state, it was hard to make a case that it was preferable. And as Jeremy Weinstein noted, insurgency-based movements that must extract resources from the populations they control are more inclined to indiscriminate violence.[22] In many cases this shifted second-wave insurgents away from the "velvet glove" approach toward the population toward a "mailed fist." ISIS is perhaps the most stunning example of reliance on extreme and widely publicized brutality.[23] Again, this element of insurgency is best conceptualized as a continuum from reliance on extreme violence (e.g., ISIS) to the minimal use of limited violence for specific political and psychological effects (e.g., the Zapatistas in Mexico).[24]

Insurgents still sought external funding and support during the second wave but in a different way. In the first wave, insurgents obtained it by affiliation with an external sponsor, usually the Soviet Union or another communist nation, and by adopting at least the rhetoric of the sponsor if not its actually policies. In the second wave, global connectivity—the internet, social media, wireless communication, methods for easy transfer of funds—and the extensive movement of people allowed insurgents to receive donations from diasporas of ethnic, racial, or sectarian groups that they were associated with or from other sympathizers. Sri Lanka's Tamil Tigers reportedly raised 80 percent to 90 percent of their budget from the Tamil diaspora.[25] A 2002 Council on Foreign Relations task force found that al-Qaeda supported itself by "charities, nongovernmental organizations, mosques, websites, intermediaries, facilitators, and banks and other financial institutions."[26] The internet and social media allowed insurgents to expand their pool of potential supporters beyond what was possible during the first wave.[27] In some cases donors did not even know that they were contributing to violent extremist movements.[28]

The need for insurgent-based organizations to be self-supporting had cascading effects. Even if they undertook crime only out of necessity, doing so changed and sometimes consumed them. Absent very strong leadership, the power and money associated with crime become alluring—it is more personally rewarding and sometimes safer to be a gangster than a guerrilla. Sendero Luminoso in Peru saw its branch involved in narcotrafficking survive long after its political-ideological element collapsed following the arrest of Abimael Guzmán, the movement's founder and leader.[29] Ostensibly political movements such as al-Qaeda in the Islamic Maghreb, the Abu Sayyaf organization in the Philippines, the Revolutionary United Front, the Lord's Resistance Army, and, in its later stages, the FARC morphed into criminal organizations with only a thin veneer of ideology or politics. Some organizations even flip the process: rather than beginning as political-ideological movements that take on the attributes of organized crime (like many bandit and pirate gangs throughout history), they begin as organized criminal gangs that adopt some of the rhetoric of political-ideological insurgency, whether to make themselves more appealing to recruits, gain the support from the local people in the areas where they operate, or simply justify what they do to themselves. Gangsters often undertake charity and public works to portray themselves as populists (e.g., Al Capone and Pablo Escobar). In fact, there is now a robust and growing analytical literature on "criminal insurgency" in which movements that begin as normal criminal gangs later take on some political or ideological attributes as a way to gain legitimacy or support.[30] Rather than a political movement compelled to enter into crime, they are criminal organizations that see an advantage in portraying themselves politically.

In the second wave, private weapons dealers largely replaced state sponsors as the provider of arms to insurgents. Weapons from the huge arms caches accumulated by Iraq's Saddam Hussein, Libya's Muammar Gaddafi, and the combatants in the Balkans wars of the 1990—many of them originating in the former Soviet bloc—often found their way to insurgent movements.[31] That said, some states continued to arm insurgents as an element of national policy. Iran's support to Iraqi insurgents is an important example.[32] More recently, the United States has armed, equipped, and trained insurgents in Syria.[33]

Second-wave insurgents, like their forebears, were skilled at innovating weapons from available materials. After all, insurgency is a strategy of desperation, which often sparks creativity. The most notorious recent insurgent innovations have been the improvised explosive devices and vehicle-borne explosive devices that caused many of the casualties in the Iraq insurgency.[34] These were constructed with everything from artillery shells salvaged from Saddam's arsenals to detonation devices using cell phones or garage-door openers. The internet amplified and accelerated this process. First-wave insurgents normally had to innovate weapons on their own; second-wave insurgents could learn how to do so from chat rooms or digitized videos.

Another defining feature of the second wave of insurgency was a shift in the dominant ideological framework from the metarevolutionary blend of Marxism and nationalism to a combination of limited-objective ethnic-sectarian-religious-based ideologies and a metarevolutionary ideology based on violent jihadism.[35] The Sri Lankan insurgency—which began during the first wave but became one of the paradigmatic conflicts of the second wave—was based on the intersection of ethnicity and religion, pitting the minority Hindu Tamils against the majority Sinhalese, who are mostly Buddhists and control the Sri Lankan state.[36] Most of the second-wave insurgencies, though, were outgrowths of the war within Islam, often combined with an ethnic or sectarian component (e.g., Afghanistan, Iraq, Egypt, Algeria, Yemen, Indonesia, Mali) or the result of conflict between Muslims within multireligious nations and the national states (e.g., Russia, Nigeria, Thailand, the Philippines).

The predominance of affinity-based new wars has made second-wave insurgencies more intractable than first-wave ones. During the first wave, a Batista or a Nguyen Van Thieu in Vietnam could give up and go into a comfortable exile. A leader facing an ethnic or sectarian insurgency is likely to be more steadfast since if he abandons the fight, his coethnics or cosectarians suffer. That accounts in part for the failure of insurgency in Sri Lanka and in Syria, where the defeat of Bashar al-Assad might mean genocide for his Alawite minority sect. In affinity-group conflict, the stakes are simply too high for the regime to surrender.

Certainly, ethnic, sectarian, religious, or racial differences in a nation do not invariably lead to conflict—much less insurgency—but they sometimes did, in part because of emulation. Over the course of the first wave, a "cult of the insurgent" developed, making insurgency seem heroic and glamorous.[37] Insurgents who failed or died early did not write about it—only the successful ones did. Hence, potential insurgents knew little of the failures and much of the successes. For leaders of ethnic, sectarian, religious, or racial groups that were treated unfairly and excluded from power, insurgency seemed to offer a solution, particularly the paradigmatic Chinese and Vietnamese ones. But global connectivity and transparency gave potential second-wave insurgents a more realistic picture of their prospects. The dark underbelly of insurgency and its frequent failure were as well-known as its successes. While it is hard to know how many potential insurgents were deterred by this, it is safe to assume that some were. That means only the most determined and violent turned to the phenomenon. This helped make hyperviolent mailed-fist insurgency more common than its velvet-glove form.

Transnationalism is common in second-wave insurgency. There were a few foreign fighters in first-wave insurgencies. For instance, Guevara, an Argentine, fought in Cuba and the Congo and died in Bolivia. But even though foreign fighters helped Marxist insurgent movements portray themselves as international to appeal to the intelligentsia and external sponsors, foreign fighters were secondary to local ones even in conflicts like the Afghanistan war against the Soviet Union, where there were many.[38] Throughout the second wave, foreign fighters became increasingly important, particularly for insurgents with a transnational ideology, such as al-Qaeda and ISIS.[39] Some first-wave insurgencies talked about international solidarity, but al-Qaeda and ISIS practiced it. The internet and social media made this possible. Insurgent movements used them not only for fundraising and intelligence gathering but also for the recruitment of foreign fighters.[40]

Transnationalism loosened the connection between insurgent organizations and a specific piece of territory. First-wave insurgencies composed largely of rural peasants as well as second-wave insurgencies based purely on ethnicity were inextricably linked to territory—often the traditional homeland of whatever group formed the core of the movement. The essentially Pashtun Taliban insurgency in Afghanistan is an example. But revolutionary insurgencies like al-Qaeda and ISIS, with both transnational ideological frameworks and composition, were not. When they opened a theater of operations, fighters tended to swarm to that location. If they lost in one place, they could move to another.[41] Their "franchise" structure facilitated this: both al-Qaeda and ISIS have a central leadership linked to but not in direct command of franchises across the Islamic world. When they were defeated in Iraq (twice), many of their leaders and fighters relocated. The same happened after ISIS's defeat in Syria.[42] Phrased differently, the first wave was composed almost exclusively of stationary insurgencies; the second wave included some stationary and some fluid ones.

Second-wave insurgents often placed greater emphasis on terrorism than first-wave ones. While first-wave insurgents used it, only a few urban-based ones relied on it. And they only succeeded when the will of the state was already fragile (e.g., the Haganah and the Irgun in the British-administered

Mandatory Palestine). During the second wave, many insurgent movements became terrorism-centric. There were two reasons for this. First, information technology and global connectivity made terrorism more effective by greatly expanding the audience it could reach. A first-wave terrorist attack in Vietnam or China would only have an immediate impact on people in close proximity. News of it might be transmitted by word of mouth, print, or broadcast media, but second-hand reports never had the same psychological impact as direct experience. In the internet age, local and global audiences can watch attacks in near-real time or even real time, thus amplifying the impact. Connectivity and information technology also allowed emulation, so understanding of terrorism techniques spread rapidly and widely. Tactical learning was faster than in the first wave. Second, terrorism, particularly suicide terrorism, requires less training than complex guerrilla operations. As insurgent-based movements relied more on foreign fighters with whom they had weaker personal ties and thus often were considered disposable, suicide terrorism was a way to extract some psychological and political value from recruits, with minimum investment either in emotional terms or in training.

The use of terrorism had another significant effect: it gave insurgents a strategic power-projection capability. The North Vietnamese never attempted to strike directly at the United States. This may have been because they concluded that it would have further antagonized Americans (a lesson perhaps learned from the Japanese attack on Pearl Harbor). This might have undercut the antiwar movement in the United States, which Hanoi considered helpful to its cause. But it is also possible that North Vietnam could not have launched effective terrorist attacks in the United States even if it wanted to. Second-wave insurgent movements like al-Qaeda used terrorism against outside nations that supported the state they were trying to overthrow. The September 11 attacks on the United States was a stark signal of this change, and many other al-Qaeda- and ISIS-linked terrorist attacks since have reinforced the point. In broad terms second-wave insurgency became transnational.

During the second wave, insurgency remained a form of proxy conflict, but it was often used by neighboring nations rather than faraway powers. Serbia supported insurgency in Bosnia; some African states backed insurgency in the Democratic Republic of the Congo, Liberia, Sierra Leone, and Spanish Sahara; Pakistan supported insurgency in Afghanistan; Russia support it in Ukraine; Iran supported it in Iraq; Turkey and other nations did so in Syria. The distinction, then, might be called "local proxyism" rather than the "global proxyism" of the first wave.[43]

THE THIRD WAVE

Insurgency's third wave is now forming: today it is inchoate, its ultimate direction unclear. If history holds, it will have some attributes of second- and even first-wave insurgency but will be different in important ways. At this point it is possible to identify trends in operational methods and tactics but not in insurgency's ideological framework or the pace and vector of its evolution. The beginning of an insurgency wave is characterized by an array of mutations. Most will be ineffective and die out. A few will prove successful; they will spawn emulation and further innovation. At some point, paradigmatic insurgencies will emerge.

A shift in the organization of insurgent movements is already under way. First-wave insurgencies aspired to become state-like, developing formal decision processes, internal hierarchy, and subunit specialization. In most cases, there was a clear paramount leader. Insurgent movements thus mirrored the state that they wanted to become. Some second-wave insurgents continued this, particularly those able to control and administer territory (e.g., the Tamil Tigers). This made sense since the state-like form of organization was specifically designed to administer large things. Insurgencies unable to control and administer territory, whether due to their own weakness or the strength of the state, often became a network of nodes (e.g., the Iraq insurgency from 2003 to 2008).[44] In the network-and-node organizational form there might be hierarchy, formal decision processes, and functional specialization within a node but no overall authority over the entire network. Hence, they are similar to the American and Sicilian mafias and the international state system. Operationally and strategically, network-and-node insurgencies function by emulation and swarming.

For the insurgents this organizational form had both advantages and disadvantages. It made them more resilient and harder to eradicate since no one mode was irreplaceable. Counterinsurgents had to take the network apart a node at a time rather than strike a single decisive blow.[45] Networked insurgencies could not be defeated through decapitation as when, for example, Shining Path fell apart after Guzmán was captured.[46] On the other hand, networked insurgencies have been unable to mobilize and concentrate enough power to defeat a state. At best, they can force the state to make concessions and integrate them into the power structure, as in Iraq.[47]

First-wave insurgents almost always sought to control and administer territory, whether a part of the nation or a nation as a whole. So, too, did most second-wave insurgents. Even ISIS wanted (but was unable to sustain) a "caliphate." Many—perhaps most—third-wave insurgents will recognize that this is infeasible. Often they will be satisfied with limited state authority and control in their operating regions, much like the criminal insurgencies in Mexico today.[48] Put differently, third-wave insurgents will deliberately engineer what are often called "ungoverned spaces." They will exercise some authority but not attempt full control and administration lest they provide targets that counterinsurgents, with their superior military capability, can strike.

This suggests that a networked organizational form, a swarming/emulation strategy, and delinkage from a specific piece of territory will characterize insurgency's third wave. Third-wave insurgents are likely to follow the current pattern of ISIS, swarming on a point of vulnerability, then dispersing if the pressure from enemies becomes too great, and later reswarming to another location when an opportunity arises and a franchise exists. Insurgents will be like flies, constantly seeking out dying or dead states.

Like some cutting-edge corporations, third-wave insurgents are likely to have a dispersed leadership with less than total control over the movement—think of al-Qaeda after the US invasion of Afghanistan with its leadership in Pakistan but its operating force elsewhere. Like al-Qaeda at that time, the franchises of third-wave insurgencies will do the movement's actual work, whether armed action, resource accumulation, recruitment, training, psychological warfare, or something else. They will increasingly rely on the virtual domain, including social media and the internet, particularly the dark web. This means that information security will be an exceptionally valuable skill for third-wave insurgents, but it will be readily available and not require a physical presence in whatever location the insurgency's leaders happen to live. Insurgency, like work, is becoming less location dependent.

The shift from guerrilla operations to terrorism will continue. Since the logic of terrorism requires increasingly fearful actions to generate the same level of response on the part of target audiences, as the audiences become accustomed to a type of attack, third-wave insurgents will seek escalated methods of terrorism, including nuclear, radiological, biological, and large-scale cyber. And insurgents will be at the leading edge of efforts to use new technology for destructive purposes, from drones and robots to artificial intelligence.[49] As always, they will innovate in this quest.

Third-wave insurgents will pursue the "weaponization of everything," searching for ways to use things and activities not designed as weapons.[50] Think of al-Qaeda's weaponization of hijacked airliners, the increasingly common use of trucks and cars for terrorism, and the kinds of aggressive information warfare conducted through cyberattacks and disinformation campaigns that exploit "fake news" and vulnerabilities on social media. In a 2015 book, Benjamin Wittes and Gabriella Blum explained:

> Modern technology enables individuals to wield the destructive power of states. Individuals . . . can potentially be attacked with impunity from anywhere in the world. . . . New technologies are able to generate and channel mass empowerment, allowing small groups and individuals to challenge states and other institutions of traditional authority in ways that used to be the province only of other states. They are growing increasingly cheap and available. They defy distance and other physical obstacles. And, ultimately, they create the world of many-to-many threats, a world in which every individual, group, or state has to regard every other individual, group, or state as at least a potential security threat.[51]

Third-wave insurgents will be masters of this phenomenon.

For third-wave insurgents, crime will continue to provide funds to buy or lease talent, recruits, weapons, information, and technology. Hence, the blending of crime and insurgency seen during the second wave will continue. Most third-wave insurgencies will devote more organizational energy to crime than politics and will form alliances with purely criminal organizations—a dark echo of the united progressive or nationalistic fronts that first-wave insurgents found useful. Put another way, first-wave insurgents were focused on the attainment of political power. Resources—money, recruits, alliances, weapons—were a means to that end. Second-wave insurgents were forced to devote more of their energy to resource accumulation. In the third wave, power will be defined more broadly. Rather than political power being clearly paramount and other forms secondary, resources and political power will be coequal. For many third-wave insurgents, resource accumulation will be a priority rather than an enabler. Politics and ideology will be used to facilitate resource accumulation rather than resources being used to facilitate promotion of political and ideological objectives. Commercial or criminal insurgency will not be a discrete type as during the second wave: all third-wave insurgencies will be commercial or criminal.

AN UNCERTAIN FUTURE

Early in insurgency's first wave, Maoist "people's war" emerged as the paradigm. Because of the growing complexity of the security environment fueled by globalization, connectivity, and the profusion of information and communication, the paradigms of the second wave were not immediately obvious. Only over time did the Tamil Tigers, the ANC, and al-Qaeda and ISIS emerge as dominant types. It is much too early at this point to conclusively identify the paradigmatic insurgencies of the third wave. Today ISIS is the closest to a paradigm. It is organized on nodes and franchises; it relies on swarming; it is deeply transnational; it is not inextricably linked to a specific piece of territory or terrain; it relies extensively on social media and the internet for resource accumulation, recruitment, psychological warfare, narrative building, and probably operational planning; it has crafted an ideology and narrative that combines historical myth, a psychologically astute framework to appeal to recruits and supporters, and an action plan; and it devotes a large amount of its effort to resource accumulation and has a multitude of ways to do this.[52] It is possible, even likely, that different paradigms will emerge, particularly if ISIS continues to fail. After all, it was an outgrowth of the second wave, so that legacy continues to encumber it. Its core ideology—violent revolutionary jihadism—has limited appeal, resonating mostly with the deeply alienated and psychologically troubled. As stories continue to come out about life in the former ISIS "caliphate," its pool of potential recruits will shrink.

Given this, new extremist ideologies—new causes and new narratives—more powerful and appealing than violent revolutionary jihadism may emerge. In some cases, they will inspire insurgencies. It is hard to predict what these new extremist ideologies will be, but it is likely that something that exists today as a protoideology will evolve into a full blown one. It may be extremist forms of racism, environmental extremism (driven by climate change), or antitechnologyism (driven by the perceived dehumanization brought by autonomous machines and artificial intelligence). An insurgency based on charismatic millenarian Christianity is not impossible—the Lord's Resistance Army might prove a portent of insurgency's third wave. It is also possible that movements that begin as criminal and take on some attributes of politics and ideology, such as Mexico's Knights Templar, will form a paradigm.[53] Ultimately the third wave, like the second, is likely to have multiple, diverse paradigms rather than a single one.

It is also too early to assess the global strategic significance of third-wave insurgencies. That depends on whether great-power conflict reemerges as some scholars and security analysts predict, and whether third-wave insurgents are able to create a viable method to undercut states and the existing power structure.

Because of connectivity and the profusion of information, the pace and complexity with which insurgency evolves will increase. There will be more mutations than in the past, although, as always, most of them will fail. And paradigms will emerge more quickly, followed by emulation and further evolution. But so long as desperate and weak organizations fight against what they consider an unjust power structure and have the tools of violence available to them, insurgency in some form will persist, evolve, and mutate. While the third wave is just coalescing, somewhere the seeds of the fourth wave are germinating.

NOTES

This chapter is solely the work of the author and does not necessarily represent the official position of the US Army War College, the US Army, or the US Department of Defense.

1 Max Boot, *Invisible Armies: An Epic History of Guerrilla Warfare from Ancient Times to the Present* (New York: Liveright, 2013).
2 Further explored in Steven Metz, "Rethinking Insurgency Revisited: Myths, Misperceptions, Mutations, and Memes," in *The Routledge Companion to Insurgency and Counter Insurgency,* ed. Paul Rich and Isabelle Duyvesteyn (New York: Routledge, 2012); Steven Metz, "Insurgency," in *Conceptualising Modern War: A Critical Inquiry,* ed. Ole Jørgen Maaø and Karl Erik Haug (London: Hurst, 2011); and Steven Metz, *Rethinking Insurgency* (Carlisle, PA: US Army War College Strategic Studies Institute, 2007).

3 E.g., Iran's national security strategy over the past few decades has been based on a form of insurgency.

4 Hezbollah is an example of an organization that adopted, refined, and later abandoned the strategy of insurgency. See Augustus Richard Norton, *Hezbollah: A Short History* (Princeton, NJ: Princeton University Press, 2007).

5 Official US military thinking has moved only partly beyond treating only revolutionary insurgency as "real insurgency." According to current joint doctrine, "two common objectives of insurgent movements are legitimacy according to public opinion and political control of a population in a particular geographic area." *Joint Publication 3–24: Counterinsurgency; 25 April 2018,* https://www.jcs.mil/Portals/36/Documents/Doctrine/pubs/jp3_24pa.pdf. This excludes insurgents simply seeking inclusion in the existing power system, those attempting to alter specific government policies, and those only attempting to weaken the state in their operating area without exercising control themselves, particularly criminal insurgencies.

6 Historian Mark Grimsley argues that the civil rights movement was an insurgency: "Why the Civil Rights Movement Was an Insurgency," Historynet, February 24, 2010, https://www.historynet.com/why-the-civil-rights-movement-was-an-insurgency.htm.

7 I argue that the ANC model of insurgency is more difficult to counter than violence-based ones in Steven Metz, "How Insurgents Could Beat the United States," *World Politics Review,* September 1, 2017.

8 Scholars and analysts often try to distinguish between an insurgency and a terrorist organization, but this is an analytically flawed approach. Insurgency is a strategy; terrorism is a tactic or operational method. Nearly all organizations using the strategy of insurgency use terrorism to some extent. For some it is of minor importance, for others a central component of their activity. Neither insurgency nor terrorism is a type of organization.

9 Some insurgency-based movements in recent years have forgotten this point, become impatient, and attempted to launch a major military offensive. More often than not, this proves disastrous to the organization. Examples are the 1968 Tet Offensive, which, while eroding domestic support for US involvement in Vietnam, virtually destroyed the Viet Cong as an organization, and the 1989 offensive by El Salvador's Farabundo Martí National Liberation Front.

10 Some variants of insurgency—specifically the Maoist—use irregular violence to address the power asymmetry and then shift to conventional warfighting, but this is only possible under rare conditions.

11 For Maoist people's war, see Steven Metz and Raymond Millen, *Insurgency and Counterinsurgency in the 21st Century: Reconceptualizing Threat and Response* (Carlisle, PA: US Army War College Strategic Studies Institute, 2004), 8–10, https://ssi.armywarcollege.edu/pubs/download.cfm?q=586, and Robert Taber, *War of the Flea* (Washington, DC: Potomac Books, 2002). Mao

himself explained it in "On Protracted War," reprinted in *Selected Works of Mao Tse-tsung,* vol. 2 (Beijing: Foreign Languages Press, 1967), 113–94, http://www.marx2mao.com/Mao/PW38.html#s1, and in his *On Guerrilla Warfare* (Champaign: University of Illinois Press, 2000). For adaptation and refinement, see Võ Nguyên Giáp, *People's War, People's Army: The Viet Cong Insurrection Manual for Underdeveloped Countries* (Honolulu: University Press of the Pacific, 1961), and Edward C. O'Down, "Ho Chi Minh and the Origins of the Vietnamese Doctrine of Guerrilla Tactics," *Small Wars and Insurgencies* 24, no. 3 (2013): 561–87. See also Boot, *Invisible Armies,* 328–46; Robert Asprey, *War in the Shadows: The Guerrilla in History* (New York: William Morrow), 229–62; and Douglas S. Blaufarb, *The Counterinsurgency Era: U.S. Doctrine and Performance, 1950 to the Present* (New York: Free Press, 1977), 1–21.

12 During the first wave, there were attempts to undertake urban-based insurgency, particularly in South America, but none succeeded. On this substrategy, see Carlos Marighella, *Minimanual of the Urban Guerilla* (1969), https://www.marxists.org/archive/marighella-carlos/1969/06/minimanual-urban-guerrilla/index.htm, and Donald C. Hodges, ed. and trans., *The Philosophy of the Urban Guerilla: The Revolutionary Writings of Abraham Guillén* (New York: William Morrow, 1973).

13 Võ Nguyên Giáp, *Big Victory, Great Task* (London: Pall Mall, 1968). The classic village-level case study of the development of an insurgent underground is Jeffrey Race, *War Comes to Long An* (Berkeley: University of California Press, 1973).

14 The most important study of political undergrounds in Maoist-style insurgency, specifically in Vietnam, is Andrew R. Molnar, *Human Factors Considerations of Undergrounds in Insurgencies* (Washington, DC: American University Special Operations Research Office, 1972).

15 Régis Debray, *Revolution in the Revolution?* (New York: Monthly Review Press, 1967); Ernesto "Che" Guevara, *Guerrilla Warfare* (New York: Monthly Review Press, 1961). Also, Paul B. Rich, "People's War Antithesis: Che Guevara and the Mythology of *Focismo,*" *Small Wars and Insurgencies* 28, no. 3 (2017): 451–87.

16 Douglas Pike, *Viet Cong: The Organization and Techniques of the National Liberation Front of South Vietnam* (Cambridge, MA: MIT Press, 1966). For a first-person perspective, see Truong Nhu Tang, *A Viet Cong Memoir: An Inside Account of the Vietnam War and Its Aftermath* (New York: Vintage, 1986). On the ultimate end of the Vietnam conflict by large-scale conventional combat, see Harry G. Summers, *On Strategy: A Critical Analysis of the Vietnam War* (Novato, CA: Presidio, 1995).

17 Thomas A. Marks and Paul B. Rich, "Back to the Future: People's War in the 21st Century," *Small Wars and Insurgencies* 28, no. 3 (2014): 409–25. For case studies, see David E. Spencer and Hugo Acha Melgar, "Bolivia, a New Model Insurgency for the 21st Century: From Mao Back to Lenin," *Small Wars and Insurgencies* 28, no. 3 (2014): 629–60; Thomas A. Marks, "Terrorism as Method

in Nepali Maoist Insurgency, 1996–2016," *Small Wars and Insurgencies* 28 no. 1 (2014): 81–118; and Namrata Goswani, *Indian National Security and Counter-Insurgency* (London: Routledge, 2014).

18 Mary Kaldor, *New and Old Wars: Organized Violence in a Global Era* (Stanford, CA: Stanford University Press, 1999); Herfried Münkler, *The New Wars* (Cambridge: Polity, 2005).

19 Andrew Terrill, *Antiquities Destruction and Illicit Sales as a Source of ISIS Funding and Propaganda* (Carlisle, PA: US Army War College Strategic Studies Institute, 2017), https://ssi.armywarcollege.edu/pubs/display.cfm?pubID=1348.

20 Colin P. Clarke, "ISIS's New Plans to Get Rich and Wreak Havoc," *Foreign Policy,* October 10, 2018, https://foreignpolicy.com/2018/10/10/isiss-new-plans-to-get-rich-and-wreak-havoc/.

21 Phil Williams, *Criminals, Militias, and Insurgents: Organized Crime in Iraq* (Carlisle, PA: US Army War College Strategic Studies Institute, 2009), https://ssi.armywarcollege.edu/pubs/display.cfm?pubID=930.

22 Jeremy M. Weinstein, *Inside Rebellion: The Politics of Insurgent Violence* (Cambridge: Cambridge University Press, 2007).

23 Steven Metz, "The Islamic State's Brutality May Not Be Its Undoing," *World Politics Review,* August 28, 2015, https://www.worldpoliticsreview.com/articles/16553/the-islamic-state-s-brutality-may-not-be-its-undoing.

24 David Ronfeldt, John Arquilla, Graham E. Fuller, and Melissa Fuller, *The Zapatista Social Netwar in Mexico* (Santa Monica, CA: RAND Corp., 1998).

25 Rüdiger Falksohn and Padma Rao, "Tamil Tigers Exploit Exiles Abroad to Fund Insurgency," *Spiegel Online,* February 14, 2008, http://www.spiegel.de/international/world/extorting-the-diaspora-tamil-tigers-exploit-exiles-abroad-to-fund-insurgency-a-535316.html.

26 Council on Foreign Relations, *Terrorist Financing: Report of an Independent Task Force Sponsored by the Council on Foreign Relations* (New York: Council on Foreign Relations, 2002), https://www.cfr.org/content/publications/attachments/Terrorist_Financing_TF.pdf.

27 Tom Keatings and Florence Keen, "Social Media and Terrorist Financing: Time for a Focused Response," *Royal United Services Institute Newsbrief* 37, no. 4 (October 2017), http://www.tomkeatinge.net/uploads/1/7/8/4/17845871/201710_newsbrief_37.4_keatinge_and_keen_final.pdf; Gabriel Weimann, *Terror on the Internet: The New Arena, the New Challenges* (Washington, DC: United States Institute of Peace, 2006); Steven Metz, "The Internet, New Media, and the Evolution of Insurgency," *Parameters* 42, no. 3 (Autumn 2012): 80–90. On the overall effect of social media on conflict, see James Jay Carafano, *Wiki at War: Conflict in a Socially Networked World* (College Station: Texas A&M University Press, 2012); David Patrikarakos, *War in 140 Characters: How Social Media Is Reshaping Conflict in the Twenty-First Century* (New York: Basic Books, 2017); and P. W. Singer and Emerson T. Brooking, *LikeWar: The Weaponization of Social Media* (Boston: Eamon Dolan, 2018).

28 Stacey Yuen, "It's Not Just Russia—Terror Financiers Are Also Using Social Media Propaganda," CNBC.com, January 1, 2018, https://www.cnbc.com/2017/12/18/social-media-propaganda-terror-financiers-operate-on-internet.html.

29 Gustavo Gorriti, *The Shining Path: A History of the Millenarian War in Peru* (Chapel Hill: University of North Carolina Press, 1999).

30 Robert Bunker and John Sullivan, eds., *Criminal Insurgents in Mexico and Latin America: A Small Wars Journal–El Centro Anthology* (Bloomington, IN: iUniverse, 2015). The concept of criminal insurgency is derived from the idea of commercial insurgency that I introduced in *The Future of Insurgency* (Carlisle, PA: US Army War College Strategic Studies Institute, 1993), https://ssi.armywarcollege.edu/pubs/display.cfm?pubID=344.

31 Elias Groll, "Where the Insurgent Groups of the World Get Their Weapons," *Foreign Policy*, June 1, 2015, https://foreignpolicy.com/2015/06/01/where-the-insurgent-groups-of-the-world-get-their-weapons/; Daniel Byman et al., *Trends in Outside Support for Insurgent Movements* (Santa Monica, CA: RAND Corp., 2001), 93–95, https://www.rand.org/content/dam/rand/pubs/monograph_reports/2001/MR1405.pdf.

32 Lionel Beehner and Greg Bruno, "Iran's Involvement in Iraq," Council on Foreign Relations Backgrounder, March 3, 2008, https://www.cfr.org/backgrounder/irans-involvement-iraq; Ed O'Keefe and Joby Warrick, "Weapons Prove Iranian Role in Iraq, U.S. Says," *Washington Post,* July 5, 2011, https://www.washingtonpost.com/world/war-zones/weapons-prove-iranian-role-in-iraq-us-says/2011/07/05/gHQAUnkmzH_story.html; Michael Eisenstadt, Michael Knights, and Ahmed Ali, *Iran's Influence in Iraq: Countering Tehran's Whole-of-Government Approach,* Washington Institute for Near East Policy, Policy Focus #111, April 2011, https://www.washingtoninstitute.org/policy-analysis/view/irans-influence-in-iraq-countering-tehrans-whole-of-government-approach.

33 Carla E. Humud, Christopher M. Blanchard, and Mary Beth D. Nikitin, *Armed Conflict in Syria: Overview and U.S. Response* (Washington, DC: Congressional Research Service, September 28, 2016), https://apps.dtic.mil/dtic/tr/fulltext/u2/1018239.pdf.

34 Clay Wilson, *Improvised Explosive Devices (IEDs) in Iraq and Afghanistan: Effects and Countermeasures* (Washington, DC: Congressional Research Service, 2007).

35 On the ideology of revolutionary jihadism, see Anonymous (Michael Scheuer), *Through Our Enemies' Eyes: Osama bin Laden, Radical Islam and the Future of America* (Washington, DC: Brassey's, 2002); William McCants, *The ISIS Apocalypse: The History, Strategy and Doomsday Vision of the Islamic State* (New York: St. Martin's, 2015); Daniel Byman, *Al Qaeda, The Islamic State, and the Global Jihadist Movement* (Oxford: Oxford University Press 2015); and Michael Weiss and Hassan, *ISIS: Inside the Army of Terror* (New York: Regan Arts, 2016).

36 The Tamil Tigers were also paradigmatic of the second wave by their reliance on terrorism as a tactic and operational method. It is also true that some first-wave insurgencies had an ethnic component or structure, as in Malaya, Peru, Guatemala, Kenya, Angola, and Zimbabwe.

37 Bruce Hoffman, "The 'Cult of the Insurgent': Its Tactical and Strategic Implications," *Australian Journal of International Affairs* 61, no. 3 (2007): 312–29. The phrase is drawn from J. Bowyer Bell, *The Myth of the Guerrilla: Revolutionary Theory and Malpractice* (New York: Alfred A. Knopf, 1971).

38 Maria Galperin Donnelly with Thomas M. Sanderson and Zack Fellman, "Foreign Fighters in History," (Washington, DC: Center for Strategic and International Studies, n.d.), http://foreignfighters.csis.org/history/case-studies.html.

39 Efraim Benmelech and Esteban F. Klor, "What Explains the Flow of Foreign Fighters to ISIS?" (working paper 22190, National Bureau of Economic Research, Cambridge, MA, April 2016, https://www.nber.org/papers/w22190).

40 Gabriel Weimann, "The Emerging Role of Social Media in the Recruitment of Foreign Fighters," *Foreign Fighters under International Law and Beyond,* ed. Andrea de Guttry, Francesca Capone, and Christophe Paulussen (New York: Springer, 2016). See also Metz, "Internet, New Media."

41 Eric Schmitt, Thomas Gibbons-Neff, Helene Cooper, and Alissa J. Rubin, "Its Territory May Be Gone, but the U.S. Fight against ISIS Is Far from Over," *New York Times,* March 24, 2019, https://www.nytimes.com/2019/03/24/us/politics/us-isis-fight.html.

42 Kathy Gilsinan, "The 'Caliphate' Is Dead but Americans Might Not Be Any Safer," *The Atlantic,* March 23, 2019, https://www.theatlantic.com/politics/archive/2019/03/us-safer-islamic-state-gone/584110/. For detailed analysis, see Colin P. Clarke, *After the Caliphate: The Islamic State and the Future Terrorist Diaspora* (Cambridge: Polity, 2019).

43 US support for the Syrian rebels was a peculiar exception, but it was motivated more by the desire to prevent ISIS and al-Qaeda from dominating the resistance than to weaken the client of an opposing nation as during the Cold War.

44 Ahmed S. Hashim, *Insurgency and Counter-Insurgency in Iraq* (Ithaca, NY: Cornell University Press, 2006); Malcom W. Nance, *The Terrorists of Iraq: Inside the Strategy and Tactics of the Iraq Insurgency* (Charleston, SC: Booksurge, 2007); Joel D. Rayburn and Frank Sobchak, eds., *The U.S. Army in the Iraq War—Volume 1: Invasion-Insurgency-Civil War, 2003–2006* (Carlisle, PA: US Army War College Strategic Studies Institute, 2019), https://ssi.armywarcollege.edu/pubs/display.cfm?pubID=1373); Joel D. Rayburn and Frank Sobchak, eds., *The U.S. Army in the Iraq War—Volume 2: Surge and Withdrawal, 2007–2011* (Carlisle, PA: US Army War College Strategic Studies Institute, 2019), https://ssi.armywarcollege.edu/pubs/display.cfm?pubID=1376.

45 For a description and analysis of how this worked in Iraq, see Stanley McChrystal, *My Share of the Task: A Memoir* (New York: Portfolio, 2013).

46 Carlos Ivan Degregori, "After the Fall of Abimael Guzmán: The Limits of Sendero Luminoso," in *The Peruvian Labyrinth: Polity, Society, Economy,* ed. Maxwell A. Cameron and Philip Maurceri (University Park: Penn State University Press, 1997), and, more generally, Steve J. Stern, ed., *Shining and Other Paths: War and Society in Peru, 1980–1995* (Durham, NC: Duke University Press, 1998).

47 Michael E. Silverman, *Awakening Victory: How Iraqi Tribes and American Troops Reclaimed al Anbar and Defeated al Qaeda in Iraq* (Philadelphia: Casemate, 2011); Austin Long, "The Anbar Awakening," *Survival* 50, no. 2 (2008): 67–94; John A. McCary, "The Anbar Awakening: An Alliance of Incentives," *Washington Quarterly* 32, no. 1 (2009): 43–50.

48 Ioan Grillo, *El Narco: Inside Mexico's Criminal Insurgency* (New York: Bloomsbury, 2012).

49 Robert J. Bunker, *Terrorist and Insurgent Unmanned Aerial Vehicles: Use, Potentials, and Military Implications* (Carlisle, PA: US Army War College Strategic Studies Institute, 2015), https://ssi.armywarcollege.edu/pubs/display.cfm?pubID=1287.

50 Yonah Jeremy Bob, "Ex-CIA Director Petraeus: Everything Can Be Hijacked, Weaponized," *Jerusalem Post,* January 30, 2018, https://www.jpost.com/israel-news/ex-cia-director-petraeus-everything-can-be-hijacked-weaponized-540235.

51 Benjamin Wittes and Gabriella Blum, *The Future of Violence: Robots and Germs, Hacker and Drones* (New York: Basic Books, 2015).

52 See David Kenner, "All ISIS Has Left Is Money. Lots of It," *The Atlantic,* March 24, 2019, https://www.theatlantic.com/international/archive/2019/03/isis-caliphate-money-territory/584911/.

53 See Robert J. Bunker and John P. Sullivan, "Extreme Barbarism, a Death Cult, and Holy Warriors in Mexico: Societal Warfare South of the Border?," *Small Wars Journal,* May 22, 2011, https://smallwarsjournal.com/blog/journal/docs-temp/769-bunkersullivan.pdf; Kate Kingsburg, "The Knights Templar Narcotheology: Deciphering the Occult of a Narcocult," *Small Wars Journal,* October 26, 2018, https://smallwarsjournal.com/jrnl/art/knights-templar-narcotheology-deciphering-occult-narcocult.

CHAPTER 7

The Ability to Adapt

NATO's Statecraft and Europe's Transformation, 1966–94

STEPHAN KIENINGER

Although it is the world's premier security alliance, the North Atlantic Treaty Organization (NATO) today faces a multitude of challenges. While NATO has seen plenty of upheaval during the seven previous decades, the alliance has always been able to adapt to changing circumstances, proving capable of finding sustainable responses to international challenges. This article provides a historian's look into NATO's adaption processes and its role in Europe's transformation during the three decades between the Harmel Report of 1967 and NATO's post–Cold War enlargement process in the 1990s. It emphasizes that the current crisis around arms control and the discussions over a decline of shared transatlantic interests had plenty of historic predecessors. NATO's reaction to these challenges was not merely short-term and problem-fixing responses. Rather, a look at NATO's history underlines that crisis and changing circumstances resulted in forward-looking and proactive NATO policies.

France's withdrawal from NATO's integrated military in 1966 had the potential to unravel NATO, but the Lyndon B. Johnson administration's careful diplomacy facilitated the reconstitution of NATO as an even more cohesive alliance, now dedicated to both deterrence and détente. The Harmel Report of 1967 was the inception of NATO's dynamic détente policy, showing that NATO's purpose was not just collective defense. NATO's second task was indeed détente—with the long-term aim of overcoming Europe's division. NATO's rationale was to perforate the Iron Curtain in an effort to soften up communism from within through the expansion of societal communication and the freer movement of people, information, and ideas, principles that were enshrined in the Helsinki Final Act of 1975. However, détente did not stop the arms race. A strong NATO defense posture remained essential. In the second half of the 1970s, the Soviet Union's buildup in SS-20 missiles led to the emergence of NATO's dual-track decision of December 1979: NATO leaders agreed to deploy new US intermediate-range weapons—cruise and Pershing II missiles—in response to the SS-20s. At the same time, NATO maintained its readiness to continue arms control negotiations with the USSR—in other words, balancing deterrence with détente in these two parallel and complementary approaches. Crafting and implementing the dual-track decision, both military and diplomatic, tested NATO's cohesion to the limit. Eventually, this mixture of solidarity and flexibility proved to be an essential combination and the solution that ultimately led to the conclusion of the Intermediate-Range Nuclear Forces (INF) Treaty in 1987, resulting in the withdrawal of all intermediate-range missiles from Europe.

NATO had a persistent purpose after the end of the Cold War. The Alliance played a pivotal role in the formation of Europe's post–Cold War security architecture. The end of the Cold War and Germany's unification did not resolve Europe's security issues. The demise of the Soviet Union and the dissolution of its empire seemed to result in the "end of history" and the ascendancy of Western liberal democracy.[1] However, the ensuing war in Yugoslavia signaled the dangers of fragmentation, ethnic violence, and a potential return to authoritarianism, and there was no script or master plan for how to replace the Cold War with a more cooperative world order. The United States was indispensable as a power broker and alliance manager at a time when the Soviet Union as the external enemy had disappeared. NATO enlargement was the most feasible way in the search for a post–Cold War order. The aim was to extend the Western space of stability eastward. NATO pursued a policy of two tracks: the aim was to open up NATO but slowly, cautiously, and combined with an expanded effort to engage Russia.

NATO's gradual approach was the means to secure Central and Eastern Europe and to support Mikhail Gorbachev's and Boris Yeltsin's reforms. By working gradually, NATO hoped to buy time and to work out a cooperative relationship with Russia.

THE HARMEL REPORT AND THE EMERGENCE OF NATO'S DYNAMIC DÉTENTE POLICY

In his compelling book *How NATO Adapts: Strategy and Organization in the Atlantic Alliance since 1950,* Seth A. Johnston suggests that NATO is unique among peer international organizations in its ability to adapt: "Unlike other enduring post–World War II institutions that continue to reflect the international politics of their founding era, NATO stands out both for the boldness of its transformations as well as their frequency over a period of nearly 70 years."[2] For its first forty years, NATO focused mainly on collective defense. But NATO's overriding strategic preoccupation did not prevent important changes from taking place within the alliance. In 1956, NATO produced *The Report of the Committee of Three on Non-Military Cooperation in NATO.* Following the 1956 Suez Crisis, NATO's North Atlantic Council sensed the need for improved nonmilitary consultation among the allies. By enhancing the nonmilitary cooperation of alliance members, the report helped to create a more balanced, inclusive, responsive, and adaptive alliance.[3]

The 1967 Harmel Report continued NATO's adaptation by encouraging the alliance to take a more cooperative approach to security issues. In considering the tasks of the alliance for the next twenty years, the report advocated a dual-track approach with a focus on defense and deterrence on the one hand and coupled détente and arms control on the other.[4] It restated NATO's basic purpose and principles but added the concept of dialogue and the relaxation of tensions between East and West. This shift had a profound and lasting impact on the alliance's strategic approach to cooperative security. Taken together, both seminal reports helped NATO adapt to the changing security environment during those periods and thereafter. Both reports contributed to NATO's institutional capacity for organizational adaptability, which has served the alliance well by broadening and deepening the alliance's political cooperation.[5]

In March 1966, Charles de Gaulle's decision to withdraw France from NATO's integrated military command sent shock waves through NATO's member states. It was a reminder of the fissures within NATO and a challenge to its very existence. Could NATO survive without a key member state's participation in the very military agreements it was founded on? Yet the alliance lived on. The withdrawal forced all member states to remove their bases from France, and NATO itself moved its headquarters from Paris to Brussels. The Johnson administration used NATO's crisis as an opportunity to reform the alliance without France. The initial US reaction to de Gaulle's challenge was firm but quiet. Historian Andreas Wenger reiterated that "Johnson was willing to abandon the hegemonic leadership style of the 1950s and to avoid a public stance against the French action. The United States would instead outwait de Gaulle, exercise its leadership within NATO as primus inter pares, and opt for greater political consultation with its allies."[6] France's withdrawal from NATO's military structures further enhanced West Germany's role, a result that caused concern among many allies. Thus, NATO had to accommodate the interests of the smaller countries to a greater degree than in the 1950s.

By December 1966, the United States and its European partners had successfully adapted NATO's military structures in response to France's pullout by reorganizing them. But de Gaulle's policy challenged NATO in yet another respect. De Gaulle's claim was that NATO had lost not only its credibility as an integrated military structure but also its legitimacy as a political forum for the coordination of its members' détente policies.[7] The Johnson administration found another proactive response to de Gaulle's challenge: In October 1966, Johnson gave a landmark address before the National Conference of Editorial Writers in New York in which he outlined his détente approach, using the term "peaceful engagement" as a new label for his policy toward the Soviet Union and Eastern Europe. Johnson emphasized his willingness to search for an attainable peace and the emergence of a new, less confrontational Euro-Atlantic security order despite the escalation of the Vietnam War and US-Soviet conflicts in other parts of the globe.[8] Envisaging Europe as the starting point in this endeavor, Johnson set out in his speech a bold concept for the transformation of Europe and the establishment of new Euro-Atlantic security structures over time. Instead of drawing up specific plans for a settlement of the German question, Johnson emphasized that it was imperative to improve the East-West environment first. The nonproliferation of nuclear weapons, balanced force reductions in Europe, and a halt of the strategic arms race were conceived as essential pieces in the puzzle to build a new Europe. Peaceful engagement constituted only one part in a larger scheme for Europe's transformation. "Making Europe whole" also necessitated a broader purpose for the alliance and support for movement toward Western Europe's integration.[9]

The rationale of Johnson's speech was also to multilateralize détente. Johnson wanted his allies to pursue their own bridge-building policies across the Iron Curtain in an effort to soften up communism from within through "bridges of increased trade, of ideas, of visitors, and of humanitarian aid."[10] Johnson believed that compared to the United States, the West European allies had more leverage to overcome the Iron Curtain due to their proximity and long-established cultural ties with Eastern Europe. Johnson and Secretary of State Dean Rusk thought that their allies had become mature enough to pursue initiatives on their own. They encouraged the West Germans to formulate a more proactive policy for dealing with the Eastern bloc. In December 1966, Johnson's peaceful engagement gained additional momentum through the establishment of a grand coalition government in Bonn. From the outset, Chancellor Kurt Georg Kiesinger and Foreign Minister Willy Brandt turned on their head the premises that had guided the policy of their predecessors. The Konrad Adenauer and Ludwig Erhard administrations had taken the position that progress toward Germany's unification was a precondition for détente, but Kiesinger and Brandt held that it was vice versa. This was a quantum leap that enabled the Americans and the Germans to think aloud and to draw up bold schemes to pursue dynamic détente diplomacies. Reviewing NATO's ministerial meeting in December 1966, Rusk reiterated:

> Brandt made a major impression on NATO in demonstrating that the new German government will not be bound by the rigid theology of the Adenauer period and is prepared to probe the possibilities of better relations with Eastern Europe, including the East Germans. This may not move us forward, but twenty years of confrontation has not done so and I believe that we should give them a chance to find out whether another approach might produce more results.[11]

At the same time, Rusk emphasized the necessity of NATO's deterrence policy: "Let us not misunderstand the basis for the prudence which has entered into the relations between East and West here in this part of the world. You're not going to get détente by giving away little countries to somebody who's got a big appetite."[12]

The rationale was that the allies should more confidently play a leading role in resolving urgent questions of European security—which they did. The Harmel Report led to initiatives on several fronts. It provided NATO the institutional mandate for an East-West détente and for negotiations with the Warsaw Pact countries over new means of cooperation across the East-West divide, ranging from renunciation of force and the inviolability of frontiers in Europe to economic cooperation, the freer movement of people, human rights, and military confidence measures. Within a number of years, these talks led to the Conference on European Security and Co-operation (CSCE) and to the Helsinki Final Act. The Western preparatory work evolved in NATO, and the coordination of Western CSCE policies equally so.[13] The Harmel Report Europeanized Europe's security issues, and this process brought a plus in security for the United States. In 1967, Dean Rusk argued that "Europe is not an innocent bystander. Europe is the issue. The Soviet Union and the United States are not going to fight each other about polar bears in the Arctic. If Europe were safe, we and the Soviet Union would have very little to fight about."[14]

NATO's work on the blueprint for its dynamic détente emerged in meetings of the Atlantic Policy Advisory Group (APAG), established in 1961 by the North Atlantic Council as a means to "provide the North Atlantic Council with studies on long-term policy problems."[15] The concept was that these informal meetings of high-ranking officials of the foreign affairs ministries would provide for wide-ranging discussions on the international situation. Starting in 1967, the American, British, and German policy planning staff held additional, trilateral mini-APAG meetings on their own to discuss the sensitive issue of the Federal Republic's new détente initiatives. In January 1967, West Germany's policy planning director, Günter Diehl, gave his curious colleagues a succinct outline of Bonn's new approach. He argued that the new Kiesinger-Brandt government was about to pursue "a dynamic rather than a defensive policy [that] was well described by the phrase 'peaceful engagement.'" Diehl explained that "things were moving under the surface and . . . the West Germans felt that they should respond to the desire in Eastern Europe for more contacts with the West."[16] The *Ostpolitik* concept was that the goal of German reunification would not be abandoned, but it could be pursued gradually after new political and security arrangements between East and West. In 1970, NATO faced the challenge to implement the concepts for the transformation of Europe that had been thought up during the previous years. From the vantage point of an eyewitness, James Goodby reminisced that, initially, "there was no substance behind this noble thought and little in the way of strategic purpose for American ideas about undercutting the status quo in Europe and French ideas about ending the Europe of blocs."[17]

It took the alliance time to elaborate on common positions for the ensuing CSCE. There was unanimity among Western delegates that the Soviets must not be allowed to have a perfunctory conference for the sake of cementing the status quo. The Soviet Union's desire to convoke the CSCE gave NATO leverage to turn the entire project to Western advantage and to work for liberalizing societal changes in the Warsaw Pact countries: NATO's rationale was to expose the people under communist rule to Western values and Western liberties and to give them a chance to compare and the opportunity to doubt. The US Mission to NATO was instructed to emphasize that "freer movement between East and West of people, ideas and information would tend to increase pressure for liberalization upon Warsaw Pact regimes and thereby dilute ideological rigidities of present policies."[18] It was argued that "nothing would do more to undermine Communist propaganda about life in the West."[19] In 1973, West German foreign minister Walter Scheel emphasized that "with our détente policy, we have opened up the way to direct encounter and competition between the societies of East and West. We have wanted this because we believe in the power of conviction of our ideals and because we trust in the inner strength of our system, which is based on democratic liberties, human rights and social justice."[20] The détente process underlined the importance of NATO's political machinery. It facilitated the growing European impact and the increasing relevance of allied consultation on all security matters in the US-Soviet relationship. The CSCE process forced the reluctant Richard Nixon and Gerald Ford administrations to endorse the dynamic Western agenda with more vigor. Secretary of State Henry Kissinger had long been unwilling to confront the Soviet leadership with ambitious Western positions on human rights and the freer movement of people, information, and ideas.[21] NATO's ministerial meetings gave the West European allies a chance to challenge Kissinger on his static view of détente and on his skepticism toward the CSCE process. In 1973, turning to

Kissinger, Dutch foreign minister Max van der Stoel reiterated that "what is at stake here is the quality of the détente as it will, I hope, develop in Europe during the years to come. If we are not prepared now to take a stand together for freedom and openness as the principles on which we wish to base future of international relations in Europe, I am afraid that it will be even more difficult for us to do so later on."[22]

The provisions of the Helsinki Final Act institutionalized the dynamic détente concept. The freer movement provisions of Basket III on the freer movement of people, information, and ideas as well as the incorporation of human rights in the declaration of principles turned out to be the ferment for a transnational network of dissidents, human rights activists, and peace movements that challenged communism in Eastern Europe and the Soviet Union until its demise.[23] NATO's détente diplomacy had been intending the dynamic Helsinki effects.[24] At the same time, it was important for NATO to avoid euphoria over détente. In 1974, West Germany's foreign minister, Hans-Dietrich Genscher, stressed that "we can't let NATO be undermined—it is the alpha and omega of our . . . security. I believe it is necessary that we look at detente in the proper light. There is no alternative to supporting it, but there is a danger of playing down the threat which exists. I speak frequently of 'realistic' detente because the Communist threat must always be kept in mind."[25]

THE EUROMISSILE CRISIS: NATO'S ADAPTABILITY AND ITS DUAL-TRACK POLICY DURING NEW INTERNATIONAL TENSIONS

In the second half of the 1970s, NATO was again adjusting and widening the scope of its political discussions. Actually, West European leaders made the case that the United States should deploy modern intermediate-range nuclear forces to Europe—missiles with sufficient range to strike Soviet territory. The deployment of Soviet SS-20 missiles highlighted the need for a modernization of NATO's deterrent. NATO addressed the growing nuclear imbalance in Europe with its dual-track decision in December 1979, offering the Warsaw Pact countries a mutual limitation of medium-range and intermediate-range ballistic missiles combined with the threat that in the event of disagreement NATO would deploy additional weapons in Western Europe.[26] NATO's dual-track policy was riddled with serious debates over NATO's credibility and its purpose. Again, NATO proved its ability to adapt. It set up two high-level expert groups—the High Level Group (HLG), which focused on the deployment question, and later the Special Group (SG), which concentrated on the arms control package—to deliberate future alliance defense and deterrence needs. The HLG and SG consisted of senior officials from national defense and foreign ministries and were chaired by a senior US official, not a NATO International Staff member. Also, for the first time, NATO as a whole took a nuclear procurement decision. Kristina Spohr points out that "both firsts were steps toward NATO's internal democratization and a reflection of the weight that was being placed on inter-allied solidarity in nuclear decision-making."[27] In 1977, West Germany's Chancellor Helmut Schmidt was the first to criticize the issue of the imbalance of what became called "Euromissiles." Schmidt wanted an unenthusiastic Jimmy Carter administration to respond firmly to Soviet nuclear policies, as the US-Soviet arms control accords did not cover nuclear weapons deployed in Europe. Schmidt's fear was that the gap in deterrence could lead to a decoupling of Europe's security.[28] He feared a "regionalization and categorical limitation of a potential conflict" to the European battlefield, leaving the territories of the superpowers unaffected.[29]

In 1978, Schmidt eventually managed to push the United States toward a compromise solution, which consisted of three steps: (1) the United States would go ahead and announce the beginning of production of its neutron bomb—a highly effective, reduced-blast, enhanced radiation weapon (ERW)—as part of a long-term modernization program for US theater nuclear forces (TNF), (2) NATO as a whole would soon after declare its willingness to negotiate for two years with the USSR over SS-20 reductions in return for not deploying ERWs, and (3) if these negotiations failed, the alliance would meet to decide on ERW deployment, with West Germany willing to act as an ERW host nation if at least one other NATO ally could be found to share the deployment burden.[30] By 1978, after Carter's unilateral deferral of production of the neutron bomb, NATO finally put cruise missiles and Pershing II missiles against the Soviet SS-20.[31] However, it was imperative for Schmidt that West German forces not be able to use them. In October 1978, he told Carter's national security adviser, Zbigniew Brzezinski, that "they could only be in U.S. hands. The Soviets should not feel that the Germans are deploying weapons which could destroy Moscow." Moreover, Schmidt insisted that deployment not be limited to the Federal

Republic. Such a singularization of West Germany would highlight its "political vulnerability."[32]

Carter doubted Schmidt's commitment. If West Germany was not prepared to accept outright the necessary deployment of ground-launched cruise missiles and Pershing IIs, Carter said, it was difficult to see why others should do so on Bonn's behalf. Carter gave priority instead to the modernization of NATO's nuclear deterrent. He considered the arms control aspect of the dual-track approach primarily as a means to garner support for deployments.[33] Carter wanted a minimum number of missiles to be deployed. From a German vantage point, though, the simultaneity in the proposed package was crucial. At NATO's summit in The Hague in 1979, a consensus seemed to emerge that the alliance had to carry out its TNF modernization in parallel to arms control talks.[34] At NATO's ministerial meeting in December 1979, US secretary of state Cyrus Vance emphasized his conviction that "the Alliance is on the right track." Vance said that "our long-term defence program, our commitment to three per cent real increases in annual defence spending, and our decision to modernize theatre nuclear weapons promise to take us into the Eighties with a sense of real security. . . . The strength of our Alliance remains the essential underpinning of our efforts to strengthen the framework for productive relations with the East. It is clear to all that we will pursue security in Europe through negotiations and through military preparedness."[35]

Schmidt believed that the Soviet Union would unlikely make all the concessions necessary to obviate NATO's TNF modernization. At the same time, his government could not go public with this presumption owing to domestic sensitivities. Schmidt's preference was a zero outcome of the dual-track process—in other words, the total removal of Soviet intermediate-range ballistic missiles and no deployment of American TNFs. Eventually, the Reagan administration adopted Schmidt's zero-zero approach in November 1981.[36] Reagan and Schmidt had differing conceptions over NATO's arms control strategy and the right mix between deterrence and dialogue with the Soviet Union. In May 1981, Reagan told Schmidt that "for us to be successful in arms control the Russians have to see that the alternative is a buildup to match theirs." Schmidt agreed but highlighted the importance of US-Soviet negotiations, arguing that "talk of such discussions is necessary for Europeans who require reassurance."[37] The most important factor for Schmidt was to have a timetable for the start of INF negotiations. In 1981, his concern was that the Soviet Union was about to win the propaganda war in Europe: "The Russians talk peace, we are talking rockets."[38] Schmidt was troubled by the growing popular suspicion in the Federal Republic that the Reagan administration was not seriously interested in arms control negotiations.[39]

In 1981, the prospects for successful INF negotiations were dim. The State Department was alarmed by the impact of the Soviet peace offensive. So far, the Reagan administration lacked a public peace strategy, owing to bureaucratic turf battles in Washington. It was only in November 1981 that Reagan finally gave a televised speech and appealed to European audiences in a dramatic address along the lines of President John F. Kennedy's 1963 appearance in Berlin. Reagan's plea for the nuclear zero option entailed a simple message: "The United States is prepared to cancel its deployment of Pershing II and ground-launched Cruise Missiles if the Soviets will dismantle their SS-20, SS-4, and SS-5 missiles." "If the Soviets agreed," he continued, "we could together substantially reduce the threat of nuclear war which hangs over the people of Europe."[40] Reagan's address on the zero option was the kind of bold plan to capture public opinion. The rationale was easy. Secretary of Defense Caspar Weinberger emphasized that "if [the zero option was] refused by the Soviets, they would take the blame for its rejection. If the Soviets agreed, we would achieve the balance that we've lost. . . . If we adopt the 'zero option' approach and the Soviets reject it after we have given it a good try, this will leave the Europeans in a position where they would really have no alternative to modernization."[41] Schmidt had already championed the zero option back in 1979. He saw it as the ideal outcome because it would remove all the Euromissiles rather than simply control their growth in balanced ways.

Deployment and negotiations were intertwined. NATO would not get one without the other. If the West did not deploy Pershing II and cruise missiles, there would be no incentive for the Soviet Union to negotiate seriously for nuclear weapons reductions. Reagan's premise was that the path to sustainable arms control would begin with an arms buildup.[42] In November 1983, the German parliament gave final authorization to install American Pershing II missiles. The challenge was the lack of leadership communication in US-Soviet relations and the absence of real high-level dialogue and understanding. Thus, it was acknowledged that the Soviet Union could misread, misinterpret, and miscalculate NATO's true intentions. There was an urgent need to restore a climate of increased confidence. The Soviets had stormed out of the INF negotiations, but President Reagan turned to Soviet secretary-general Yuri Andropov, requesting him to return his delegation.[43] NATO reiterated its willingness for serious negotiations time and again.[44] Canada's prime minister, Pierre Elliott Trudeau, emphasized that "people want their leaders to carry a big stick but to talk softly in their dealings with the Russians. They want to hear something about mutual trust, and the ability to live in peace with the Soviet Union, provided that she did not use force. . . . People would not buy unilateral disarmament. But they did want their leaders to 'bust their asses' to reach agreement with the Soviet Union."[45] Eventually, NATO's dual-track approach facilitated the conclusion of the INF Treaty in 1987. It became one of the most successful arms control treaties of all time as it both eliminated an entire category of nuclear weapons and reduced the likelihood of a surprise nuclear strike.

At the same time, the INF Treaty triggered an intra-alliance debate over NATO's short-range nuclear forces (SNF), which had a range under five hundred kilometers and were not included in the INF Treaty. The SNF debate signaled both the limits of multilateral cooperation in NATO and the ability to resolve the contested issue in a different international setting after the fall of the Berlin Wall. Initially, NATO's plan had been to modernize its SNF, which consisted of Lance missiles: they were needed for deterrence as long as the Warsaw Pact maintained a massive advantage in conventional forces in Europe. After the INF Treaty, NATO sought an analysis of what it needed for its security. German policymakers were concerned about the prospect that the only weapons left in Europe might be stationed in and targeted at East and West Germany.[46] "The shorter the missile, the deader the German" quickly became an aphorism in Germany.[47] German policymakers rejected SNF modernization and instead wanted the George H. W. Bush administration to respond to Gorbachev's arms control proposals.[48] The Helmut Kohl government was suspected to have neutral tendencies. Kohl had serious clashes with British prime minister Margaret Thatcher, who argued that "NATO could not be a shell. It had to modernize its weapons, otherwise the US would sooner or later withdraw its troops from Germany."[49] In August 1989, Bush's national security adviser, Brent Scowcroft, noted that "Germany's repudiation of the Alliance position on SNF was unprecedented. It threatens the very basis of extended nuclear deterrence—on which the security of NATO and Europe rests—and may also signal stronger pressure from the FRG toward the denuclearization of Europe."[50]

Finally, NATO's May 1989 summit brought a compromise: it delayed modernization and maintained the option for deployment. NATO showed resolve and found a way to be open to Gorbachev's arms control agenda. Scowcroft thought that "the SNF negotiations would, in the current political climate, create almost irresistible pressures for a 'third zero,' eliminating missile systems from 0–500 km range. This would in turn hasten the denuclearization of Europe. We prefer to await further progress in conventional arms control and rely on unilateral restructuring of SNF forces."[51] Eventually, the solution for NATO's SNF problem was not in the nuclear field but in the area of conventional arms control. NATO's aim was to eliminate the asymmetries in conventional forces as a way to put off the need to modernize its Lance SNF. President Bush used NATO's May 1989 summit for proposal to cut US and Soviet troops by 20 percent. This would require NATO to withdraw about thirty thousand troops. The decisive aspect was that it would require the Soviet Union to withdraw roughly 325,000 troops from Eastern Europe. In 1990, there was no longer a need for SNF modernization after the conclusion of the Treaty on Conventional Forces in Europe (CFE) between NATO and the Warsaw Pact. Both sides agreed to abandon their capacities for surprise attacks and large-scale military offensives in Europe.

NATO'S NEW DUAL-TRACK POLICY: ENLARGING NATO AND ENGAGING RUSSIA

In the first half of the 1990s, when NATO was preparing to extend its membership eastward, Russian officials began to claim that the entry of former Warsaw Pact countries would violate a solemn "pledge" not to include any former communist countries in the alliance.[52] The declassification of documents from all sides bear out that neither the United States nor any other Western country had pledged not to expand NATO beyond Germany.[53] There was clearly no promise to freeze NATO's borders;[54] Western policymakers did not mislead Gorbachev.[55] NATO and the West did not take advantage of Russia's weakness in the post–Cold War years. Michael Mandelbaum makes an ungrounded claim arguing that NATO's open-door policy damaged beyond repair US efforts to transform Russia from enemy to partner.[56] Rather, NATO undertook comprehensive efforts to create a cooperative environment in its post–Cold war relations with Russia. In parallel to enlargement, NATO was building a strategic framework to bring Russia into the family of nations through the 1990s. The aim was to open up NATO but slowly, cautiously, and combined with an expanded effort to engage Russia. NATO's objective was to frame the strategic relationship with Russia on a win/win premise as opposed to a win/lose framework, allowing both sides to manage their disagreements. NATO's gradual approach was the means to secure Central and Eastern Europe and to support Gorbachev's and Yeltsin's reforms.[57] Second, by working gradually, NATO hoped to buy time to work out a cooperative relationship with Russia. The emergence of the North Atlantic Cooperation Council (NACC) in November 1991 and the Partnership for Peace (PfP) in January 1994 reflected NATO's gradual approach.[58]

Both initiatives were designed to give the Central and Eastern European (CEE) countries a perspective for closer association and eventual NATO membership.[59] At the same time, both endeavors were intended to include Russia in the future European security system. After the fall of Berlin Wall, NATO's enlargement was not yet on the agenda. The NATO membership of unified Germany was the issue of the day—and it was imperative for NATO to adapt itself and to change its doctrine. The process of NATO's transformation was initiated at the North Atlantic Council summit in London in June 1990. "We must build a transformed alliance for the new Europe of the 21st century," President Bush said then. In the same vein, Prime Minister Thatcher emphasized that NATO's "signal from this meeting must continue to be one of resolve in defence, resolve and unity in defence coupled with willingness to extend the hand of friendship to Eastern Europe and the Soviet Union."[60] Indeed, at the London summit, NATO extended a "hand of friendship" to the Warsaw Pact countries, inviting them to form a new relationship and to establish regular diplomatic liaison with NATO in an effort to think aloud with each other during a historic period of change. This involved meetings between the ambassadors of the CEE countries in Brussels and NATO secretary-general Manfred Wörner and his staff for Eastern Europe and the Soviet Union.[61]

Initially, the CEE countries sought only closer ties with NATO, not membership. However, against the backdrop of the ensuing war in Yugoslavia and the coup against Gorbachev in August 1991, the political leaders of the CEE countries were afraid of a security vacuum developing in their region. Starting in 1990, Czechoslovakian president Václav Havel, Polish president Lech Wałęsa, and Hungarian prime minister József Antall articulated their desire to develop the closest possible relations with NATO. Equal security was also a precondition for them in their endeavor to join the European Community. But from their vantage point, only NATO was able to provide the kind of hard security they were seeking. The August 1991 coup in the Soviet Union highlighted the urgency to build a foundation for a new peace order in Europe based on cooperative security while Gorbachev was still in power. It underlined the need to construct a new security system in an effort to provide the CEE countries a prospect for closer ties with the West going beyond NATO's hand of friendship. President Bush seized two initiatives to address both challenges. First, following the aborted coup in Moscow, he proposed a unilateral move on nuclear weapons. Bush was eager to make progress while he still had Gorbachev as a partner.[62] His proposals entailed the idea of getting rid of all tactical nuclear weapons (except air-launched ones). Other parts of the Bush initiatives took bombers and missiles off alert and canceled some nuclear modernization programs. The purpose of the Bush initiative was to signal to the leaders and the people of the Soviet Union that NATO's policy would enhance their security and build stability.[63]

Bush's second initiative was aimed at the transformation of Europe's security architecture. In October 1991, Secretary of State James Baker and Foreign Minister Genscher issued a joint declaration highlighting their ambition to create a "Euro-Atlantic Community that extends East from Vancouver to Vladivostok." The Baker-Genscher declaration signaled the establishment of the NACC, whose aim was to institutionalize NATO's partnership programs with the former Warsaw Pact countries and the Soviet Union.[64] The NACC was explicitly not about increasing NATO's membership and thereby extending NATO's security guarantee eastward. NATO's enlargement was still not on the public agenda, although the Bush administration discussed its rationale and modalities behind closed doors in Washington.[65] In November 1991, Bush's National Security Council (NSC) team argued that "while we cannot state so publicly, our main aim remains drawing the main Central European countries . . . closer to NATO."[66] NATO did not make a decision for the fast track to enlargement. Congress and public opinion in the United States would not have endorsed new commitments after the dissolution of the Soviet Union and the end of the

Gulf War. Moreover, a fast move on NATO enlargement might "redivide" Europe. As David Gompert of the Bush NSC staff wrote in January 1992, there would be "difficulty in drawing the line as to whom is in and out, and ramifications of isolating Russia, Ukraine and the Islamic states of the CIS."[67]

There were three scenarios for the future: First, the NACC could remain merely a liaison program—with an uncertain future. Second, the NACC could over time turn into a forum for political consultations and crisis management. The question here was whether or not the United States would be willing to resolve conflicts outside of NATO territory. Third, as Gompert wrote in January 1992, the NACC could be "a waystation to NATO membership." Thus, as Gompert pointed out, "the Poles, Hungarians, Czechs and others would know there would be an end-point (but not a clearly defined one) and therefore would not grow impatient with the NACC or with its unwieldy number of participants."[68] By the end of March 1992, Bush's NSC advisers were arguing that the United States should "signal" to the Eastern Europeans that they "may become eligible" for NATO membership.[69] By June 1992, there was a growing consensus within the Bush administration toward "opening up the Alliance to new members," although the details had yet to be "worked out."[70] But the year 1992 was not the right time for a public discussion on NATO enlargement. The Soviet Union had just collapsed, and the Bush administration was not sure whether the Soviet nuclear weapons could be brought under control and whether the USSR's dissolution was going to be peaceful at all or would be like Yugoslavia's. It was not viewed as a good time at all to provoke the Soviet Union—not because the West accepted that the Soviet Union had any power of veto over this, but rather because provoking the Soviets during this extremely delicate phase would have been risky. In February 1992, Russia's domestic situation and its economic reform were clearly the most pressing item on the agenda of President Bush's first summit meeting with Yeltsin.[71] The debate on NATO's opening was postponed until 1993, when President Bill Clinton continued the search for a post–Cold War order.

However, NATO enlargement was not yet on Clinton's agenda. The focus of his diplomacy was on Russia and contacts with Boris Yeltsin. It was argued that "the ever-expanding partnership between the U.S. and Russia [should] not be endangered by hasty decisions about NATO expansion to the East. . . . Now is not the time to move forward on alliance membership for any of the former Warsaw Pact states (including Russia)."[72] The Clinton administration was divided over NATO enlargement. The Department of Defense wanted to kick the can of NATO enlargement down the road. In contrast, Undersecretary of State Lynn Davis and Steve Flanagan of the State Department's Policy Planning Staff were in favor of NATO's enlargement, seeing an urgent need for a fundamental transformation of NATO and a new vision for America's role in post–Cold War Europe. Davis and Flanagan envisioned NATO's January 1994 summit as an ideal opportunity to articulate a bold US strategy: "The fundamental task for the President is to develop a rationale for why Americans still need to play a major role in Europe's evolution, beyond support for reform in Russia. The answer is that American leadership will be required both to build democracy and to prevent the dangers of revived nationalism."[73] German defense minister Volker Rühe came out as the first Western policymaker to argue in favor of NATO's enlargement. On March 26, 1993, he gave a landmark speech at the International Institute for Strategic Studies in London. Rühe emphasized that "the Atlantic Alliance must not become a 'closed shop.' I cannot see one good reason for denying future members of the European Union membership in NATO."[74] Secretary of Defense Les Aspin and Chairman of the Joint Chiefs of Staff John Shalikashvili were opposed. Their primary concern was that a positive offer had also be made to the Russians in order to mitigate Yeltsin's problems. The Clinton administration was divided: in October 1993, Assistant Secretary of State for Political-Military Affairs Thomas Gallucci noted that "the primary difference [was] over whether NATO would commit at the January NATO summit to expansion, or simply hold out the vague possibility."[75] The concept for the PfP packed both ideas into a single concept envisioning the search for Europe's post–Cold War order to be a longish process. The PfP squared a number of circles. It avoided the creation of new front lines across Europe and would be open to the neutral and nonaligned nations as well as the CEE nations, including Russia and Ukraine. The PfP could be portrayed as a stepping-stone to full NATO membership at some later date, and it put enlargement at the end, rather than the beginning, of a long-term process. The PfP had many virtues and combined "three seemingly objectives," as the US ambassador to the United Nations, Madeleine Albright, noted, "to revitalize NATO, to avoid antagonizing Russia by feeding nationalist tendencies, and to calm growing fears in Central and Eastern Europe."[76]

On January 11, 1994, NATO formally launched the PfP at its Brussels summit. Policymakers in the CEE countries had considerable reservations. After the summit, Clinton traveled to Prague to defend the PfP in meetings with Havel and Wałęsa, where he declared that it was no longer a question of whether NATO would enlarge but how and when and tried to assuage them that the PfP did not shelve the idea of NATO enlargement. What was uncertain, however, was whom exactly NATO would deem ready to join. Clinton argued that "what he especially likes about the PfP . . . is that it lets us begin right now joint training and exercising and the introduction of NATO troops into CEE and establish a dual-track that will lead to NATO membership. On the other hand, it does not draw another line dividing Europe a few hundred miles East."[77] The PfP had yet another advantage: it combined a parallelism between containment and engagement in NATO's approach toward Russia. In January 1994, Secretary of State Warren Christopher and Clinton's Russia adviser, Strobe Talbott, argued that "one of the best things about PfP was that it could go in either direction: it could lean forward to accept Russia if the 'good bear' emerges, but could also lead to a post–Cold War variant of containment to confront a post–Cold War variant of Russian expansionism."[78] Thus, NATO enlargement was a hedge and an insurance policy against the return of a more aggressive Russian foreign policy and the further rise of nationalism in the country.

Yeltsin did not want NATO to treat Russia as just one among the many PfP countries. He wanted a special NATO-Russia partnership going beyond assurances that Russia was eligible to join the alliance someday. Yeltsin saw Russia as a major international player. He depreciated the PfP and instead focused on bilateral US-Russia diplomacy. "There should be "a kind of a cartel of the U.S., Russia and the Europeans to help to ensure and improve world security," Yeltsin emphasized. "Russia has to be the first country to join NATO. Then the others from Central and Eastern Europe can come in," he said. Finally, "in truth," Yeltsin added," Russia is not yet ready to join NATO."[79] In fact, Yeltsin's position amounted to the desire to have veto power over NATO enlargement. The PfP hurt his feelings. In May 1994, he told Kohl that he insisted on "a statement or 'protocol' that makes clear that Russia is different from all other countries joining PfP—'a great country with a great army with nuclear weapons.'"[80]

Russia's European strategy was based on the expectation that sovereign nation-states would determine Europe's future. Time and again, Yeltsin stressed bilateral relations with big European member states. There was a permanent Russian reluctance to deal with NATO and the European Union as institutions. Russian policymakers did not sufficiently understand the inner workings of the European Union as a postmodern empire with supranational institutions. Russia rejected a postmodern European order and the emergence of a highly developed system of mutual interference in each other's domestic affairs and security based on openness and transparency. Nor did Yeltsin grasp the essence of NATO's effective rules-based multilateralism taking into account the interests of its smaller members. In the post–Cold War period, Russian policymakers, including Yeltsin, had a flawed understanding of how Europe's security structures would look like in the twenty-first century. "In part," as Clinton told Kohl in December 1994, "Yeltsin has a real concern. The Russians don't understand how everything will look 10–15 years from now."[81]

NOTES

1 Francis Fukuyama, *The End of History and the Last Man* (New York: Free Press, 1992).

2 Seth A. Johnston, *How NATO Adapts: Strategy and Organization in the Atlantic Alliance since 1950* (Baltimore: Johns Hopkins University Press, 2017), 184.

3 For the text of the report, see https://www.nato.int/cps/en/natohq/topics_65237.htm. For the context, see Gustav Schmidt, ed., *A History of NATO: The First Fifty Years,* vol. 1 (New York: Palgrave Macmillan, 2001).

4 See Timothy Andrews Sayle, *Enduring Alliance: A History of NATO and the Postwar Global Order* (Ithaca, NY: Cornell University Press, 2019).

5 For the context, see Helga Haftendorn, *NATO and the Nuclear Revolution: A Crisis of Credibility, 1966–1967* (Oxford: Clarendon, 1996); Gregory Pedlow, ed., *The Evolution of NATO Strategy 1949–1969* (Brussels: Historical Office Supreme Headquarters Allied Powers Europe, 1997); Thomas A. Schwartz, *Lyndon Johnson and Europe: In the Shadow of Vietnam* (Cambridge, MA: Harvard University Press, 2003); Lawrence S. Kaplan, *NATO Divided, NATO United: The Evolution of an Alliance* (Westport, CT: Praeger, 2004); and Andreas Wenger, Christian Nuenlist, and Anna Locher, eds., *Transforming NATO in the Cold War: Challenges beyond Deterrence in the 1960s* (London: Routledge, 2006).

6 Andreas Wenger, "Crisis and Opportunity: NATO's Transformation and the Multilateralization of Detente, 1966–1968," *Journal of Cold War Studies* 6, no. 1 (2004): 22–74, 39.

7 See Frédéric Bozo, *Deux strategies pour l'Europe: De Gaulle, les États-Unis et l'Alliance Atlantique* (Paris: Plon, 1996), and Maurice Vaisse, *La Grandeur: Politique étrangère du Géneral de Gaulle, 1958–1969* (Paris: Fayard, 1998).

8 See Thomas A. Schwartz, "Lyndon Johnson and Europe: Alliance Politics, Political Economy, and 'Growing Out of the Cold War,'" in *Beyond Vietnam: The Foreign Policies of Lyndon Johnson,* ed. H. W. Brands (College Station: Texas A&M University Press, 1999), 37–60.

9 Lyndon B. Johnson, Remarks in New York City before the National Conference of Editorial Writers, October 7, 1966, *Public Papers of the Presidents of the United States: Lyndon B. Johnson, 1966,* book 2 (Washington, DC: Government Printing Office, 1967), 1125–30.

10 Johnson had coined the term "bridge building" in his January 1964 address at the dedication of the George C. Marshall Research Library, May 23, 1964. See *Public Papers of the Presidents of the United States: Lyndon B. Johnson, 1963–1964,* book 1 (Washington, DC: Government Printing Office, 1964), 708–10. For the context, see Stephan Kieninger, *Dynamic Détente: The United States and Europe, 1964–1975* (Lanham, MD: Rowman & Littlefield, 2016).

11 Rusk to the Department of State (Personal for the President), telegram, December 16, 1966, in *Foreign Relations of the United States, 1964–68,* ed. Charles S. Sampson, vol. 13, Western Europe Region (Washington, DC: Government Printing Office), 517.

12 Verbatim Record of the North Atlantic Council in Ministerial Session, December 15, 1966, in C-VR(66)69, NATO Archives.

13 See James E. Goodby, *Europe Undivided: The New Logic of Peace in U.S.-Russian Relations* (Washington, DC: United States Institute of Peace Press, 1998), and Kenneth Weisbrode, *The Atlantic Century: Four Generations of Extraordinary Diplomats Who Forged America's Vital Alliance with Europe* (New York: Da Capo, 2009).

14 Verbatim Record of the North Atlantic Council in Ministerial Session, December 13, 1967, in C-VR(67)50, NATO Archives.

15 The meetings were usually held twice a year, in the spring and the autumn, over several days, in an isolated location of a member country conducive to fruitful exchanges.

16 Memo from Miriam Camps, the director of the State Department's Policy Planning Council, on the Interagency Planning Group Meeting with Diehl and British Policy Planning Director John Thomson, January 26, 1967, Records of the Department of State, record group (RG) 59, Records of the Policy Planning Council, 1965–68, box 393, National Archives and Records Administration (hereafter NARA).

17 Goodby, *Europe Undivided,* 53.

18 Department of State to US Mission at NATO (No. 177967), telegram, October 29, 1970, RG 59, Central Files, 1970–73, box 2263, NARA.

19 Springsteen and Kirchschläger, September 28, 1970, memcon, RG 59, Central Files, 1970–1973, box 1705, NARA.

20 Verbatim Record of the North Atlantic Council in Ministerial Session, June 14, 1973, in C-VR(73)36, part II, NATO Archives. For the context, see Oliver

Bange and Gottfried Niedhart, eds., *Helsinki 1975 and the Transformation of Europe* (New York: Berghahn Books, 2008).

21 See Jussi M. Hanhimäki, "'They Can Write It in Swahili': Kissinger, the Soviets, and the Helsinki Accords, 1973–75," *Journal of Transatlantic Studies* 1, no. 1 (2003): 37–58.

22 Verbatim Record of the North Atlantic Council in Ministerial Session, December 10, 1973, in C-VR(73)74, part I, NATO Archives.

23 See Sarah B. Snyder, *Human Rights Activism and the End of the Cold War: A Transnational History of the Helsinki Network* (Cambridge: Cambridge University Press, 2011), and Michael Cotey Morgan, *The Final Act: The Helsinki Accords and the Transformation of the Cold War* (Princeton, NJ: Princeton University Press, 2018).

24 Thomas A. Schwartz, "Legacies of Détente: A Three-Way Discussion," *Cold War History* 8, no. 4 (November 2008): 513–25.

25 Ford, Kissinger, and Genscher, memcon, September 26, 1974, Records of the Department of State, RG 59, Records of the Office of the Counselor, entry 5339 (Helmut Sonnenfeldt) 1955–1977, box 5, NARA. See also https://www.fordlibrarymuseum.gov/library/document/0314/1552808.pdf.

26 See Leopoldo Nuti, ed., *The Crisis of Détente in Europe: From Helsinki to Gorbachev 1975–1985* (London: Routledge, 2009); Leopoldo Nuti, Frédéric Bozo, Marie-Pierre Rey, and Bernd Rother, eds., *The Euromissile Crisis and the End of the Cold War* (Stanford, CA: Stanford University Press, 2015); and Kristina Spohr, *The Global Chancellor: Helmut Schmidt and the Reshaping of the International Order* (Oxford: Oxford University Press, 2016).

27 Kristina Spohr, "Conflict and Cooperation in Intra-Alliance Nuclear Politics: Western Europe, the United States, and the Genesis of NATO's Dual-Track Decision, 1977–1979," *Journal of Cold War Studies* 13, no. 2 (Spring 2011): 39–89, 40.

28 On October 28, 1977, Schmidt used the Alistair Buchan Memorial Lecture at the International Institute for Strategic Studies as a means to highlight his criticism. The address in printed in *Survival* 20, no. 1 (1978): 2–10. For the context, see Helmut Schmidt, *Menschen und Mächte* (Berlin: Siedler Verlag, 1987).

29 Schmidt to Leber, note, October 6, 1977, in *Akten zur Auswaertigen Politik der Bundesrepublik Deutschland* (hereafter *AAPD*) *1977*, 1331. For the context, see Klaus Wiegrefe, *Das Zerwürfnis: Helmut Schmidt, Jimmy Carter und die Krise der deutsch-amerikanischen Beziehungen* (Berlin: Propyläen Verlag, 2005).

30 See Van Well and Aaron, memcon, January 30, 1978, in *AAPD 1978*, 138–43.

31 See Kristina Spohr, "Germany and the Politics of the Neutron Bomb 1975–1979," *Diplomacy and Statecraft* 21, no. 2 (2010): 259–85.

32 Brzezinski and Schmidt, memcon, October 3, 1978, in Jimmy Carter Library, National Security Affairs 7, box 33. For the German record, see *AAPD 1978*, 1451–62.

33 See Special Coordination Committee, April 12, 1979, Nuclear Vault, National Security Archive, Nuclear Vault, http://nsarchive2.gwu.edu/nukevault/ebb301/doc07.pdf.

34 See Assistant Secretary Blech to the Foreign Office, note, May 30, 1979, in *AAPD 1979*, 736–44.

35 Verbatim Record of the North Atlantic Council in Ministerial Session, December 13, 1979, in C-VR(79)40, part I, NATO Archives.

36 For the context, see Strobe Talbott, *Deadly Gambits: The Reagan Administration and the Stalemate in Nuclear Arms Control* (New York: Alfred A. Knopf, 1984).

37 Reagan and Schmidt, memcon, May 21, 1981, Executive Secretariat, NSC, Subject File, Reagan Memcons, box 48, Ronald Reagan Library (hereafter RRL).

38 Heads of State, G7 Meeting in Montebello, memcon, July 19, 1981, in *AAPD 1981*, 1145.

39 Tim Geiger and Jan Hansen, "Did Protest Matter? The Influence of the Peace Movement on the West German Government and the Social Democratic Party, 1977–1983," in *Nuclear Threats, Nuclear Fear and the Cold War of the 1980s*, ed. Eckart Conze, Martin Klimke, and Jeremy Varon (Cambridge: Cambridge University Press), 290–315.

40 Ronald Reagan Remarks to Members of the National Press Club on Arms Reduction and Nuclear Weapons, November 18, 1981, https://www.reaganlibrary.gov/research/speeches/111881a.

41 Minutes of a National Security Council Meeting, October 13, 1981, in *Foreign Relations of the United States, 1981–1988*, ed. James Graham Wilson, vol. 3, *Soviet Union, January 1981–January 1983* (Washington, DC: Government Printing Office, 2016), 313.

42 See James Graham Wilson, *The Triumph of Improvisation: Gorbachev's Adaptability, Reagan's Engagement, and the End of the Cold War* (Ithaca, NY: Cornell University Press, 2014).

43 Ronald Reagan to Yuri Andropov, letter, December 28, 1983, in Executive Secretariat, Head of State File, RRL.

44 See Stephan Kieninger, *The Diplomacy of Détente: Cooperative Security Policies from Helmut Schmidt to George Shultz* (London: Routledge, 2018).

45 Note by Robert Armstrong of a Meeting at the World Economic Summit in Williamsburg, Virginia, May 29, 1983, in Records of the Prime Minister's Office (hereafter PREM), vol. 1009, 19, The National Archives (hereafter TNA), Kew, www.margaretthatcher.org/document/139339.

46 See Mary Sarotte, *1989: The Struggle to Create Post-Cold War Europe* (Princeton, NJ: Princeton University Press 2009), 26–27.

47 Hugh Faringdon, *Strategic Geography: NATO, the Warsaw Pact and the Superpowers* (London: Routledge, 1989), 30.

48 See Kristina Spohr, *Post Wall, Post Square: Rebuilding the World after 1989* (London: William Collins, 2019), 44–46.

49 Kohl and Thatcher, memcon, February 29, 1989, in PREM 19/2697, TNA, https://www.margaretthatcher.org/document/212213.

50 Scowcroft to Bush, "Dealing with the Germans," memo, August 7, 1989, in Brent Scowcroft Collection, USSR Chronological Files, SNF Files, 91120–004, Soviet Power Collapse in Eastern Europe—SNF—May 1989 (1), George Herbert Walker Bush Presidential Library (hereafter GHWBL).

51 Scowcroft to Bush, "Short-Range Nuclear Forces and NATO's 'Comprehensive Concept,'" memo, n.d., Brent Scowcroft Collection, USSR Chronological Files, SNF Files, 91120–002, Soviet Power Collapse in Eastern Europe—SNF—April 1989 (1), GHWBL.

52 For a debate on this issue, see Mark Kramer and Joshua R. Itzkowitz Shifrinson, "Correspondence: NATO Enlargement—Was There a Promise?," *International Security* 42, no. 1 (Summer 2017): 186–92. See Mary E. Sarotte, "Not One Inch Eastward? Bush, Baker, Kohl, Genscher, Gorbachev, and the Origin of Russian Resentment toward NATO Enlargement in February 1990," *Diplomatic History* 34, no. 1 (January 2010): 119–40, and James Goldgeier, "Promises Made, Promises Broken? What Yeltsin Was Told about NATO in 1993 and Why It Matters," *War on the Rocks,* July 12, 2016, https://warontherocks.com/2016/07/promises-made-promises-broken-what-yeltsin-was-told-about-nato-in-1993-and-why-it-matters/.

53 See Mark Kramer, "The Myth of a No-NATO-Enlargement Pledge to Russia," *Washington Quarterly* 32, no. 2 (Spring 2009): 39–61, and Kristina Spohr, "Precluded or Precedent-Setting? The NATO Enlargement Question in the Triangular Bonn-Washington-Moscow Diplomacy of 1990–1991," *Journal of Cold War Studies* 14, no. 4 (October 2012): 4–54.

54 See "Mikhail Gorbachev: I Am against All Walls," interview, Russia Beyond, October 16, 2014, https://www.rbth.com/international/2014/10/16/mikhail_gorbachev_i_am_against_all_walls_40673.html, and Steven Pifer, "Did NATO Promise Not to Enlarge? Gorbachev Says 'No,'" *Up Front* (blog), Brookings Institution, November 6, 2014, https://www.brookings.edu/blog/up-front/2014/11/06/did-nato-promise-not-to-enlarge-gorbachev-says-no/.

55 In February 1990, Secretary of State James Baker started the effort to obtain Mikhail Gorbachev's consent to NATO membership of unified Germany. Baker asked Gorbachev whether he would rather see an independent Germany outside of NATO, with no US forces on its territory, or a united Germany tied to NATO but with assurances that "there would be no extension of NATO's jurisdiction for forces of NATO one inch to the East." Baker, Gorbachev, and Shevardnadze, memcon, February 9, 1990, National Security Archive, Soviet Flashpoints, box 38, https://nsarchive2.gwu.edu//dc.html?doc=4325679-Document-05-Memorandum-of-conversation-between. Joshua Shifrinson portrays Baker's remarks as a promise not to enlarge NATO. See Joshua Itzkowitz Shifrinson, "Deal or No Deal? The End of the Cold War and the U.S. Offer to Limit NATO Expansion," *International Security* 40, no. 4

(Spring 2016): 7–44. However, the question of NATO enlargement came up only in ways as it was related to the NATO membership of unified Germany. The CEE countries were still members of the Warsaw Pact—and Gorbachev could not even imagine they would someday aspire to join NATO. Money was the first carrot for obtaining Gorbachev's consent; NATO's reform was the second one. Gorbachev got both. He never asked for a commitment not to expand NATO.

56 See Michael Mandelbaum, *Mission Failure: America and the World in the Post-Cold War Era* (New York: Oxford University Press, 2016). For Mandelbaum's contemporary critique, see "Preserving the New Peace: The Case against NATO Expansion," *Foreign Affairs* 74, no. 3. (May/June 1995): 9–13.

57 Hal Brands, *Making the Unipolar Moment: U.S. Foreign Policy and the Rise of the Post–Cold War Order* (Ithaca, NY: Cornell University Press, 2016); Jeffrey Engel, *When the World Seemed New: George H. W. Bush and the End of the Cold War* (Boston: Houghton Mifflin Harcourt, 2017); Spohr, *Post Wall, Post Square.*

58 See Stephan Kieninger, "Opening NATO and Engaging Russia: NATO's Two Tracks and the Establishment of the North Atlantic Cooperation Council in 1991," in *Open Door: NATO Enlargement and Euro-Atlantic Security in the 1990s,* ed. Daniel S. Hamilton and Kristina Spohr (Washington DC: Brookings Institution Press, 2019), 57–69.

59 For the context, see James Goldgeier, *Not Whether but When: The U.S. Decision to Enlarge NATO* (Washington, DC: Brookings Institution Press, 1999); Ronald Asmus, *Opening NATO's Door: How the Alliance Remade Itself for a New Era* (New York: Columbia University Press, 2002); Strobe Talbott, *The Russia Hand: A Memoir of Presidential Diplomacy* (New York: Random House, 2002); and James M. Goldgeier and Michael McFaul, *Power and Purpose: U.S. Policy toward Russia after the Cold War* (Washington, DC: Brookings Institution Press, 2003).

60 Verbatim Record of the North Atlantic Council Meeting with the Participation of the Heads of State and Government, July 5, 1990, C-VR (90)36, part I, NATO Archives, https://www.nato.int/nato_static_fl2014/assets/pdf/pdf_archives/20141218_C-VR-90-36-PART1.PDF.

61 See Stephen J. Flanagan, "NATO from Liaison to Enlargement: A Perspective from the State Department and the National Security Council 1990–1999," in Hamilton and Spohr, *Open Door,* 93–114.

62 See George Bush and Brent Scowcroft, *A World Transformed* (New York: Alfred A. Knopf, 1998), 404–5.

63 Bush and Gorbachev, telecon, September 27, 1991, https://bush41library.tamu.edu/files/memcons-telcons/1991-09-27--Gorbachev.pdf. For the background, see Svetlana Savranskaya and Thomas Blanton, *Unilateral U.S. Nuclear Pullback in 1991 Matched by Rapid Soviet Cuts,* Briefing Book no. 561, September 30, 2016, https://nsarchive.gwu.edu/briefing-book/nuclear-vault-russia-programs/2016-09-30/unilateral-us-nuclear-pullback-1991-matched.

64 See Joint Statement by Secretary of State James A. Baker III and Hans-Dietrich Genscher, Minister for Foreign Affairs of the Federal Republic of Germany, Washington, DC, October 2, 1991, in *American Foreign Policy: Current Documents, 1991,* ed. Paul Claussen and Evan M. Duncan (Buffalo, New York: William S. Hein, 2008), 216–18. For the context, see Robert Hutchings, *American Diplomacy and the End of the Cold War: An Insider's Account of U.S. Policy in Europe, 1989–1992* (Washington, DC: Woodrow Wilson Center Press and Johns Hopkins University Press, 1997).

65 See Stephen J. Flanagan, "NATO and the East: From Liaison to Security Partnership," *Washington Quarterly,* Spring 1992, 141–51; Liviu Horovitz, "The George H. W. Bush Administration's Policies vis-à-vis Central Europe: From Cautious Encouragement to Cracking Open NATO's Door," in Hamilton and Spohr, *Open Door,* 71–92; Joshua R. Itzkowitz Shifrinson. "Eastbound and Down: The United States, NATO Enlargement, and Suppressing the Soviet and Western European Alternatives, 1990–1992," *Journal of Strategic Studies,* April 1, 2020, https://www.tandfonline.com/doi/abs/10.1080/01402390.2020.1737931.

66 Lowenkron through Gompert to Scowcroft, "Follow-Up to NATO Summit," memo, November 15, 1991, National Security Council Files (NSC), Nicholas Rostow Files, Subject Files, CF01329–005, GHWBL.

67 Lowenkron through Gompert to Scowcroft.

68 Lowenkron through Gompert to Scowcroft.

69 Gompert, "Implications for NATO of Expanded WEU Membership," memo, March 26, 1992, NSC, David C. Gompert Subject Files, CF01301–009 European Strategy [Steering] Group (ESSG), GHWBL.

70 Edward A. Hewett, "Memo for Scowcroft: Prime Minister Major and NATO Membership," June 5, 1992, NSC, Nicholas Rostow Subject Files CF01329–005 NATO (1), GHWBL.

71 Bush and Yeltsin, memcon, February 1, 1992, NSC, Nicholas R. Burns and Ed Hewett Files, CF01421–009, GHWBL.

72 US Embassy Moscow to Secretary of State (No. 31886), "NATO Expansion: Now Is Not the Time," telegram, October 8, 1993, case M-2017–12019, doc. C06554765, State Department Virtual Reading Room, released through the Freedom of Information Act (hereafter FOIA) on May 21, 2018, https://foia.state.gov/Search/Search.aspx.

73 Davis and Flanagan to Christopher, "Strategy for NATO's Expansion and Transformation," memo, September 7, 1993, https://nsarchive2.gwu.edu//dc.html?doc=4390816-Document-02-Strategy-for-NATO-s-Expansion-and.

74 Volker Rühe, "Shaping Euro-Atlantic Policies: A Grand Strategy for a New Era," *Survival* 35, no. 2 (Summer 1993): 131. On Rühe's thinking, see Ulrich Weisser, *Sicherheit für ganz Europa: Die Atlantische Allianz in der Bewährung* (Stuttgart: Deutsche Verlags Anstalt, 1999), and Ronald Asmus, Stephen Flanagan, and Richard Kugler, "Building a New NATO," *Foreign Affairs* 72, no. 4 (September/October 1993): 28–40.

75 Gallucci through Davis to Christopher, "Your October 6 Lunch Meeting with Secretary Aspin and Mr. Lake," memo, October 5, 1993, https://nsarchive2.gwu.edu//dc.html?doc=4390819-Document-05-Your-October-6-Lunch-Meeting-with.

76 Albright for the President, the Vice President, the Secretary of State and the National Security Adviser, "Subject: PfP and Central and Eastern Europe," memo, January 26, 1994, 16, https://clinton.presidentiallibraries.us/items/show/57563.

77 Clinton and Havel, memcon, January 11, 1994, https://nsarchive2.gwu.edu//dc.html?doc=4390825-Document-11-The-President-s-Meeting-with-Czech. For the background, see Michael Zantovsky, "In Search for Allies: Vaclav Havel and the Expansion of NATO," *World Affairs* 177, no. 4 (November/December 2014): 47–58, and Jan Havranek and Jan Jires, "Vaclav Havel and NATO: Lessons of Leadership for the Atlantic Alliance," in Hamilton and Spohr, *Open Door*, 173–95.

78 Christopher to Department of State (Secto-10020), "Secretary's Meeting with Foreign Ministers of Hungary, Poland, Slovakia, and the Czech Republic," telegram, January 16, 1994, case M-2017–11649, doc. C06548772, State Department Virtual Reading Room, released through FOIA on May 8, 2018, https://foia.state.gov/Search/Search.aspx.

79 Moscow to White House and Secretary of State (No. 1457), "President's Dinner with President Yeltsin, January 14, 1994," telegram, January 20, 1994, case F-2017–13804, doc. C06694488, State Department Virtual Reading Room, released through FOIA on March 29, 2019, https://foia.state.gov/Search/Search.aspx.

80 Helmut Kohl's national security adviser Joachim Bitterlich gave the US ambassador to Germany, Richard Holbrooke, and Undersecretary of Defense Frank Wisner a briefing of Yeltsin's visit in Bonn. See US Embassy Bonn to Secretary of State (No. 11493), "Subject: May 12 Kohl/Yeltsin Talks," telegram, May 13, 1994, 28, https://clinton.presidentiallibraries.us/items/show/100538.

81 Clinton and Kohl, memcon, December 1994, 166, https://clinton.presidentiallibraries.us/items/show/57651.

CHAPTER 8

Russia and the Erosion of the Liberal Order

JENNIFER BRUSH

This chapter builds on the experiences of a retired diplomat of the US Foreign Service, the Organization for Security and Cooperation in Europe (OSCE), and the United Nations (UN). I have been retired from the Foreign Service for six years. My comments are based solely upon my personal views and do not represent the views of the Department of State or of the US government. Russian threats to our democracy are serious, ongoing, and are not being addressed adequately at the national or state levels. I want to describe why Russia is so intent upon destroying our democracy and, indeed, the international liberal world order but also how Russia is carrying out its mission.

THE PEACE DIVIDEND

Russian leader Vladimir Putin has a visceral hatred of US democracy and is making remarkable progress at undermining US leadership around the world. He believes the greatest sin visited upon Russia was the breakup of the Soviet Union. Over the past two-plus decades, he has endured a series of perceived insults to Russia for which he pledges revenge. Revenge to Putin means destroying the liberal world order created after World War II, which began as punishment to Nazi Germany but which has transmogrified into Russian containment.[1]

Bill Clinton was elected US president in 1992 and dedicated himself to pursuing the "peace dividend" following the breakup of the Soviet Union. The United States poured billions of dollars into Russia to pursue economic and democratic reform. We were seized with the idea that the Russian people, once freed from communism, would naturally embrace democracy and market forces. Economically, we attempted to wean Russia off its dependence on its extractive industries in order to create a diversified economy. Tragically, the divesting of state-owned enterprises led to the creation of an oligarch economy. Very little of the billions given to Russia actually improved the life of the average Russian or contributed to a democratic, market-oriented society. The peace dividend was a bust; oligarchs enriched themselves and leapt to new levels of kleptocracy as average Russians sank into more squalor. Putin considered the influx of Western money and values an insult, although he became one of the world's richest men because of it.

NATO/EU Expansion

In the 1990s, former Warsaw Pact members clamored to join the North Atlantic Treaty Organization (NATO) to prevent returning to Russian servitude. The State Department began a delicate dance of NATO expansion, welcoming former Warsaw Pact members while trying to reassure Moscow that NATO expansion was not a threat to Russia. Although a special NATO committee was established to cooperate with Russia and the Partnership for Peace was launched, Russia considered NATO expansion an existential threat to its security. I was studying at Princeton University for my master's degree in public policy during this time and read Russian news sites and blogs, in Russian, to better understand how this "nonthreatening" NATO expansion was playing in Russia. Nationalist websites relentlessly depicted blood-soaked scenarios, guaranteeing to the Russian public that NATO wanted nothing more than the annihilation of Russia and Russians.

Putin's foreign minister, Sergei Lavrov, most recently updated his anti-NATO talking points at the prospect of Macedonia becoming the alliance's thirtieth member. On February 20, 2019, he claimed, "The West is advancing its brazen policy of dragging this region into NATO in total disregard of the countries' people, in addition to ignoring the lessons of history or simple diplomatic courtesies."[2] The likelihood of Russia allowing other former Soviet republics—such as Moldova, Ukraine, Georgia, Armenia, and Azerbaijan—to join is now remote.

Putin consistently conflates membership in the European Union (EU) with membership in NATO, and Russian-language media rarely distinguish between the two. Fighting EU expansion is the front line for fighting NATO expansion. Russia took its battle to Georgia and Ukraine. In 2008, Russia invaded Georgia. This was prompted by increasing Russian frustration with Georgian pro-Western leader Mikheil Saakashvili, who defeated pro-Russian president Eduard Shevardnadze in 2003 in the "Rose Revolution," a political movement Putin associates with US interference and meddling. Since 2008, residents of the breakaway, nonrecognized republics of Abkhazia and South Ossetia have lived in an increasing hell of isolation, deprivation, and massive emigration.

In 2013, while Ukraine was chairman in office of the OSCE, Russia ordered President Viktor Yanukovych to backtrack on accepting an EU stability and association agreement. As the OSCE Ministerial Council met in Kyiv in December of that year, massive crowds were gathering in its Independence Square (Maidan Nezalezhnosti) to protest Yanukovych, Russia, and the Ukrainian security forces' violent crackdown of previous protests. Unfortunately for Ukraine, it was followed as chairman in office by a crazy-quilt chairmanship shared by Switzerland and Serbia, neither of which were inclined—or equipped—to take on Russian aggression. Russia entered this vacuum by invading Crimea in February 2014.[3]

I was ambassador of our OSCE mission in neighboring Moldova at the time and immediately dispatched two of our most senior military advisers to Crimea to assess the situation. At the time, news reports about Crimea cited spontaneous activities by "little green men"—Russian soldiers fighting alongside Ukrainian separatists in uniforms but without insignia. Our observers, UK and Polish colonels fluent in Russian and expert in Russian military uniforms and equipment, were stopped at the "border" of Crimea by these forces for hours.[4] This was fortuitous for our observers, as they were able to return to Moldova fully confident in reporting that the uniforms and equipment in question were directly from the Russian military. Russia eventually dropped the little green men fiction and subsequently claimed Crimea as Russia.

Crimea was widely considered the gem of the Black Sea; with its holiday villages and beaches, it was a regional tourist destination. But the 2014 tourist season in Crimea was a disaster, with empty hotels and restaurants.

A Radio Free Europe / Radio Liberty report from that year chronicled the 35 percent drop in tourism revenues as a result of the annexation. One native lamented, "The last time tourism was this bad was in 1970 when we had a cholera epidemic."[5]

By his activities in Georgia and Ukraine, Putin continues to demonstrate his disdain for the welfare of his people, as he single-mindedly pursues his task of preventing EU and NATO expansion in the near abroad. Through his annexation of Crimea, Putin violated the liberal order, including the UN Charter, the Helsinki Founding Agreement of the OSCE, and various other international and bilateral agreements governing Russian relations with Ukraine.

This is why US president Donald Trump's naked land grab for Greenland in August 2019 was more than a sick joke. It is no coincidence that Trump announced his plans for Greenland as he was inviting Russia back to the Group of Seven (G7), the major political forum for the world's most industrialized economies. Russia had been kicked out in 2014 for invading Crimea, a fact Trump ignored, or forgot, when he said on August 21, three days before the next G7 summit, that Russia should return to the group unconditionally. Naturally, our allies are nervous that Trump has embraced, or at least forgiven, Russia's encroachments on its neighbors. US Russia experts are now very concerned about Russian intentions vis-à-vis our Scandinavian allies. Russian military activity in the Baltic Sea has increased, and Russia is making aggressive moves about lucrative Arctic resources, now more readily available as a result of global warming. Lusting after neighboring territory apparently no longer is forbidden, but its prevention was a major cornerstone of the post–World War II liberal world order.

NATO Bombing

In the late 1980s and early 1990s, as the EU was declaring the post-Soviet period "the EU era," Yugoslavia was falling apart. I was posted to Belgrade when Slobodan Milošević came to power. I witnessed and reported to the State Department on Milošević's systematic eradication of any elements of a liberal society, beginning with the press and universities, purging them of intellectuals who disagreed with his nationalist plans and then cracking down on anyone who exercised the freedom of assembly to oppose his agenda.

In an odd quirk for me, in 1987, I was the only Bosnia expert in the entire US government, so I was a frequent visitor to the region. Bosnians then trembled at the thought of the emerging Serbian nationalist Milošević bringing his brand of politics into Bosnia-Herzegovina. As the editor of the Sarajevo daily *Oslobođenje* told me in 1989, "If one drop of blood is shed here, it will be a bloodbath." I was redirected from a tour in Poland to Bosnia-Herzegovina in 1991 to assess the potential for the overflow of violence from the war in Croatia. I penned a number of reports recording my chilling meetings in which local Serbs all read from identical scripts citing the threat of the Vatican, Islamic Jihad, and the Trilateral Commission. Muslim and Croatian groups told me they knew they were about to be slaughtered. Serbs had already kicked them out of the security services and encouraged them to leave Bosnia. Both groups pleaded for UN peacekeepers, which I faithfully reported back to Washington. No, I was told—peacekeepers do not prevent war; they come in to clean up after a war. The subsequent Serbian invasion of Bosnia-Herzegovina was no surprise.

UN peacekeepers subsequently performed abysmally, leading up to the Srebrenica massacre in 1995, during which Dutch peacekeepers stood by helplessly as Serbs slaughtered eight thousand Bosnian men and boys. Srebrenica was too much for the international community. NATO ordered air strikes on Bosnia to bring the Serbs to the negotiating table, and we got the much-flawed Dayton Accords. The Russians vigorously opposed this NATO out-of-theater activity.

I had also been assigned to Kosovo in 1993 to assess the overflow of violence from Bosnia into Kosovo and had reported that violence was inevitable. After Dayton, Serbs turned to Kosovo, and after a couple of years of escalating violence and failed negotiations, NATO bombed Serbia proper in 1999. Putin was incensed, crying foul about NATO out-of-theater activities and lack of a UN umbrella. He has never let go of his objections, most recently using them as a rallying cry for his visit to Belgrade on January 20, 2019, when he repeated that the 1999 NATO bombing was a turning point in US-Russian relations and should make Serbia avoid closer ties with the West.[6]

Transnistria

Conflict resolution in Moldova resulted in another black eye for Putin. Following the collapse of the Soviet Union, there was a brief skirmish between the Moldovan army and forces of the breakaway, Russian-speaking area of Transnistria in 1990. Fewer than one thousand people were killed before the Russians intervened and established a (non-UN) peacekeeping force along the banks of the Dniester River. In 2003, Putin adviser Dmitry Kozak presented a peace plan that both sides deemed acceptable. Solving this dilemma would have been a coup for Putin and would have burnished his peacemaking credentials in the international arena. As Putin was flying to the United States for a summit with George W. Bush, his foreign minister was en route to the Moldovan capital of Chisinau to sign the plan. But the United States, at the last minute, balked at the plan and convinced Moldovan president Vladimir Voronin not to sign. When news got to Putin, he allegedly reversed his transatlantic flight, canceled his visit to Washington, and angrily returned to Moscow.

2011 Russian Presidential Election

More recently, Putin became incensed when Secretary of State Hillary Clinton declared his 2011 election "dishonest and unfair."[7] Although the Mueller Report is ambiguous about President Trump's relationship with Putin, there is no doubt about Putin's animosity toward both Clintons, with special animus toward Hillary.

LIFE IN RUSSIA

Demographics

Russian poverty and backwardness should be just as much an insult to Putin's leadership as NATO and EU "encroachment," but he is content to keep his power through his boldness on the international stage rather than by doing much about Russia's abysmal demographics and economy. Anti-Americanism is Putin's best campaign tool. Russia's domestic problems are numerous and serious:

- Russia's low birth rate and high death rate have significantly reduced Russia's population, which has declined from 148.6 million in 1993 to between 139 million and 143 million today. Emigration vastly exceeds immigration, with a net loss of over one million from 1991 to 2015.[8]
- According to the *Moscow Times,* Russia has the second-highest abortion rate in the world. In 2015, officially 930,000 abortions were performed, although the total annual number could have been twice as high, experts say.[9]

- The Central Intelligence Agency's World Factbook lists Russia as 155th in the world for life expectancy. Average male life expectancy at birth is 66.3 years.[10] Most studies point to heavy vodka consumption as the main source of Russia's abysmal male life expectancy.[11] But other factors contribute, as well, according to the World Health Organization, including heart disease in general, accidents, violence, and suicide. Smoking rates are among the highest in the world (twice as high as in the United States). Environmental conditions, especially in the workplace, are often poor. Many Russians' diets are harmful and the quality of the health-care system is low.

Adoptions

Adoptions are another window onto Russian life. Russian children are orphaned, abandoned, or taken from nonviable parents at alarming rates. Alcoholism and drug use account both for babies with disabilities and children given over to orphanages and foster care. Conditions in orphanages are inhumane. Following the collapse of the Soviet Union, conditions in the orphanages were made known to the public, and Americans rushed in to adopt. By some estimates, Americans adopted over sixty thousand Russian children.[12] Given the supply of Russian orphans, US adoptions were a useful release valve for Russia's social problems.

Adoptions ended in 2012 with the Magnitsky Act, a series of sanctions passed by Congress to protest the death in prison of Russian lawyer Sergei Magnitsky, who had been conducting a tax fraud case involving high-ranking Kremlin officials. Three weeks after the act passed, Putin put a ban on adoptions, even though hundreds of cases were in process, with American parents and Russian orphans having already met and the paperwork begun.

The Russian version of the story is different. Putin called the adoption ban the "Dimi Yakovlev Act," after an adopted toddler who died in an overly heated car in the United States. The Russian press breathlessly reported on the 2010 case of a seven-year-old Russian adoptee who was returned to Russian alone on a one-way ticket because he had exhibited "violent and psychotic" behavior. According to a *CNN* story on the incident, unbeknownst to his American parents, the child had already burned down a building in Russia before he was adopted, and while in the United States he had threatened to kill family members and burn down the family home.[13]

Because of the continued demand by American parents to adopt Russian children and the continued supply of abandoned Russian children, Russian adoptions remain an open sore in our bilateral relationship. Russians continue to lobby to have the Magnitsky sanctions lifted with the understanding that the adoption ban would be lifted.

This is why, in 2016, there was no "innocent" meeting about adoptions between members of the Trump campaign and a Russian lawyer with close ties to the Kremlin. Putin was desperate to get rid of the sanctions and, during the campaign, saw a Trump win as his best chance. It is quite likely, however, that neither Donald Trump Jr. nor Jared Kushner understood the link between adoptions and sanctions, which is why Trump Jr. subsequently said the meeting "went nowhere but [he] had to listen." Paul Manafort, also present, had to have understood the linkage. The purported goal—the active seeking-out of damaging information on Hillary Clinton—has its own set of implications.[14]

The Economy

The massive US investment in Russian economic reform failed to improve the lives of average Russians. Impoverished and bereft of hope, and having access only to Putin's controlled media, average Russians blame the West and capitalism for their poverty:

- According to the World Economic Forum, Russia contributes 1.8 percent of the world's gross domestic product (GDP). The United States contributes 24.32 percent, and China 14.84 percent, as the world's two largest producers. Over 50 percent of Russia's GDP comes from extractive industries—oil, gas, and uranium.[15]
- Putin pledged to cut poverty in half during his 2018 election campaign. According to Radio Free Europe / Radio Liberty, approximately 19.8 million Russians—or 14 percent of the population—lived in poverty in 2018. More Russians have been slipping into poverty on the back of the Western sanctions and low oil prices that have battered the country's energy-dependent economy.[16]

The one bright spot in the Russian economy? Soybeans. According to David Dodson, a Republican who ran unsuccessfully in 2018 in the GOP primary in Wyoming for the US Senate and now lectures at the Stanford Graduate School of Business, Ohio's farmers' soybean losses, due to the China tariffs, have benefited Russia, already China's largest trading partner. While Russia's total soybean exports to China remain low, at about 1 percent, Russia shares a twenty-six-hundred-mile border with China and is already expanding agriculture infrastructure to take advantage of the nearby Chinese market. In response to the trade war, Russia has accelerated that expansion, opening up arable land to foreign investors, half of which is expected to go to Chinese investors. Russia has nearly doubled soybean exports to China during the past two years.[17] It is unclear if Russia oligarchs own any of the formerly collectivized arable land that is now being sold to the Chinese, but it is likely.

Human Rights

Many Russians have opposed Putin's authoritarian and antidemocratic lock on power. They have not fared well.

In 2004, pro-West Ukrainian presidential candidate Viktor Yushchenko was poisoned with dioxin, horribly disfiguring him. Former Russian military intelligence officer Sergei Skripal and his daughter were poisoned by a military-grade chemical agent in England in 2018. Jailed opposition leader Alexei Navalny was mysteriously poisoned in late July 2019 and possibly again in August 2020. Other opponents have met mysterious deaths. Alexander Litvinenko was poisoned by radiation in London in 2006. Putin's most powerful rival, Boris Nemtsov, was murdered in front of the Kremlin in 2015.[18]

Unable to improve standards of living or the lives of average Russians, Putin has stoked hatred of the United States via mass and social media. Any Putin victory over the United States is met with an increase in his popularity. Even if many Americans still do not believe it, the overwhelming majority of Russians are convinced their crafty leader controlled the outcome of the 2016 US presidential election.[19]

RUSSIAN INTERFERENCE IN THE 2016 ELECTION

The Mueller Report states in meticulous detail how Russia meddled in our 2016 presidential election with the clear goal of getting Donald Trump elected. Putin's goal in getting Trump elected was to destroy democratic institutions and establish a new Russian-controlled world order. This world order would be dominated by autocratic kleptocrats. Putin is desperate to lift US sanctions, not to help Russia's economy but because the sanctions directly target him and his oligarchs. Both before the election and throughout his presidency, Trump has flirted with lifting sanctions.

Candidate Clinton helped with the Russian efforts by her extraordinary carelessness in using an email server from her private home and by her hubris in assuming the Democratic Party mantle without a vibrant Democratic primary. She herself bore significant responsibility for losing the election. I wrote to friends working on her campaign warning that Clinton's message was not resonating in Ohio. I saw little effort made to appeal to Midwestern concerns. Scheduling the 2020 Democratic Party Convention in Wisconsin speaks volumes about the party's realization that the Midwest counts. Presidential candidates from the Midwest have had an impact on the debate.

Russian Meddling

Federal and state efforts to combat Russian meddling, even though the Mueller Report and our intelligence agencies have thoroughly detailed methods, have been inadequate. "Moscow Mitch" McConnell acquired his odious nickname by preventing Senate discussion of concrete legislation to secure our elections (though he has subsequently reversed his position). As surreal as it sounds, serious pundits have posited that Republicans believe themselves unable to win in 2020 *without* Russian meddling.

Putin used, and continues to use, classic spycraft to meddle in our elections, including personal contacts and "active measures" such as *kompromat,* disinformation, and the hacking of computer systems.

Personal Contacts

The extent of personal contacts between the Trump circle and the Russians outlined in the Mueller Report is astonishing. It is mind-boggling that public officials such as National Security Adviser Michael Flynn had such extensive prior contacts with the Russians. The extent of Trump campaign officials' contacts with high-ranking Russian officials sent a barrage of red flags into the air. I asked myself over and over, What were they thinking? Russians dangled lucrative promises of dirt on Hillary Clinton, and this appears to have been motivation enough to deal with a Russian leadership whose sole foreign policy was to destroy the liberal world order.

Kompromat

The kompromat—damaging information—on Trump is neither mysterious nor surprising. There may very well be a bedroom video tape, but that is more salacious than pertinent. The real kompromat on Trump is the money trail between him and Russia's oligarchs. Trump's passion to build a Trump Tower in Moscow is well documented. Trump was disappointed that his arrangement with the oligarchs who helped him stage the 2013 Miss Universe pageant in Moscow did not result in a meeting with Putin to finalize a tower deal. Trump was prepared to offer Putin a penthouse.[20]

The Russian oligarch money coming into this country is equally troubling. According to a Bloomberg news investigation, Trump acquired his capital for Trump Tower in Manhattan from Russian investors. Their money flooded into Trump projects from 2001 to 2007, helping Trump weather the real estate collapse. First son Donald Trump Jr. is proud of the Russian money; in 2008, he said, "We see a lot of money pouring in from Russia."[21]

And the money keeps coming. Notorious Russian oligarch and Putin confidant Oleg Deripaska is reportedly planning to build a $1.7 million aluminum plant on top of an abandoned strip mine in Kentucky—Mitch McConnell's Kentucky. Deripaska was under sanctions until McConnell gathered enough votes in the Senate in February 2019 to block continuation of the sanctions.[22] Deripaska is well known in Europe for running into the ground an aluminum plant in Montenegro and then helping to plan an unsuccessful coup to plant a pro-Russian prime minster there in order to prevent Montenegro from joining NATO. I am reminded of Trump's dismissive treatment of the Montenegrin prime minister at the 2017 NATO summit and his subsequent comment in 2018 that he would be unhappy defending "tiny" Montenegro and questioning whether the country's "very aggressive people" could draw NATO into a war with Russia.[23]

More unsettling are Trump's views on democracy and authoritarianism. In him, Putin found a willing ally to assault the liberal world order. Within his first months in office, Trump managed to insult NATO, the EU, and Canada and Australia, two of our strongest allies. And then he took on Denmark, calling comments of Prime Minister Mette Frederiksen "nasty" when she simply rebuffed his suggestion that the United States buy part of her country.[24]

In Russian spycraft, there are, in addition to unwilling accomplices, three types of "assets": fellow travelers, "useful idiots," and willing accomplices. Trump can fit into any of these categories. Although "fellow traveler" originally meant a follower of communism, the counterpart in current Russian thinking would be a fellow adherent to autocratic kleptocracy. The most generous of categories is that he is just a useful idiot—that he is unwittingly being manipulated by Putin as a result of his narcissism. Now he has slipped into far more dangerous territory and acts more as a willing accomplice. Trump's preference for Putin's analyses of world events over the expertise of his intelligence experts is damning.

Disinformation

In February 2013, Russian general Valery Gerasimov published an article titled "The Value of Science Is in the Foresight" in the weekly Russian trade paper *Military-Industrial Kurier.* Gerasimov took tactics developed by the Soviets, blended them with strategic military thinking about total war, and laid out a new theory of hybrid warfare. He wrote: "The very 'rules of war' have changed. The role of nonmilitary means of achieving political and strategic goals has grown, and, in many cases, they have exceeded the power of force of weapons in their effectiveness."[25]

Facebook and other social media are still reeling over the discovery that many of its Facebook accounts can be traced back to Russian troll farms. These organizations, owned by Putin's fellow oligarch Yevgeniy Prigozhin, were responsible for fear mongering on Facebook and disseminating fake news there and elsewhere on the internet about Hillary Clinton. This included the infamous "Pizzagate" episode in which a man traveled hundreds of miles to a pizza parlor in Washington, DC, and opened fire because he had believed a Russian troll farm's Facebook post that Clinton was running a child trafficking ring there. Although Facebook is becoming more proficient about scouting out fake Facebook accounts, Russian trolls continue with their work. The troll farms specifically targeted the African American vote with posts discouraging them from voting. One account, "Blacktivist," sent out messages on the Democratic candidate such as "No lives matter to Hillary Clinton. Only votes matter to Hillary Clinton." Another account, "Black Matters," posted on Facebook: "Cops kill black kids. Are you sure that your son won't be the next?"[26] Most recently Russian troll farms have been credited with spreading antivaccination conspiracy theories.[27]

Hacking

The Mueller Report also fully documents the extent and methods of Russian computer hacking of our political parties and government institutions.[28] The

Obama administration fought the hacking without seeming to be partial to the Hillary Clinton campaign. In June 2016, the United States formally accused Russia of hacking. Putin again got lucky when this news was released on the same day as the infamous *Access Hollywood* tape was released.

US intelligence knew that Russian hackers had penetrated the Democratic National Committee and the Clinton campaign, and yet, during the campaign, candidate Trump famously urged them to do more. Release of DNC and Clinton campaign emails by Julian Assange and WikiLeaks was devastating for the Clinton campaign.

As US intelligence learned more about Russian hacking, it offered to help states maintain the security of their voting systems, an offer that Ohio refused. I see that the Mike DeWine administration is now accepting federal assistance in protecting the Ohio voting system, and I welcome that.

The Russian hacking of the 2016 election has been compared to Pearl Harbor and September 11, but our response has been, at best, lukewarm.[29] Intelligence officials regularly report to Congress on the threat and efforts to thwart it, but without a presidential push to counter the threat, their efforts are gelded.

On November 2, 2018, I attended a meeting of a select group of academics, members of nongovernmental organizations, and businesspeople to hear Rep. David Joyce of Ohio's Fourteenth Congressional District. After clearly identifying myself as a Russia expert and senior US diplomat, I asked Representative Joyce whether he thought the federal and state governments had done enough to counter the Russian cyber-security threat. Joyce literally flipped his hand to dismiss my question, saying, "Everyone does it. We do it too." I reminded Joyce of my background and stated emphatically that this is not what the United States does. "Okay," he said, "if we don't do it, we get someone to do it for us." This flippant and ignorant response demonstrated to me the depth of denial the Republican Party has about Russia's role in getting Donald Trump elected. I asked Joyce again, in 2019, at a Chamber of Commerce event about election security, and he mumbled something about paper ballots but clearly was not focused on the issue.

Our real national emergency is not just Russia's success in getting a willing accomplice elected to the most powerful position in the world but even more that we have a US president intent upon destroying the liberal world order so many of us labored to build after the devastation of World War II. The current administrations in Washington and Columbus clearly do not see it in their political survival to take the Russian attacks on our democracy seriously.

WHAT IS TO BE DONE?

These are my recommendations for how we can stand up to the ongoing Russian-directed destruction of the liberal world order.

- Learn Russian. When I was at the University of Washington, the Defense Department gave me a scholarship to study Russian. Since my college years, Russian-language enrollments have fallen by almost 40 percent, according to the Modern Language Association.[30] Kenston High School in northeastern Ohio teaches Russian; I would encourage other high schools to offer Russian as well. The Foreign Service offers an incentive for Russian speakers to join the State Department. The Foreign Service Institute teaches Russian, but there is no substitute for a sound academic grounding.
- Be critical of your news sources. Social media is self-selecting: you choose what you want to know and from whom you want to receive your information. Now we know that social media remains heavily influenced by Russian and other bots that are seeking to form our opinions in a dangerous way. I continue to believe the major news outlets, and National Public Radio and the Public Broadcasting Service provide balanced and unbiased approaches to the news. The BBC, Reuters, Agence France-Presse, and even Al Jazeera are useful. There is also no substitute for reading academic texts. There is so much available on Russia and its intentions.
- And last, vote. The future of the liberal world order depends upon American citizens putting aside their differences and voting for democracy.

NOTES

1 On Putin's rise and government style, see Fiona Hill and Clifford G. Gaddy, *Mr. Putin: Operative in the Kremlin* (Washington, DC: Brookings Institution Press, 2013).

2 Christina Maza, "Russia Complains U.S. Is 'Dragging' European Countries into NATO, Even as Neighbors Move to Join Alliance," *Newsweek,* February 20, 2019,

https://www.newsweek.com/russia-us-dragging-european-countries-nato-join-alliance-1337890.

3 For the most recent OSCE statements and deliberations on Russian aggression in Ukraine and Crimea, see 1233rd Plenary Meeting of the Permanent Council, OSCE, https://www.osce.org/node/424496.

4 John R. Haines, "How, Why, and When Russia Will Deploy Little Green Men and Why the U.S. Cannot," Foreign Policy Research Institute, March 9, 2016, https://www.fpri.org/article/2016/03/how-why-and-when-russia-will-deploy-little-green-men-and-why-the-us-cannot/.

5 Stas Yurchenko, Usein Dzhabbarov, and Claire Bigg, "Tourist Season a Washout in Annexed Crimea," Radio Free Europe/Radio Liberty, June 5, 2014, https://www.rferl.org/a/tourist-season-washout-in-annexed-crimea/25446604.html.

6 "Ahead of Serbia Visit, Putin Claims, U.S. Is Playing Destabilizing Role in Balkans," Radio Free Europe/Radio Liberty, June 16, 2019, https://www.rferl.org/a/putin-serbia-interviews-us/29712614.html.

7 Michael Crowley and Julia Ioffe, "Why Putin Hates Hillary," Politico, July 25, 2016, https://www.politico.com/story/2016/07/clinton-putin-226153.

8 Olga Chudinovskikh and Mikhail Denisenko, "Russia: A Migration System with Soviet Roots," Migration Policy Institute, May 18, 2017, https://www.migrationpolicy.org/article/russia-migration-system-soviet-roots.

9 Ola Chichowlas, "Russia's Abortion Debate is Back," *Moscow Times,* September 29, 2016, https://www.themoscowtimes.com/2016/09/29/russias-abortion-debate-is-back-a55545.

10 Central Intelligence Agency, "Russia," The World Factbook, https://www.cia.gov/library/publications/the-world-factbook/geos/rs.html.

11 Rachel Nuwer, "Why Russian Men Don't Live as Long," *New York Times,* February 17, 2014, https://www.nytimes.com/2014/02/18/science/why-russian-men-dont-live-as-long.html.

12 Sarah Wildman, "Putin Is Angry about U.S. Sanctions—and Russian Orphans Are Paying the Price," *Vox,* July 20, 2017, https://www.vox.com/world/2017/7/20/15984378/putin-trump-jr-magnitsky-act-orphans-adoption.

13 Alan Duke, "Grandmother: Adopted Boy Sent Back to Russia was Violent," *CNN,* April 10, 2010, http://www.cnn.com/2010/US/04/09/us.russian.adoption.return/index.html.

14 Jo Becker, Matt Apuzzo, and Adam Goldman, "Trump's Son Met with Russian Lawyer after Being Promised Damaging Information on Clinton," *New York Times,* July 9, 2017, https://www.nytimes.com/2017/07/09/us/politics/trump-russia-kushner-manafort.html?action=click&module=RelatedCoverage&pgtype=Article&region=Footer.

15 Alex Gray, "The World's Ten Biggest Economies in 2017," World Economic Forum, March 9, 2017, https://www.weforum.org/agenda/2017/03/worlds-biggest-economies-in-2017/.

16 "Number of Russians in Poverty Hits Decade-High," Radio Free Europe/ Radio Liberty, April 6, 2017, https://www.rferl.org/a/recession-sanctions-left-20-million-russians-living-poverty-2016-up-300000-2015/28413387.html.

17 Dave Dodson, "Ohio Farmers Have Already Lost President Trump's Trade War," Cleveland.com, July 31, 2019, https://www.cleveland.com/opinion/2019/07/ohio-farmers-have-already-lost-president-trumps-trade-war-dave-dodson-opinion.html?fbclid=IwAR10gOwbeI55nHJjEETqG7JHSc YIXNbZqMy8zcuDoDsyQVipulYK8RtWhzM.

18 Anna Nemtsova, "Mikhail Khodorkovsky, Putin's Most Powerful Critic-in-Exile, Says He's Living under a Kill Order," *Daily Beast,* October 1, 2018, https://www.thedailybeast.com/mikhail-khodorkovsky-putins-most-powerful-critic-in-exile-should-fear-for-his-lifebut-doesnt.

19 Elena Chernenko, "What Makes Putin So Popular at Home? His Reputation Abroad," *New York Times,* March 26, 2018, https://www.nytimes.com/2018/03/16/opinion/putin-popular-russia-election.html.

20 Jon Swaine and Shaun Walker, "Trump in Moscow: What Happened at Miss Universe in 2013," *The Guardian,* September 18, 2017, https://www.theguardian.com/us-news/2017/sep/18/trump-in-moscow-what-happened-at-miss-universe-in-2013.

21 Caleb Melbi and Keri Geiger, "Behind Trump's Russian Romance, There's a Tower Full of Oligarchs," *Bloomberg Businessweek,* March 16, 2017, https://www.bloomberg.com/news/articles/2017-03-16/behind-trump-s-russia-romance-there-s-a-tower-full-of-oligarchs.

22 Charles P. Pierce, "Surely, It's a Coincidence That a Firm Tied to a Russian Oligarch Is Pouring Millions into Kentucky," *Esquire,* April 24, 2019, https://www.esquire.com/news-politics/politics/a27259438/oleg-deripaska-kentucky-aluminum-mitch-mcconnell-rand-paul/.

23 Alexander Smith, "Trump Calls Out 'Very Aggressive' Montenegro in Latest NATO Jibe," *NBC News,* July 18, 2018, https://www.nbcnews.com/news/world/trump-calls-out-very-aggressive-montenegro-latest-nato-jibe-n892311.

24 Scott Neuman and Sasha Ingber, "Trump Skips Visit to Denmark, Calls Danish Leader 'Nasty' for Greenland Sale Rebuff," NPR, August 21, 2019, https://www.npr.org/2019/08/21/752989771/trump-to-skip-visiting-denmark-after-prime-minister-says-greenland-not-for-sale.

25 Molly K. McKew, "The Gerasimov Doctrine," *Politico Magazine,* September/October 2017, https://www.politico.com/magazine/story/2017/09/05/gerasimov-doctrine-russia-foreign-policy-215538.

26 Agence France-Press, "Russian Trolls Aimed to Deter Black U.S. Voters: Study," Yahoo! News, December 17, 2018, https://news.yahoo.com/russian-troll-farm-aimed-discourage-black-us-voters-164311410.html;_ylt=AwrE1yAb9F5d2aQAbSFXNyoA;_ylu=X3oDMTEyM WhkazFlBGNvbG8DYmYxBHBvcwMzBHZoaWQDQjcyMzBfMQRzZW

MDc3I-. For a wider lens on the December 2018 reports, see Mark Hosenball, "Russia Used Social Media for Widespread Meddling in U.S. Politics," Reuters, December 17, 2018, https://www.reuters.com/article/us-usa-trump-russia-socialmedia/russia-used-social-media-for-widespread-meddling-in-u-s-politics-reports-idUSKBN1OG257.

27 Lia Eustachewich, "Russian Trolls Blamed for Spreading Anti-Vaccination Propaganda," *New York Post,* February 15, 2019, https://nypost.com/2019/02/15/russian-trolls-blamed-for-spreading-anti-vaccination-propaganda/.

28 Dana Farrington, "READ: The Full Mueller Report with Redaction," NPR, April 18, 2019, https://www.npr.org/2019/04/18/708850903/read-the-full-mueller-report-with-redactions.

29 Mark Hertling and Molly K. McKew, "Putin's Attack on the U.S. Is Our Pearl Harbor," *Politico Magazine,* July 16, 2018, https://www.politico.com/magazine/story/2018/07/16/putin-russia-trump-2016-pearl-harbor-219015.

30 Modern Language Association, Language Enrollment Database, 1958–2016, https://apps.mla.org/cgi-shl/docstudio/docs.pl?flsurvey_results.

CHAPTER 9

Erosion of the Liberal Order?

MARY NOLAN

Any discussion of the history of international cooperation and world order since 1945 inevitably concludes with reflections on the future. Hence, the concluding panel of the 2019 Baker Peace Conference was aptly titled "Erosion of the Liberal Order?" This question hovers indecisively between pessimism and optimism. It immediately conjures up a host of anxiety-inducing images: Prime Minister Victor Orbán proudly proclaiming Hungary a model of illiberal democracy; populist parties, such as the Alternative for Germany and the French National Front (renamed the National Rally), gaining support with each regional and national election, while their counterparts in places such as Austria are in the government. There is Brexit, which has called into question the future of the European project of integration that has been so central to the post–World War II order.[1] On this side of the Atlantic, President Donald Trump embraces unilateralism and nationalism as the way to "Make America Great Again." He disparages America's long-standing and loyal European allies and threatens them with tariffs and sanctions. At the February 2019 Munich Security Conference, Vice President Mike Pence proudly conveyed Trump's greetings, only to be met with stony silence from America's allies.[2] Across the Atlantic World, xenophobia, anti-Semitism, and Islamophobia are on the rise, promoting efforts to close borders and limit migration. Globalization is increasingly attacked from right and left, even as the sorts of neoliberal domestic policies that have been integral to it continue to be implemented in most states, fueling growing inequality and insecurity. And one could list many more examples.

Yet there is an optimistic question mark in the panel's title that warns against deterministic gloom. Is the post–World War II liberal order, in its international dimensions and in the national economic and political arrangements that were integral to it, eroding? Should Europeans and Americans seek an alternative? Or is this just a bad patch—and not the first one—in what is still an essential transatlantic relationship to which both sides are committed and to which they do not see a realistic alternative? Over the past few years, politicians and pundits have debated these questions obsessively and inconclusively, while pollsters try to make sense of contradictory data about concerns shared by Europe and the United States on the one hand and increasingly frayed cooperation on the other hand.

I come down on the side of those pessimistic about the future of the liberal international order and the transatlantic relationship central to it. As this chapter will argue, the postwar liberal order and international cooperation central to it are eroding for multiple reasons. The values central to them are being called into question by many on both sides of the Atlantic. The international institutions established after 1945 and the multiple international conventions and treaties signed over the next several decades are likewise coming under increasing attack. These challenges did not emerge only in the last decade but rather have developed cumulatively and unevenly among nations since the 1970s. Of equal importance, the domestic economic and political institutions and arrangements that sustained the transatlantic relationship and fostered international cooperation in the first postwar decades have altered fundamentally. These changes in institutions, values, and the global economic and political context, too, began in the 1970s, intensified after the end of the Cold War and the collapse of the Soviet Union, and accelerated rapidly in the wake of the 2008 Great Recession and 2015 migration crises.

It is not only the values, institutions, and economic and political structures and policies that have changed. The world that Americans and Western Europeans were trying to order after 1945 bears little resemblance to ours today in terms of the distribution of economic and political power and the ideologies and economic theories at play. Some of the pressing issues—a global refugee crisis, for example—that were addressed then through international cooperation (sometimes successfully, sometimes not) were similar to those we face now, while others are markedly different. Global warming is a key case. There appears to be no simple return to the status quo ante of the liberal order as it existed in the second half of the twentieth century. The new global economy, shifting domestic political alignments, and new transnational problems such as climate change and millions of displaced people and refugees call for international cooperation every bit as much as did the aftermath of the Great Depression, World War II, and decolonization after 1945. A stable world order capable of addressing these issues can only be built on a much more inclusive basis than the American-dominated transatlantic one that followed World War II. And it can only be built if dangerous trends toward nationalism, authoritarianism, and racism can be reversed and if diplomacy and dialogue replace confrontation and bullying.

These arguments will be developed not by recounting key moments of cooperation or conflict nor by focusing on how particular American and European leaders understood the liberal world order. Rather, I want to tease out the economic structures and policies and the domestic political constellations that were central to the establishment of the post-1945 world order, the values that sustained it, and the problems it was able to address. I will then sketch how these structures, political orders, and practices have eroded in ways that greatly weakened the postwar liberal order and international cooperation and prevented it from reforming itself and responding to a host of new challenges.

PILLARS OF THE POSTWAR ORDER

The world of 1945 was shaped and scarred by two decades of brutal fascist rule in Europe and East Asia, two world wars, a global depression, and the bloody beginning of decolonization with the partition of the Indian subcontinent. These took a devastating toll on human lives, economies, state structures, and moral values. There was only one hegemonic power economically, the United States, even though the Soviet Union was a military rival. Fascism had been eliminated as a political ideology, state form, and variety of capitalism, leaving only communism as an alternative to liberal or social democratic capitalism. After tentative wartime efforts at collaboration in constructing the economic and international postwar order, the unequal superpowers attempted to construct alternative communist and democratic capitalist world orders and systems of international cooperation. On both sides of what quickly became the Cold War divide, the United States and the Soviet Union sought to promote economic reconstruction and modernization and transform the economies and polities of allies and satellites along democratic capitalist or communist lines. Nations large and small sought to reintegrate, partially or wholly, the global economy after the currency blocs, tariff barriers, and autarky of the interwar years and to replace the failed League of Nations with a more robust international organization.[3]

American architects of a new liberal order attempted to address these problems, first through the creation of new international political institutions—the United Nations (UN) and its associated organizations such as the International Labor Organization and the United Nations Economic, Scientific and Cultural Organization. Second, they, along with their British allies, replaced the dead and discredited gold standard with the new international financial architecture of the Bretton Woods monetary system. As designed by Harry Dexter White and John Maynard Keynes, its pillars were the International Monetary Fund (IMF) and the World Bank (initially called the International Bank for Reconstruction and Development), and the dollar, exchangeable for gold, replaced the British pound as the anchor currency of global finance. Third, a new military alliance, the North Atlantic Treaty Organization (NATO), was established. Its aim was, as its first secretary, Lord Ismay, quipped in 1957, "to keep the Russians out, the Americans in, and the Germans down."[4] The most egregious war criminals were punished, and the Universal Declaration of Human Rights and the Convention against Genocide were endorsed by the UN member states. The United States strove to teach Western Europeans the importance of international law, international institutions, and multilateral cooperation—even if the United States often acted unilaterally. Think, for example, of the Truman Doctrine or the Marshall Plan, where the United States justified acting outside international organizations on the grounds that swift interventions were necessary to combat the threat of communism and protect the American economy.[5]

The United States rallied European support for a new liberal economic order not by appeals to an abstract internationalism or cosmopolitanism but rather by creating a transatlantic consensus around anticommunism and the containment and isolation of the Soviet Union. Washington aided economic reconstruction and modernization in Western Europe via the Marshall Plan and encouraged American foreign direct investment (FDI) by banks and multinational corporations. Government officials and businesspeople alike endorsed European integration, seeing it as beneficial not only to European countries but to American economic interests as well. On both sides of the Atlantic, Keynesianism in the form of deficit spending was adopted, but in Europe more corporatist forms of bargaining among capital, labor, and the state developed, and there was much more direct state intervention in the economy. Western Europeans and Americans implemented much more expansive social policies, although the United States lagged behind its poorer European counterparts in crucial areas such as health care and social housing. Yet the underlying goals of these new economic and social policies were the same on both sides of the Atlantic: to prevent both depression and the egregious inequality and insecurity of earlier decades and secure the future of capitalism. American occupation forces sought to guide West German political democratization in particular, and US government agencies worked overtly and covertly to discourage countries such as France and Italy from supporting communist parties or allowing them into the government. Through a great variety of study trips, educational exchanges, and nongovernmental organizations, American officials, politicians, and academics preached the virtues and practices of American democratic capitalism to Western Europeans of varied ages, professions, and political allegiances.[6]

The United States was the undisputed hegemon in the transatlantic relationship and new liberal order.[7] Its economic prowess was embodied in Fordist mass production, technological innovation, unmatched productivity, and high wages—for white workers at least—that enabled the mass consumption of durable goods on an entirely new scale. Its military might, conventional and nuclear, was unchallenged. The United States benefited from widespread European admiration for its political values, global presence, and popular culture. For its part, Western European countries benefited from the American military presence and security shield, which allowed them to devote themselves to the daunting tasks of reconstruction, modernization, and coming to terms politically and morally with war, collaboration, racial persecution, and genocide. They were willing to be the junior partners in an American empire built largely by invitation in Western Europe but supplemented by American pressure, threats, and covert intervention when necessary.[8]

From both an American and a Western European perspective, the liberal order functioned relatively well in its first postwar decades. Western Europe experienced unprecedentedly high growth rates and developed, albeit on a more modest scale, consumer economies of an American sort. The US economy flourished, even as politicians worried about a growing trade imbalance with Europe due to the cost of stationing American troops there, American FDI, and Europeans' preference to trade among themselves rather than buy American. The result was a gold drain from Fort Knox to various Western European central banks.[9] Despite repeated Berlin crises and fears of Soviet hordes pouring through the Fulda Gap, peace prevailed in Europe (although not outside) due in part to the nuclear arms balance and doctrine of mutually assured destruction. Despite its growing membership as newly independent states in Asia and, above all, Africa joined, the UN still seemed amenable to US and European interests or at least susceptible to pressure from them. The Bretton Woods system promoted financial stability, economic growth, expanded trade, and efforts at Third World development, even as it disproportionately benefited the developed transatlantic world and Japan.

The degree of transatlantic harmony in these years should not be exaggerated, however, for there were ongoing points of disagreement and divergence. After the famous Berlin Airlift of 1948–49, the United States strongly defended the four-power occupation of Berlin but took no concrete actions to support the 1953 uprising in East Berlin or to block the construction of the Berlin Wall in 1961, much to the dismay of West Berliners and West Germans. European contributions to shared defense was a recurring sore point then as now, with special pressure being put on West Germany to make offset payments to help cover the costs of the large number of US troops stationed there. The Germans paid resentfully, and Chancellor Ludwig Erhard, a loyal Christian Democratic ally of the United States, lost the election in 1966. The United States encouraged West German remilitarization, which was strongly opposed by many within Germany and feared by many outside. NATO remained central to the transatlantic partnership, and the European Community (EC) failed to develop its own European Defense Community, but in 1966 France withdrew from the unified NATO military command and developed its own nuclear weapons program despite American opposition.[10]

Decolonization was a repeated source of contention. Europe disliked America's wartime anticolonial rhetoric; Winston Churchill immediately exempted himself from the anticolonial clauses of the 1941 Atlantic Charter he had coauthored, and Charles de Gaulle was determined to reassert French rule in North Africa and Indochina. The United States sought an elusive middle way between immediate decolonization and indefinite perpetuation of European colonial rule. In general, the United States pushed for decolonization if the actual or imagined threat of communism was deemed slight, thus supporting Indian independence and opposing a Dutch return to Indonesia. If the threat was more serious or the economic cost to Europe and the goal of free market global capitalism greater, the United States allowed colonial rule to continue—for example, the British in Malaysia and all powers in sub-Saharan Africa. The United States and Britain cooperated in a coup against the democratically elected government in Iran in 1953 in order to defend Western oil interests. But when the British and French acted militarily and unilaterally to reassert their influence in Egypt, the United States responded with diplomatic anger and devastating attacks on the British pound until its will prevailed.[11] American politicians and pundits complained that the United States never got as much European support for its wars in Korea and Vietnam as it deserved. Despite these disagreements on the details of the transatlantic relationship, in the thirty years of the postwar boom / *Wirtschaftswunder* / *les trente glorieuses,* few on either side of the Atlantic questioned the stability and overall desirability of the liberal postwar order. It provided the central organizational and political framework within which the United States and Western Europe dealt with the twin challenges of the Cold War and decolonization.

THE TROUBLED 1970S AND 1980S

In the 1970s and 1980s, however, many of the foundational policies and premises of the liberal order—international and national—began to weaken. Erosion began first on the economic front.[12] America was no longer the sole economic superpower, for the European Economic Community / Common Market, with six members in the late 1960s and nine by the early 1970s, was almost as large, modern, and productive. As its membership expanded, cooperation deepened, and Europe looked inward as much as across the Atlantic. So, too, did the United States. In 1971, President Richard Nixon unilaterally and without even informing the Europeans decided to abandon the Bretton Woods monetary system and the convertibility of dollars for gold, essential pillars of the postwar international economic architecture. As Nixon so colorfully put it, Europeans "enjoy kicking the United States around. . . . European leaders want to screw us and we want to screw them in the economic arena."[13] (Trump is not the first American president to adopt the stance of angry victim of an ungrateful Europe.) While the destruction of the Bretton Woods system caused economic hardship and fluctuating exchange rates for the EC in the short run, it led the Western Europeans to increasingly coordinate their currencies in the long run, a process that culminated in the creation of the euro by century's end.

The postwar boom, which had been fueled by reconstruction, industrialization, modernization, and urbanization, gradually slowed, and the once booming economies on both sides of the North Atlantic began to suffer from the new disease of stagflation—an unhappy mix of slower growth, rising unemployment, and higher inflation, for which countercyclical government spending and welfare programs provided no cure. Fordism, which centered on the mass production of standardized consumer durables from cars to televisions and had been the core of the American economy since the 1920s, faced unprecedented competition from Japan and then the economies of the Four Asian Tigers: Hong Kong, Singapore, South Korea, and Taiwan. Outsourcing and deindustrialization began not only in the United States but in Europe as well, albeit later and more slowly. Politicians and economists turned away from Keynesianism and experimented with a range of policies that coalesced by the 1980s into a neoliberal consensus around privatization, trade liberalization, deregulation, balanced budgets, and the free flow of capital across national borders. On both sides of the Atlantic, politicians, businesspeople, and academics anguished about what the Trilateral Commission called the "crisis of democracy." In the wake of the tumultuous 1960s, the United States, Western Europe, and Japan were ostensibly becoming ungovernable because too many demands were being made by too many social actors who displayed too little discipline. Expertise and seniority needed to be restored, it was argued; efficiency should take priority over the pursuit of equality. People should develop realistic expectations.[14] This was a far cry from the heady promises of the first postwar decades when a powerful America urged Europe to become like it through hard work and emulation.

Western European and US leaders came to disagree quite publicly on a host of issues. Détente was among the most contentious, with the

United States, propelled by Henry Kissinger, envisioning it as the business of the two superpowers and a way to get more security at lower costs and to stabilize the postwar order. Europeans Eastern and Western envisioned détente as a way for the nonsuperpowers to renegotiate relations across the Iron Curtain and gain more economic and political autonomy. Germany's engagement with the east (*Ostpolitik*) and the Helsinki Accords were at the heart of this project, and while bridge builders in the State Department supported them, Nixon and Kissinger did so only reluctantly and belatedly.[15] There were disagreements between Europe and the United States (and within Europe as well) about how to respond to the 1973 oil crisis and the rise of Organization of the Petroleum Exporting Countries. The placement of intermediate-range Pershing II missiles and cruise missiles (the so-called Euromissiles) sparked massive protests across Europe, turning angry citizens against compliant European governments and the United States. In the end, some European governments accepted the missiles, but they did not comply with US sanctions against Poland for repressing protest in the early 1980s.

As transatlantic economic tensions mounted in early 1970s, Kissinger unilaterally called for a New Atlantic Charter and proclaimed 1973 "the Year of Europe." His actions were not well received. German chancellor Willy Brandt objected to the term "Atlantic Charter" as the original had targeted Germany. British prime minister Edward Heath complained that "for Henry Kissinger to announce a Year of Europe without consulting any of us was rather like my standing between the lions of Trafalgar Square and announcing that we were embarking on a year to save America."[16] America longed for the dominance and deference it had enjoyed in the 1950s and 1960s but could not re-create it. Europe enjoyed somewhat more autonomy but could not become the independent global presence it longed to be. And as the Cold War ebbed and flowed, it continued to make alternatives to the transatlantic relationship unthinkable.

Less noticed in the 1970s and 1980s, but very consequential thereafter, were three complex changes going on outside the transatlantic world. The first was globalization, which transformed European and American economies by increasing international trade and creating new competition from successful economic powers, first Japan and then South Korea and the other Asian Tigers. This encouraged the financialization of Western European and especially American economies as well as privatization and deregulation. The second was the beginning of the transformation of China, which was recognized as a future challenge by the United States in the early 1970s and launched its economic reform program under Deng Xiaoping at decade's end.[17] The third was the emergence of Islamic fundamentalism, with particular hotspots in Iran and Afghanistan. All were to profoundly challenge the liberal world order within and among nations.

AFTER THE COLD WAR

Fast-forward to 1989, a year that marked the triumph of the liberal order and yet simultaneously undermined still more of its premises. The United States was now the only superpower, liberal democracy had no ideological competitors (although liberal democratic states faced plenty of nonideological authoritarian ones), and capitalism of an increasingly neoliberal variety reigned supreme. But would Europe matter to America outside of a Cold War context? In December 1989, Secretary of State James Baker insisted, with an arrogance meant to be reassuring, that "the United State is and will remain a European power."[18] Yet by mid-1990, even before the Soviet Union had collapsed, the United States was involved in the Gulf War, and from then on the Middle East was a major, if not the major, preoccupation for every president.[19]

NATO had kept the Russians out and the Americans in but not the Germans down. Did it still have a purpose, and if so, what was its new mission to be and who would be a part of it? Expansion eastward, which occurred much faster than the growth of the Common Market, and involvement in Bosnia and Kosovo provided initial but not unproblematic answers. The EC still failed to develop a common security policy and military force. It transformed itself into the European Union (EU), many of whose members shared a common currency, the euro, although not a shared banking system or tax and fiscal policies. It expanded southward and eastward, and while new member states initially benefited, the seeds of the post-2008 debt crises were laid in these years. Throughout the 1990s, Europe became every bit as self-absorbed as the United States was, for German reunification proved costly, the transition from socialism to capitalism in Central and Eastern Europe was slow and difficult, and the development of liberal democracies proved partial at best.

Over the next decade and a half, trade, investment, cultural products, and people moved back and forth across the Atlantic in ever greater numbers as the economies became, for better or worse, ever more entangled. But cooperation on issues of foreign policy and defense proved more contentious. Take the Gulf War. Europeans initially advocated diplomacy but came to see war as necessary. While the British and French sent troops to aid the Americans, other nations sent only money or matériel and medical supplies—much to Washington's disappointment. As the EU and the UN became involved in the bloody disintegration of Yugoslavia, America claimed not to have a dog in that fight, to paraphrase Baker. In the wake of the Srebrenica massacres and mass rapes, however, the United States did step in, brokered the Dayton Accords, and controlled the NATO forces thereafter. Europe, lacking its own integrated military force, still needed the United States.[20]

Europe rallied behind the United States after the 9/11 attacks, invoking for the first time Article 5, NATO's self-defense clause. America preferred to fight alone, however, requesting help only for peacekeeping and reconstruction in Afghanistan. NATO's presence remains as protracted as the war itself. The Iraq War proved much more divisive, for many Europeans doubted the American claim that Saddam Hussein had weapons of mass destruction. Of the European allies, only Britain, Denmark, Portugal, Poland, and Spain sent troops. Millions of Europeans took to the streets on February 15, 2003, to protest the impending war. American politicians and pundits criticized Europeans as weak, immoral, emasculated. In reply, Jürgen Habermas and Jacques Derrida, leading European philosophers, issued the manifesto "February 15, or, What Binds Europeans Together." They condemned American unilateralism and the illegal preemptive invasion of Iraq and defended the European preference for diplomacy and the distinctive European social model as well. They criticized the United States for withdrawing from the Kyoto Accord on global warming and for refusing to sign either the land mine treaty or the Convention on the Elimination of All Forms of Discrimination against Women.[21] Europeans were now trying to teach internationalism and multilateralism to their former teachers—with little success. Mutual vitriol declined in the subsequent years of endless war and endless, rather futile reconstruction that followed, but mutual mistrust by no means disappeared. The constraining and containing context of the Cold War was gone, and neither Islamic fundamentalism nor the war on terror proved a unifying substitute.

ECONOMIC CRISIS AND POLITICAL POLARIZATION

Fast-forward again to the 2008 financial crisis and its messy aftermath of bank bailouts and housing foreclosures, of austerity and social policy cuts, of youth unemployment and growing precarity. What had begun as a banking crisis became in many parts of Europe a sovereign debt crisis, and the market was given priority over the state, ostensibly apolitical expertise over democratic politics, and shareholders over other stakeholders. The response of national governments, the EU, and the IMF benefited banks and businesses but not homeowners or employees. A crisis that initially seemed to call neoliberal policies and practices into question ended up reinforcing them. In Europe and America, politicians, bankers, business leaders, economists, and the IMF repeatedly invoked Margaret Thatcher's famous assertion that "there is no alternative."[22]

Economic crises, the responses to them, and their ongoing detrimental effects undermined many people's faith in their national political parties and policies, in the EU, and in the economic globalization that was integral to the liberal order. Crises and responses fueled a disintegration of the postwar political party system that had begun with the demise of communist parties and then many socialist ones in countries such as France and Italy. After 2008, the center-right and center-left parties that had been the mainstay of the liberal order at home and abroad saw their base of support erode. Christian Democrats and Social Democrats in Germany, for example, suffered repeated electoral losses to left, Green, and new right parties. In the United States, the Republican Party changed many of its long-held beliefs and policies as it shifted dramatically to the right. Most troubling has been the rise of new right-radical populist movements in the United States and virtually every European country. These new parties claim to represent the people against elites, even as they serve corporate and banking economic interests. They embrace a my-county-first nationalism that is ethnically based, racist, antifeminist, and both anti-Semitic and Islamophobic. Although they run candidates for elections and play by the parliamentary rules of the game, if in power they erode democratic forms and norms. For example, Viktor Orbán, the prime minister of Hungary since 2010 and head of the right-wing party Fidesz, has altered electoral laws, limited press freedoms, and revamped the judiciary so as enhance the power of his party and create a self-proclaimed "illiberal democracy." Right-radical populists ranging from

Fidesz and Law and Justice in Poland to the Alternative for Germany and the French National Rally have no commitment to the post–World War II liberal order in its domestic instantiations or to international cooperation. Right-radical populists are, to be sure, well networked with one another and share many common goals, but they seek to promote national goals first and then, at most, European or white and Western ones. They see little useful or salvageable in the EU, NATO, or the UN.[23]

IS THE POSTWAR ORDER HISTORY?

A majority of Europeans value the transatlantic relationship but believe it is increasingly endangered, while Americans, insofar as they pay attention to it, either believe all is well or any problems are solely the fault of Europe. Those still committed to the institutions and values of the liberal order find it increasingly difficult to cooperate on old problems as well as new ones. The fault lies primarily but not exclusively with the United States. As *New York Times* columnist Roger Cohen so aptly noted, "Trump has never encountered a multilateralism he does not loathe."[24] Nor, one should add, an international agreement he did not want to shred or leave. Take the Iran nuclear deal. The Europeans defend it, arguing that Iran was in compliance—or was until the United States unilaterally withdrew from the accord, imposed sanctions, and threatened harsh punishments to any European businesses that try to trade with or invest in Iran. The private SWIFT system that facilitates international money transfers has caved in to American threats and excluded all Iranian banks.[25] European efforts to set up an international payments system, Instrument in Support of Trade Exchange (INSTEX), as an alternative have failed, and in any case few European corporations are willing to risk losing their American trade and profits.[26] Should the United States try regime change via military means in Iran, something National Security Adviser John Bolton and Secretary of State Mike Pompeo seemed to passionately desire, Europeans would likely not endorse the move or cooperate. But nor could they stop such an effort. Or take climate change. Here again Europeans are united in support of the 2016 Paris Agreement, but the United States, again acting unilaterally, has initiated its withdrawal. Without a major polluter cooperating, the chances of avoiding catastrophic warming are greatly diminished. Efforts to strengthen Euro-American economic ties have failed due to European opposition to many deregulatory aspects of the proposed Transatlantic Trade and Investment Partnership on the one hand and President Trump's imposition of tariffs on European steel and aluminum with threats of more to come on the other. Predictably, retaliatory EU tariffs on American goods have followed.[27]

But it is not merely a case of the liberal order being endangered by a widening Atlantic. As can be seen with Hungary, Poland, and the United Kingdom, divisions within Europe about liberalism and about international or intra-EU cooperation are growing steadily. Take China. The United States and multiple EU countries all have complex economic relationships with China. All are suspicious—rightly or wrongly—of Chinese aspirations and policies; all are ambivalent about recognizing that China is now a power of equal economic might and global influence with the EU and with the United States. Yet each country pursues its own interests via bilateral means. The recent case of Italy joining China's Belt and Road Initiative is instructive. Other EU countries and the United States urged Italy not to sign on, but the Italian government rightly remarked that its critics had much more trade and investment with China than did Italy, a country in need of infrastructure projects that the EU and United States would hardly fund.[28]

Refugees are another source of intra-European and transatlantic tension. The refugee crisis that began in 2015 and persists on a smaller scale down to the present can only be solved on a European-wide or even global basis, but so far it has proven impossible to get EU states to agree on shared quotas or criteria for aiding those refused entry or returned. Each state is acting alone and punitively, just as the United States is on its southern border. The post–World War II refugee crisis, one of a magnitude and global scale comparable to the present one, was dealt with through international institutions—or partially so, for the only refugees cared for were those in Europe and Mandatory Palestine, even though the crisis was acute in both India and China.[29] Nonetheless, that earlier refugee experience shows that global refugee crises, created today by wars in the Middle East involving Europe and the United States, civil wars in Africa, decades of US interventions in Central America, and the devastating effects of climate change, can only be solved through international cooperation.

The liberal order constructed after 1945 has not been able to deal with problems such as China, Iran, climate change, and the new refugee crisis. This is because the global economic and political context in which that order developed has changed and so too have many of the key political movements, economic policies, and values that sustained it. That order was built on US leadership and European ambivalence about being an equal global player. That order was too Euro-America centric, too trapped in the ethnic and racial hierarchies of the colonial era, too unwilling to treat those outside the Global North as equal partners. The liberal order reflected the transition from the British-dominated long nineteenth century to the American-dominated twentieth. The latter is now over, and it is an open question whether the twenty-first century will be multipolar or Chinese.

Can a new world order and forms of international cooperation adequate to the world in which we live and the problems we face be built? I am a historian, professionally preoccupied with the past, not the future. Nonetheless it seems appropriate to conclude with the Italian philosopher-politician Antonio Gramsci's recommendation: Pessimism of the intellect; optimism of the will. Pessimism of the intellect so as to recognize the magnitude and complexity of the challenges we face and an optimism of the will, because if we fail to defend liberal values, international law, social and economic justice, and human rights and to restore effective international cooperation, there may not be a world left to order.

NOTES

1 In September 2020, when this essay was completed, the British government was threatening to alter the Brexit treaty it had signed and a no-deal exit remained a possibility. Even though there was in the end an agreement on the Brexit process, the broader point still stands.

2 "Vice President Pence's Remarks at Munich Security Conference," February 15, 2019, C-SPAN, https://www.c-span.org/video/?c4780657/vice-president-pence-greeting-president-trump-met-silence-munich-security-conference.

3 For the different paths to modernization and world order, see, e.g., Odd Arne Westad, *The Global Cold War: Third World Interventions and the Making of Our Time* (Cambridge: Cambridge University Press, 2005), 1–72.

4 Geoffrey Wheatcroft, "Who Needs NATO?," *New York Times,* June 15, 2011, https://www.nytimes.com/2011/06/16/opinion/16iht-edwheatcroft16.html.

5 The analysis of the construction of the postwar order is developed at length in Mary Nolan, *The Transatlantic Century: Europe and America, 1890–2010* (Cambridge University Press, 2012), 171–201. See also Elizabeth Borgwardt, *A New Deal for the World: America's Vision for Human Rights* (Cambridge, MA: Harvard University Press, 2005); Melvyn P. Leffler, *For the Soul of Mankind: The United States, the Soviet Union and the Cold War* (New York: Hill and Wang,

2007); and Mark Mazower, *Governing the World: The History of an Idea* (New York: Penguin, 2012), 191–241.

6 Nolan, *Transatlantic Century,* 201–6. See also Victoria de Grazia, *Irresistible Empire: America's Advance through Twentieth-Century Europe* (Cambridge, MA: Belknap Press, 2005), 336–457, and David W. Ellwood, *The Shock of America: Europe and the Challenge of the Century* (Oxford University Press, 2012), 215–440.

7 Daniel J. Sargent, "Pax Americana: Sketches for an Undiplomatic History," *Diplomatic History* 42, vol. 3 (2018): 357–76.

8 Geir Lundestad, "Empire by Invitation? The United States and Western Europe, 1945–52," *Journal of Peace Research* 23, no. 2 (September 1986): 263–77; *"Empire" by Integration: The United States and European Integration, 1945–1957* (Oxford: Oxford University Press, 1998).

9 Francis J. Gavin, *Gold, Dollars and Power: The Politics of International Monetary Relations, 1958–1971* (Chapel Hill: University of North Carolina Press, 2004), 33–116; Diane B. Kunz, *Butter and Guns: America's Cold War Economic Diplomacy* (New York: Free Press, 1997), 149–79.

10 Nolan, *Transatlantic Century,* 213–21.

11 Nolan, 221–25.

12 For an introduction to the multiple crises—economic, political, and cultural—in the 1970s, see *The Shock of the Global: The 1970s in Perspective,* ed. Niall Ferguson, Charles S. Maier, Erez Manela, and Daniel J. Sargent (Cambridge, MA: Belknap Press, 2010).

13 Herbert Zimmermann, "Unraveling the Ties That Really Bind: The Dissolution of the Transatlantic Monetary Order and the European Monetary Cooperation, 1965–1973," in *The Strained Alliance: United States-European Relations from Nixon to Carter,* ed. Matthias Schulz and Thomas A. Schwartz (Cambridge University Press, 2010), 136.

14 Michel Crozier, Samuel P. Huntington, and Joji Watanuki, *The Crisis of Democracy* (New York University Press, 1975).

15 Angela Romano, *From Détente in Europe to European Détente* (Brussels: Peter Lang, 2009); Jussi Hanhimaki, "'They Can Write It in Swahili': Kissinger, the Soviets, and the Helsinki Accords, 1973–75," *Journal of Transatlantic Studies* 1, no. 1 (2003): 37–58; Stephan Kieninger, *Dynamic Détente: The United States and Europe, 1964–1975* (Lanham, MD: Lexington Books, 2016).

16 Daniel Möckli, "Asserting Europe's Distinct Identity: The EC Nine and Kissinger's Year of Europe," in Schulz and Schwartz, *Strained Alliance,* 199–202.

17 Jeffry A. Frieden, *Global Capitalism: Its Fall and Rise in the Twentieth Century* (New York: W. W. Norton, 2006), 363–434.

18 James Baker, "Upheaval in the East," *New York Times,* December 13, 1989, https://www.nytimes.com/1989/12/13/world/upheaval-east-excerpts-baker-s-speech-berlin-us-role-europe-s-future.html?.

19 Andrew J. Bacevich, *America's War for the Greater Middle East: A Military History* (New York: Random House, 2016).
20 Nolan, *Transatlantic Century,* 332–37, 357–62.
21 Jürgen Habermas and Jacques Derrida, "February 15, or, What Binds Europeans Together: Plea for a Common Foreign Policy, Beginning in Core Europe," in *Old Europe, New Europe, Core Europe: Transatlantic Relations after the Iraq War,* ed. Daniel Levy, Max Pensky, and John Torpey (London: Verso, 2005), 3–13.
22 For the most comprehensive discussion of the 2008 crisis, see Adam Tooze, *Crashed: How a Decade of Financial Crises Changed the World* (New York: Viking, 2018).
23 The literature on right-radical populism and the current crisis of liberal democracy is voluminous and growing. The most comprehensive introduction is Cas Mudde, ed., *The Populist Radical Right: A Reader* (London and New York: Routledge, 2017).
24 Roger Cohen, "Munich or a Requiem for the West," *New York Times,* February 15, 2019, https://www.nytimes.com/2019/02/15/opinion/munich-trump-europe-iran.html.
25 SWIFT stands for the Society for Worldwide Interbank Financial Telecommunication.
26 Siobhan Dowling, "INSTEX: Doubts Linger over Europe's Iran Sanctions Workaround," *Al Jazeera,* July 1, 2019, https://www.aljazeera.com/ajimpact/instex-doubts-linger-europe-iran-sanctions-workaround-190701095202660.html.
27 "Tariff Wars: Duties Imposed by Trump and U.S. Trading partners," Reuters, August 1, 2019, https://www.reuters.com/article/us-usa-trade-tariffs-factbox/tariff-wars-duties-imposed-by-trump-and-u-s-trading-partners-idUSKCN1UR5YD.
28 Noah Barkin, "China Backlash: Toward a Transatlantic Agenda?," June 13, 2019, American Institute for Contemporary German Studies, https://www.aicgs.org/publication/china-backlash-toward-a-transatlantic-agenada. Frederiga Bindi, "Why Did Italy Embrace the Belt and Road Initiative?," Carnegie Endowment for International Peace, May 20, 2019, https://carnegieendowment.org/2019/05/20/why-did-italy-embrace-belt-and-road-initiative-pub-79149.
29 Peter Gatrell, *The Making of the Modern Refugee* (New York: Oxford University Press, 2015).

POSTSCRIPT

INGO TRAUSCHWEIZER

Reflecting on the state of the world and its foundational institutions in the summer of 2020 in the context of the coronavirus pandemic could lead to conclusions that are overly pessimistic. And yet the points offered by two seasoned observers of transatlantic relations on the state of NATO—that America's allies had begun to seriously doubt Washington's leadership and that the alliance had "preexisting conditions" before 2020—ring true for most international organizations.[1] It may well be that the Donald Trump administration's policies turn out to be more ordinary than radical in the sense that actions and outcomes do not match public pronouncements.[2] It is clear, however, that a combination of nativist rhetoric and mercurial mood swings broadcast in White House press briefings and on Twitter has undermined trust among Europeans—and many US citizens too—for the foreseeable future. In addition, Trump's decisions to abandon the Paris Agreement, withdraw from the Iran nuclear deal, and cast doubt on whether the United States would act on NATO's Article 5—the commitment to defend allies—could hardly be qualified as ordinary measures.[3] Yet the nationalist turn taken by Trump hardly stands out as unique at the end of a decade defined at least in part by fraying democratic norms in states such as Hungary and Poland, by mounting frustrations with the European Union in most members states, and accentuated by Brexit as much as by autocratic leaders in Beijing and Moscow who do not subscribe to Western conceptions of universal values or global institutions. The liberal order propagated after World War II and largely maintained throughout the Cold War era has been fraying.

Some of the issues are not new. Within NATO, for example, as shown in the chapters by Seth Givens and Stephan Kieninger, burden-sharing in military and financial terms has been contested from the first days of the alliance some seventy-two years ago. In fact, disagreement over who ought to pay and how much has been a more consistent theme than containment of the Soviet Union, détente, or eastward expansion since the end of the Cold War. In the economic realm, too, bloc thinking was embedded in the early Cold War—perhaps a logical outgrowth of the grand alliance of World War II—and once the Marshall Plan and its component pieces were in place, integrating a "Western" (European and transatlantic) economy did not supersede national interest even as the steps taken in the late 1940s and 1950s deepened both the East-West and North-South divides, points explored in the chapters by Armin Grünbacher and Alanna O'Malley.

Grünbacher noted that the finer points of European and transatlantic economic cooperation still have not been studied in a global context. O'Malley, assessing the Congo Crisis of the 1960s, showed the inherent weakness of the United Nations, an organization that was not designed to act decisively to enhance stability, security, or prosperity without the consent and backing of its predominant members. This was hardly confined to Africa or the 1960s, and it forced relatively wealthy and developing states outside of Europe and the main Cold War alliances to chart their own course—notably in the equally indecisive Non-Aligned Movement—and as "middle powers" (to use the parlance of political science and international relations studies) or "neighborhood powers."[4] Laura Seddelmeyer considered that process in Australia in the wake of the Vietnam War; one could also look at Latin America, especially as military dictatorships came to define regional politics in the 1960s and 1970s and South American leaders entered into tacit anticommunist coalitions.[5] From the vantage point of 2020, one may well get the impression that international organizations—indeed, the entire UN framework—are bound to face fierce resistance either from Washington, Moscow, or Beijing or from groupings of smaller, less powerful states.

It would be a mistake to view the UN framework exclusively as a top-down means for great powers to shape world politics. Part of the reason for the frustrations felt in the capitals of the most powerful states is precisely that they cannot dictate policy directions to world organizations. An illustration of this may be found in the recent attack by the Trump administration (strongly backed by Britain) on the World Health Organization and its role in helping to cover up supposedly much higher figures of covid-19 cases and deaths in China and the plea by Russian foreign minister Sergei Lavrov not to play politics with a crisis that requires a global response.[6] More generally, despite a seemingly sturdy institutional framework, there is no global strategy in place to address the most critical issues of our time that require more than national responses—most prominently, climate change, mass movement of refugees and migrants, and global public health.[7] These are not, however, signs of impending systemic failure. Instead, world organizations have served as platform for debate, and militarily, economically, or politically weaker states and nonstate actors such as those depicted in Steven Metz's chapter found ways to utilize the UN and other forums to broadcast their messages in battles for public opinion. The most prominent examples include the Algerian National Liberation Front in the 1950s and early 1960s and the Vietnamese communists, typically with Hanoi putting forward the National Liberation Front as a supposedly independent southern opposition movement. Both won their wars, against France and the United States, respectively, because they were able to integrate a strategy built on military perseverance and successful public relations.[8]

Even though the conclusions drawn in this volume, particularly by Mary Nolan in her reflections on the trajectory of the transatlantic community and the decline in shared values and by Ambassador Jennifer Brush in her firsthand observations of Vladimir Putin's (and Russia's) foreign policy and the challenges it has posed to a liberal international order in the past decades, point to a world order at sea, depicting a liberal system in disrepair and nothing else in place to provide stability, the longer-term perspectives provided in these pages also allow for a more optimistic reading. Nolan concluded that the transatlantic century is over and American world leadership is at an impasse, but as Elizabeth Borgwardt noted, the institutions put in place by New Dealers and their friends and allies in the mid-1940s—in the political, economic, legal, and military realms—always had a pragmatic bent and offered sufficient ambiguity for such different actors as the United States and the Soviet Union to join in a global community. By its very nature, this meant that the system could not be overly prescriptive or rigid. It has been defined by generally shared values, by an agreement in principle that stability, security, and prosperity ought to be fundamental rights (or, at least, aspirations) of all mankind, and even though there was never widespread agreement on some of the terms or on the pathways, the post-1945 framework nevertheless persisted through proxy wars and major crises of the Cold War and through the early decades of the war on terror. The strength and weakness of the system thus have the same roots, and the ambiguity built in should allow political leaders to exercise good will and restore a global framework that will help guide constructive steps forward. In other words, this was never meant to be a world state but rather a meeting place for contingent actors.

Taken together, these nine chapters offered a plea to policymakers and ordinary people to keep that in mind and not to assume that institutions have singular purposes, that people make choices even if they often turn on the system—as has been practiced for many years by European leaders who cast blame on their own collective decisions in Brussels when trying to appeal to national constituencies. The liberal postwar order was intended as a collective endeavor between states and peoples. It has been imperfect, but it is not written in stone that it is bound to fail, and it looks fairly good when compared to the decades of war that came before. It is—or at least should be—a negotiation space, not a means to impose leadership of a small handful of great powers. Below the surface, and often hidden from sensationalist headlines and short attention spans, trade negotiations and international as well as transnational conversations continue, often with stabilizing effects. Much like the optimism that marked the end of the Cold War (at least in the United States) was misplaced, so is the doom-and-gloom pessimism three decades later. If the current pandemic offers any instant lessons, one may well be that much of the world continues to hope for American leadership within the liberal international framework.[9] As of mid-April 2020, the Trump administration's announcement to withhold US contributions to the World Health Organization drew immediate criticisms from within (e.g., the American Medical Association) and without (e.g., UN secretary-general António Guterres, the African Union, and the foreign ministries of China and Germany).[10] The specter of a post-American, postliberal world does not seem to appeal to all that many leaders and observers around the globe, especially since powers such as China that could perhaps lead—from a material point of view—do not have the faith of much of the rest of the world and may in fact be economically dependent on the persistence of global trade underwritten by the United States.[11]

NOTES

1 Philip H. Gordon and Jeremy Shapiro, "The Atlantic Alliance Had Preexisting Conditions: The Pandemic Will Worsen Them," *War on the Rocks,*

April 13, 2020, https://warontherocks.com/2020/04/the-atlantic-alliance-had-preexisting-conditions-the-pandemic-will-worsen-them/?fbclid=IwAR1iFwgx1dhp7slXIXBxExwo-gSWLjdi1wgLYRsoMsze__P9d784BwBXoPs.

2 Jon Herbert, Trevor McCrisken, and Jon Andrew Wroe, *The Ordinary Presidency of Donald J. Trump* (London: Palgrave, 2019).

3 Gordon and Shapiro, "Preexisting Conditions."

4 See, e.g., Carsten Holbraad, *Middle Powers in International Politics* (London: Macmillan, 1984); Eduard Jordaan, "The Concept of a Middle Power in International Relations: Distinguishing between Emerging and Traditional Middle Powers," *Politikon: South African Journal of Political Studies* 30, no. 1 (2003): 165–81; and Allan Patience, "Imagining Middle Powers," *Australian Journal of International Affairs* 68, no. 2 (2014): 210–24.

5 Hal Brands, *Latin America's Cold War* (Cambridge, MA: Harvard University Press, 2010).

6 Vladimir Isachenkov, "Russia's Foreign Minister Rejects Suggestion of Using the Pandemic to Expand Political Influence," *Time*, April 14, 2020, https://time.com/5820490/russia-foreign-minister-coronavirus-unity/.

7 For the nationalist turn and its limitations, see, e.g., Kapil Kommiredi, "Modi's India Isn't Prepared for the Coronavirus," *Foreign Policy*, April 10, 2020, https://foreignpolicy.com/2020/04/10/modis-india-isnt-prepared-for-the-coronavirus/, and Garvan Walshe, "Viktor Orban Can't Eradicate the Coronavirus by Decree," *Foreign Policy*, April 14, 2020, https://foreignpolicy.com/2020/04/14/hungary-viktor-orban-authoritarianism-cant-eradicate-coronavirus-by-decree/.

8 Matthew Connelly, *A Diplomatic Revolution: Algeria's Fight for Independence and the Origins of the Post-Cold War Era* (New York: Oxford University Press, 2002); Pierre Asselin, "Revisionism Triumphant: Hanoi's Diplomatic Strategy in the Nixon Era," *Journal of Cold War Studies* 13, no. 4 (Fall 2011): 101–37; Pierre Asselin, "'We Don't Want a Munich': Hanoi's Diplomatic Strategy, 1965–1968," *Diplomatic History* 36, no. 3 (June 2012): 547–81; Pierre Asselin, *Vietnam's American War: A History* (Cambridge: Cambridge University Press, 2018).

9 Philip H. Gordon, "'America First' Is a Dangerous Fantasy in a Pandemic," *Foreign Affairs*, April 4, 2020, tps://www.foreignaffairs.com/articles/2020-04-04/america-first-dangerous-fantasy-pandemic?utm_campaign=fb_daily_soc&utm_source=facebook_posts&utm_medium=social&fbclid=IwAR1hY8tLDERoDwFsookmPt5_n1bu46Z33XVa5Q4iYjzRKGF8OoWc2esqR-4; Karen Donfried and Wolfgang Ischinger, "The Pandemic and the Toll of Transatlantic Discord," *Foreign Affairs*, April 18, 2020, https://www.foreignaffairs.com/articles/united-states/2020-04-18/pandemic-and-toll-transatlantic-discord?utm_medium=social&utm_campaign=fb_daily_soc&utm_source=facebook_posts&fbclid=IwAR1pcNzow2aR4W-gbYeY3g6yPENhyfhv3lImX_pa6ryQ_MCTNjypmaqB-uY.

10 "World Leaders Denounce Trump's Cuts to WHO Funding," *New York Times,* April 15, 2020, https://www.nytimes.com/2020/04/15/world/coronavirus-news.html?action=click&module=LiveUpdates&pgtype=Homepage&action=click&module=Spotlight&pgtype=Homepage#link-50593e90. On the folly of nationalist and bellicose responses to the coronavirus crisis, see also Mark Hannah, "Stop Declaring War on a Virus," *War on the Rocks,* April 17, 2020, https://warontherocks.com/2020/04/stop-declaring-war-on-a-virus/.

11 Gordon H. Chang, "China Is Flailing in a Post-Coronavirus World," *Strategika,* no. 64, April 23, 2020, https://www.hoover.org/research/china-flailing-post-coronavirus-world; Michael Green and Evan S. Medeiros, "The Pandemic Won't Make China the World's Leader," *Foreign Policy,* April 15, 2020, https://www.foreignaffairs.com/articles/united-states/2020-04-15/pandemic-wont-make-china-worlds-leader?utm_source=linkedIn_posts&utm_medium=social&utm_campaign=ln_daily_soc; H. R. McMaster, "How China Sees the World," *The Atlantic,* May 2020, https://www.theatlantic.com/magazine/archive/2020/05/mcmaster-china-strategy/609088/.

CONTRIBUTORS

ELIZABETH BORGWARDT is an associate professor of history and law at Washington University. She has published widely on human rights ideas and institutions, including *A New Deal for the World: America's Vision for Human Rights* (Harvard University Press, 2005).

JENNIFER BRUSH is a retired ambassador. She spent twenty-eight years in service to the United States and the United Nations, with particular expertise on the former Soviet Union and the Balkans. Among other high-profile appointments, Brush led the OSCE Mission in Moldova (2012–14) and served as deputy special representative of the UN secretary-general to the UN peacekeeping mission in Kosovo (2014–15). Prior to that, she served as Balkans Director for the State Department (2010–12).

SETH GIVENS is a historian at the US Marine Corps History Division. Givens, who is working on books on Berlin in the Cold War and on the Marines in the Iraq War, won the 2018 Cold War Essay Prize of the John A. Adams Center for Military History and Strategic Analysis. His article "Liberating the Germans: The US Army and Looting in Germany during the Second World War" appeared in *War in History* in January 2014.

ARMIN GRÜNBACHER is a senior lecturer in modern history at the University of Birmingham. Grünbacher is the author of *Reconstruction and Cold War in Germany: The Kreditanstalt für Wiederaufbau, 1948–1961* (Ashgate, 2004), *The Makin`vg of German Democracy: West Germany during the Adenauer Era, 1945–1965* (Manchester University Press 2010), and *West German Industrialists and the Making of the Economic Miracle: A History of Mentality and Recovery* (Bloomsbury, 2017).

STEPHAN KIENINGER is an independent historian and former fellow at Johns Hopkins University's School of Advanced International Studies and the Berlin Center for Cold War Studies. Kieninger is the author of *The Diplomacy of Détente: Cooperative Security Policies from Helmut Schmidt to George Shultz* (Routledge, 2018) and *Dynamic Détente: The United States and Europe, 1964–1975* (Rowman & Littlefield, 2016).

STEVEN METZ is a professor of national security affairs at the US Army War College and a fellow at the Quincy Institute for Responsible Statecraft. Metz has published widely on contemporary military issues and US wars in the twenty-first century. His books include *Iraq and the Evolution of American Strategy* (University of Nebraska Press, 2008) and *Learning from Iraq: Counterinsurgency in American Strategy* (Strategic Studies Institute, 2014).

MARY NOLAN is an emeritus professor of history at New York University. She has published in a wide range of fields: Europe and America in the twentieth century, the Cold War, the history of human rights, the global economy in twentieth century, modern German history, and European women's history. Nolan's books include *Visions of Modernity: American Business and the Modernization of Germany* (Oxford University Press, 1994) and *The Transatlantic Century: Europe and America, 1890–2010* (Cambridge University Press, 2012).

ALANNA O'MALLEY is Professor of United Nations Studies in Peace and Justice at Leiden University. She is a historian focusing on the United Nations, decolonization, the Congo, and the Cold War. Her first book, *The Diplomacy of Decolonisation: America, Britain and the United Nations during the Congo Crisis 1960–64,* was published by Manchester University Press in 2018 and was named as one of the top twenty best new diplomacy books to read in 2020 by BookAuthority.

LAURA M. SEDDELMEYER is an assistant professor of history at Lycoming College. She is completing a book that examines Australia's place within a changing global environment by questioning how the British withdrawal from east of the Suez Canal and changes in American policy toward Asia affected the close relationship between English-speaking allies in the 1960s and 1970s.

INGO TRAUSCHWEIZER is a professor of history and the director of the Contemporary History Institute at Ohio University. He has previously coedited *Failed States and Fragile Societies: A New World Disorder?* (Ohio University Press, 2014) in the Baker Series in Peace and Conflict Studies, and he is the author of *The Cold War U.S. Army: Building Deterrence for Limited War* (University Press of Kansas, 2008) and *Maxwell Taylor's Cold War: From Berlin to Vietnam* (University Press of Kentucky, 2019).

INDEX

D